EDWARD GOODMAN

A Study of Liberty
and Revolution

I cannot understand the captiousness of our Government in liking to persecute the rising generation who must needs breathe the air of the present century rather than of the past. It would be so easy to gratify their aspirations and to win their love.

Cardinal Matsai-Ferretti, afterwards (1846–78) Pope Pius IX

DUCKWORTH

Published in association with the Acton Society Trust

First published in 1975 by
Gerald Duckworth & Company Limited,
The Old Piano Factory,
43 Gloucester Crescent, London NW1

© 1975 Edward Goodman

ISBN 0 7156 0870 3

Printed by Bristol Typesetting Co. Ltd.,
Barton Manor, St. Philips, Bristol.

FOR THE MEMBERS
OF THE
ACTON SOCIETY
and in particular
N.M.   P.T.K.
G.C.

Vos autem hortor . . . ut ea [virtute] excepta
nihil amicitia praestabilius putetis

Cicero, *De Amicitia*

Contents

Preface

The world is restless; the spirit of its people, stirred. From Japan to China, across the hills and plains of India, beyond to the countries of eastern and western Europe, then to Britain and over the Atlantic to the Americas, there is a movement in the minds of people, taking many forms, but at heart a protest against the materialistic, utilitarian kind of world to which they are expected to conform. They see a world shaped by the productive processes rather than by the rounded needs of human personality and human community. The particular statements and actions of those who make up this protest are often at variance with each other, often contradict the ends they seek and sometimes seem to be over-simplified. This hardly matters. It is the movement itself that is really significant. At bottom it is a spiritual movement that finds echoes in the minds of a great many people of all ages, especially those with religious, neo-Marxist and liberal affiliations. It is a movement made up of sensitive, radical and sometimes revolutionary people who, in spite of their convictions, are unable to commit themselves to the aims, methods or policies of orthodox communism. In this respect, many of them regard features of the soviet system – the repression of personal freedom, the concentration of power and its emphasis on the productive process – as no less objectionable than any other evil in the rest of the world.

People are searching to rediscover human significance of an altogether more simple and intimate level than can be understood either by technologists, the ordinary run of politicians, or revolutionary writers overloaded with sophisticated logics and confusing vocabularies. Human life and human society must regain balance and proportion. Solutions to the problems of mankind must be sought in terms of value and personality.

These are the general sentiments that preoccupy those whose views I am describing. But sentiments are not enough. If the enemy is the Establishment or whatever we like to call it, it cannot be overcome by thoughtless violence which will be bound to lead to a tyranny of the Left or Right. A false philosophy must be replaced by a way of thought that is true or at least more true. We must begin by looking anew at our own conception of freedom and, by applying that to the conditions of our society, gradually work out the policies of an altogether more human and creative outlook. We must reject the present mechanistic theories of social development and reaffirm the value of an outlook deliberately thought out to meet the conditions and challenges of the time.

Outlooks do determine behaviour. Very often, too, in seeing and rejecting attitudes that have become decadent, people do make explicit their own choices and values, both social and individual; and by virtue of this, they alter their own ways of life which in turn influence patterns of mass behaviour – the basis of social change.

These are the themes of this book. They are themes in which we are all involved; scholars, general readers, scientists, philosophers, novelists, busy men and women, dramatists, journalists and the like. I am appealing, therefore, to a wide range of readers, and, in order to reach them all, I have written as simply as possible, avoiding the technical language of any one discipline. In spite of this, I have not always found it easy to reach every level of reader at the same time, so that I have sometimes had to repeat the same thought in different forms.

In Parts I and II, I describe the outlook that has led to our present condition and the narrow and sometimes negative concepts of human freedom that underlie it. We must understand before we can effectively challenge. In Part III, I try to show how we may offer society a framework that will relate a wider, more positive conception of human freedom to the needs of the community, which, in the words of the Communist Manifesto, shall be 'an association in which the free development of each will lead to the free development of all'. In this part also I have turned to a consideration of the actual conditions in which each man lives out his life and the actual constraints that limit him –

the natural as well as the artificial boundaries of his life. Finally I have put forward some practical recommendations. In all this I have tried to show that the idea of liberty, conceived as the policy of freedom and justice working together, is itself, in times such as these, the justification for a policy of continuing revolution not needing the support of any sophisticated logic or dialectic.

Throughout I have used the writings of Acton. This is not simply because several of the chapters were first conceived as papers for the Acton Society; it is also because I find in Acton a writer on freedom who stood at the confluence of the older natural law and natural rights traditions of political thought, with their self-assertive revolutionary axioms, and the more modern 'human condition' modes of expression.

For this second reason Acton's writings provide a good framework in which to begin searching for the common ground between Christian, Marxist and liberal traditions of political thought. This is certainly no easy task and has to be undertaken in a spirit which recognises that all these traditions are continuously moving forward in face of new conditions and new challenges : one also which prompts members of each school of thought to begin thinking about the use of a common vocabulary. Acton, I believe, would have recognised the value of starting with a critical consideration of such expressions as the essentially, the distinctively and the fully human as terms in which to describe the new, more genuine valuations which so many people hope will replace the materialism, artificiality and predominantly commercial attitudes that characterise present-day industrial societies, exemplified in both the monopoly capitalism of the West and the state capitalism of the East.

In writing about the outlooks I condemn as well as the ones I esteem, I have referred to the actual texts of few writers except Acton. This is because outlooks do not recall the words of their heroes. They consist of a popular distillation of the writings that influenced serious thought at least two generations before, together with the folk memory of the few colourful personalities to whom have been attributed the credit for progressive attitudes. I have, therefore, reduced footnotes to the minimum (again with the exception of Acton, from whom in Chapters 8 and 16 I have quoted extensively both in the text and in footnotes), but for each chapter I have given a bibliography of the works I have consulted as well as a more general list of books that make points similar to and comparable with mine.

In Part IV, in which I put forward some conclusions, I have kept to the plan of the rest of the book and sketched each chapter as an agenda for the discussion of a new outlook rather than as a definitive set of ideas.

Acknowledgments

Inevitably a book such as this, the final writing of which has taken much less time than all the thoughts and discussion of issues and previous drafts which have gone into it, has incurred for me enormous debts of gratitude. First, there are my parents, part of whose natures I share and who have given me many advantages in life. Then there are all who have taught me and those who have allowed me to attend their seminars, and all the authors of the books I have read. Then, there are those of my friends who have been patient enough to discuss draft chapters with me. In this connection I have to thank Joseph Agassi, Bernard Crick, Ernest Gellner, Lucien Foldes, Maurice Goldsmith, Bhikhu Parekh, Andrew Goodman and John Vaizey. I remember with gratitude too both the late J. B. Morrell and the late Sam Coleman.

There are those in my home to whom I am especially grateful; who have tolerated, in the best sense of toleration, my obsession with the problems I set myself. Nor can I forget anyone who has struggled with my handwriting and who has typed for me. There is only space to mention Mrs Wendy Ramsden, Miss Diane Moir, Mrs Brenda Pridel, Mrs Patrica Lightfoot, Mrs Amy Whittemore and the lady I call Providence at the Secretarial Assistance Service, Chelsea, also Jackie Eames of the Acton Society staff.

Finally there are members of the Acton Society and my friends who have urged me to this day and discussed my themes in much detail and great patience – Nathanial Micklem, Gillian Carter and Joseph Agassi. Most of all in this respect, and for going over several drafts most encouragingly, critically and constructively, I must thank Preston King: my debt to him is a special one. With Krishan Kumar I have much enjoyed discussing the implications of the concepts of 'revolution' and 'the revolution', and he has given invaluable help with the proofs and the index.

I had hoped, in order to illustrate my special view of human personality and fellowship, to say, contrary to usual practice, that all these people are responsible for what I have written. That may be so. But this final version I have worked on alone until the last draft, which Maurice Goldsmith, Trevor Smith and Susan Rayner have kindly read with much patience, and made many helpful suggestions for improvements for which I am immensely grateful.

The quotation on the title page is taken from Bishop David Matthew's book, *Lord Acton and his Times* (London, 1968) p 141. It comes from an account of a conversation described in *The Memoirs of Count Giuseppe Pasolini*, compiled by his son, pp 2–3.

Rignana, Italy   E.G.
January 1974

Abbreviations

In referring to the works of John Emerich Edward Dalberg-Acton, first Baron Acton, I have adopted the following abbreviations, used by G. E. Fasnacht in *Acton's Political Philosophy* (London, 1952).

Add. Additional Manuscripts, Cambridge University Library
FR *Lectures on the French Revolution* (London, 1910)
HE *Historical Essays and Studies* (London, 1907)
HF *History of Freedom and Other Essays* (London, 1907)
LMG *Letters of Lord Acton to Mary Gladstone* (London, 1913)
LMH *Lectures on Modern History* (London, 1930)

At all times sincere friends of freedom have been rare, and its triumphs have been due to minorities, that have prevailed by associating themselves with auxiliaries whose objects often differed from their own; and this association, which is always dangerous, has been sometimes disastrous, by giving to opponents just grounds of opposition, and by kindling dispute over the spoils in the hour of success. (Acton, HF)

Introduction

The Disappointments of Liberty in the Twentieth Century

It is not difficult, with the aid of newspaper libraries, private documents and books written at that time, to put oneself in the shoes of the men of liberty and radical temper in the years between 1900 and 1906 and to share their anticipation of the century then beginning. Nor is it difficult to imagine, were they to be brought back to life today, their perplexity at the fact that almost everything that has happened since in the fields of ideas and politics has gone against their firmest beliefs and expectations. More astonishing than the extraordinary material changes wrought by technology, they would find the fact that there had been no continuation of the revolution of liberty that transformed the nineteenth century. They would see that even those parts of their policies and programmes which have been carried out have produced consequences they would abhor.

It is worth, in our imagination, reliving their spirit of triumphant confidence by retrospectively and vicariously, as it were, participating in some of their hopes. They were, at the beginning of the century, a strong and apparently united force representative of nearly all the elements of the alliance that had marched together for more than two hundred years under the flag of freedom. They were relaxing in the hours of victory,[1] occupying the foothills of liberty, able to look back on the seventeenth and eighteenth centuries and to see the enormous advances that had been made. Political and civil liberty seemed safe, toleration secure. The private power of most corporations and monopolies had either been broken or rendered harmless. Almost everywhere the conviction was gaining ground that rulers, however designated, held power on behalf of the ruled. The legal framework had been built and the lines of future progress laid down. Civilisation seemed very strong.

Ahead they could see the terrain they were about to cross. There were, no doubt, differences of opinion about the details and about the means they should employ to overcome some of the more obvious hazards. But about their objectives, and the certainty of obtaining them, there was general agreement. There would be a century of peace and of reconciliation during the course of which the ideas of justice, liberty, compassion and enlightenment would be carried to the ends of the earth. Attention would at once be turned to the lot of the workers : indeed, one newspaper was about to organise a 'Sweated Industries Exhibition'[2] which was to give point to these intentions. There was also great concern for the people still living under despotism overseas, in Russia for example, and the Balkans; their exiles and refugees were welcomed and fêted. They discussed with the refugees how to replace these regimes of oppression by free and democratic ones. They were critical, too, of their own country's colonial administration and saw in missionary effort, in education, in justice and eventually in democratic processes, the answers to much that worried them.

They were mostly practical men – an alliance of Liberals, Radicals, Fabians, Whigs, Nonconformists and Evangelicals; but all for the moment joined together under the Liberal banner. All that they had won had been backed by solid material progress. This would continue and be consolidated in solid principles of social justice. A book such as L. T. Hobhouse's *Elements of*

1. In the parliament of 1906 the Liberal and Labour parties, independently of the Irish Nationalists, had a majority of 273 over the Conservative and Liberal Unionist opponents.
2. The *Daily News* 'Sweated Home Industries Exhibition' opened 2 May 1906; see also Nathaniel Micklem, *The Box and the Puppets* (London, 1955), Chapter 1.

Social Justice,[3] although written a little later, should be read to see how simple these problems seemed and how trivial appeared the differences of opinion that might exist between the members of the alliance. The aims of Liberalism and Fabianism would easily combine in a new philosophy of social purpose.

Nor were these practical men conceited. Their objectives were important to them; yet theirs was not the gospel of final salvation. 'Time makes ancient good uncouth.' They were prepared for other generations to find more apt words and fitter policies to express them. Of one thing, however, they were sure beyond any possibility of revision, and this was the conviction, which they shared with almost all other sections of enlightened opinion at the beginning of the twentieth century, that every man living, besides possessing religious, political and civil liberty, should become increasingly free, within a community of moral purpose, to develop the skill of his body and to improve the power of his mind in order to realise the good of his own person. In this way they reflected the neo-Hegelian idealism of T. H. Green, Bosanquet and other Oxford thinkers, which was a major influence.[4]

These thoughts had many forms of expression, though, sadly, the issues thrown into prominence by each different expression were not as keenly debated as they might have been. Out of these unresolved difficulties has emerged much of the century's confusion and bewilderment of purpose. For different members of the alliance the future of liberty meant different things. Indeed, many of the most serious-minded were more than a little confused about what their deepest standards really were. Lowes Dickinson's *Modern Symposium*, published in 1905, illustrates this point wittily. W. H. Mallock's *New Republic*, written in 1877, is not only more penetrating, but also shows for how long the moral and intellectual differences had really existed. Supreme, and in reality most influential of all, were the Utilitarian experts and advisers of the alliance; for example, the Webbs and Haldanes, but also many others, who believed that catch-words, slogans and even the ideas underlying them mattered little.

3. L. T. Hobhouse, *Elements of Social Justice* (London, 1921).
4. See for example, T. H. Green, *Lectures on the Principles of Political Obligation* (London, 1882).

Society had only to be efficiently administered for men to have all the goods they required to make them contented and happy.

These were not differences that at the beginning of the century were apparent to the members of the alliance themselves nor could they diminish the confidence of this radical generation. Indeed, they were seen as no more than alternative ways, perhaps sophisticated ways, of describing and of approaching the theme expressed more simply by the tiny but very active minority that had once led them and still formed their most committed part. Acton, indeed, had called them 'sincere friends of freedom', an expression which we find today awkward, and, perhaps, embarrassing. To these men the idea of liberty required no justification or slogan. It was a self-evident value of human life that guaranteed also the conditions for the great masses of people increasingly to live good and useful lives and soon to earn enough for everyone to follow his own chosen ends. All these partisans of freedom could look back on the century before as one of political achievement for liberty and democratic principles; the one ahead would be one of economic triumph for the same principles. These would enable their successors to reshape the established order as the material and technical means became available for them to do so.

If we wish to share the excitement and the sense of anticipation of the members of the alliance of liberty at the beginning of the century, we must understand that this was the terrain they were preparing to cross and these were the distant mountains they hoped their column would one day reach. But :

> And long the way appears, which seemed so short
> To the unpractised eye of sanguine youth;
> And high the mountain-tops, in cloudy air,
> The mountain-tops where is the throne of truth,
> Tops in life's morning sun so bright and bare.
> Unbreachable the fort
> Of the long-batter'd world uplifts its wall.[5]

UNEXPECTED WAR AND LIBERAL RETREAT

Very little of this happened, and much else has. Few, if any,

5. Matthew Arnold, 'Thyrsis', l. 141.

can still see the mountain tops or even the ways that lead to the foothills before them. If the men of the 1906 generation of Liberal and Radical leaders and their active supporters could be restored to life now, their disappointment at the failure of their vision would be immense. Historians will eventually write the impartial story of the collapse of their dominion and of all its causes. We are as yet too close to them and their aspirations to be objective. We can only state those facts which stand out like gravestones in the stretch of time between 1914 and 1945 – the Great War itself, the 12,000,000 slaughtered; the millions of refugees; the loss of so many young men who might have helped another generation of liberty; the great Russian Revolution and the other revolutions in every continent since; the vengeful Treaty of Versailles with its intricate legacy of reparations, debts, inflation and misery – especially in the countries of the former Austro-Hungarian Empire; Conservative governments in Great Britain almost without interruption until 1945; the withdrawal of the United States of America from the League of Nations, which its president had founded; the failure of Great Britain and France to support the sanctions clauses; the rise of fascism and the savage sweep of nazi power; Hitler's march into the Rhineland, Austria and Czechoslovakia : the wars in Manchuria and Abyssinia : the civil war in Spain, and the tragic desertion of its democratic government by the other democratic powers of Europe; the Stalinist regime in Russia; the persecution of the Kulaks and the purges; the concentration camps in Germany and the Soviet Union; the 1939–45 war; the systematic execution of 6,000,000 Jewish people; and the use of two atom bombs that all but obliterated life in two very large Japanese cities.

Humanly speaking, it is most difficult to say that these catastrophes could all have been prevented. Reflection will tell us of the immense reservoirs which have overflowed and flooded this century with evil. Yet there are many evil developments which many will consider to have been avoidable. It is often argued, for example, that after 1919 Britain and France were too weak industrially and militarily to play their parts in rebuilding an international order and in resisting the aggression of the Axis power that inhibited Britain and France; nor was it merely exhaustion after the First World War, for Germany, Italy and Japan had no less reason to be exhausted. At least as important was the fact that the content of liberal and democratic ideas had undergone profound changes that became immediately apparent following the close of the First World War. Liberty became a conservative and defensive principle. The rights it had won were converted into walls behind which Britain, France and the United States withdrew from world affairs. None of these countries, nor indeed any industrially advanced democracy, could any longer provide a relevant and rigorous example of social and economic advance which a turbulent world required and sought.

Since 1914 a reaction against the whole structure of advanced liberal thought had taken place.[6] Although the record of the small British Liberal Party in foreign affairs, especially its almost solitary stand against appeasement and fascism in the 30s, was good (the stand much later against the Smith regime in Rhodesia can be compared), the term 'liberal' as a school of political thought and activity came slowly to be regarded as little more than a reflection of the willingness of a few just men and 'do-gooders' to stay together and compromise with other parties at the centre of domestic politics. And this was at a time when the politicians and political groups most conspicuous in the public eye were moving to more extreme positions. By far the most effective contributions of the liberal tradition to public life have been outside the realm of party politics. In activities on behalf of political prisoners and the persecuted, and in voluntary organ-isations of many kinds, its spirit has been as active as ever. But everywhere else the reaction against the expression of liberal attitudes has been strong, even amongst those on the Left; and this has had the effect of modifying many of the previous achieve-ments of the great liberal revolutionary movements of the past.

Now, in the 70s, one of their greatest achievements of all is in jeopardy – the general recognition that civilisation of the quality and human concern enjoyed in the West is always a fragile fabric that can only survive if those who enjoy power, leadership and responsibility in it and who have control over the use of the force needed to sustain it are sensitive to the whole range of human values, and if they are willing to pay as much attention

6. George Dangerfield, *The Strange Death of Liberal England* (London, 1935).

to the just claims of wronged minorities as they are to the clamourings of majorities.

COUNTER-REVOLUTION

During the 1920s and 30s and again in the 50s something like a slow counter-revolution took place. Although the law and parliamentary government remained exalted and the great safety valves of free speech and of representative government continued to be cherished, democratic government shifted the concentration of its policies from individual effort to achievement through the agency of bureaucratic and corporate organisations. It forsook the old claims of improving the quality of individual life and of strengthening small purposive or local groups; and even more evident, it reversed the principle, so strong in the nineteenth century, that power should be decentralised and carry with it personal duties. The ownership of wealth became progressively divorced from its responsible control, whilst its control became more concentrated than its ownership had ever been. Opportunities for individual freedom, responsibility and initiative were thus diminished, and in time the word 'freedom' itself came to be regarded as a 'right-wing' or 'reactionary' slogan. Individuals were expected to put forward their demands through collective bodies which represented their interests; employers' organisations, trade associations, professional bodies and, of course, trade unions and dozens of others. The power of these bodies grew hardly less than those of the industrial corporations. Through all of them, bargains were struck.

All the many new classes which were created by these changes had interests besides wages or salaries to protect. They nearly all feared the consequences of the rapid pace of change and attempted to keep as much of its direction as possible within such control as they had. Managers, for example, did not want their basic industries to be so drastically reorganised that they would lose their jobs, any more than shareholders wanted to see their original capital scrapped and replaced by new and more efficient machines, or the workers to have to find new occupations or to leave their crumbling but much loved homes. All classes and categories in this period were essentially conservative, feared the logic and rigours of a competitive economy and welcomed high tariffs to protect whatever standard of living they had.

Hence there was a sullen compact between the classes that survived strikes and bitter words.

Such was the beginning in the late 20s and early 30s of the counter-revolution. Its subsequent course was greatly helped, and to some extent determined by, two factors not foreseen by the radical generation at the beginning of the century. One was the mechanical revolution, which, aided by a new, well-conceived nation-wide electricity system, brought into existence many new industries besides transforming many of the more prosperous old-established ones. The other was the defection of the Utilitarians from the alliance of liberty. It was they who in government, journalism, the influential clubs and latterly in the universities provided most of the expertise and influences that settled the course of the counter-revolution. They planned its new impersonal structures, staffed its centralised administrations and provided it with a pragmatic basis devoid of beliefs and but faintly tinged with values. Arguments in their mouths became pronouncements of the obvious or the inevitable which only the intellectually uninformed would wish to discuss.

On this new tide, by the end of the 30s and again after the Second World War, the large corporations reached the ports for which they had already set their heavy power-steered rudders. At first inconspicuously and then with the blarings of publicity, they took advantage of all the psychological fears and economic incompetence of the times to force through amalgamation after amalgamation and later, when conditions became more propitious and merchant bankers' money more easily available, merger after merger, until they became more powerful in their own realms than any corporation in the land had ever been. Their chosen destination was nothing less than the total domination of the economy and the complete winning over of society to commercial values. The advent of television greatly helped their purposes. It was not until the 60s that they achieved almost total victory, and even now the question is raised of how long it will take the league of five hundred leading industrial companies to become the league of one hundred. And then ?

The physical consequence of these developments was a startlingly swift transformation of the country. In Britain, for example, London and possibly three or four important provincial towns became 'headquarter cities'. Not only did the large corporations move their administrative and executive staffs to these centres; so also did government departments, financial institutions and professional firms – all swollen to meet the new needs of the times. The impressive buildings they occupied gave to those working in them a sense of vicarious importance. Away from the headquarter cities were the factories and subsidiary firms they controlled; the older ones in the places that had been built in the nineteenth century and the new ones in well-defined areas, most of them close to old towns deserted by their old elites. All these became no more than 'branch and factory towns'. In each of their High Streets, parades of multiple shops and stores came to occupy the positions of most importance, either taking over the old respected tradesmen's businesses or building ugly new parades. The old traders moved down the scale of social significance, but the new branch managers of the chain stores were not encouraged or financially able to occupy the positions of social responsibility and leadership they had vacated, and were unable to devote themselves to local interests as their predecessors had done.

Fifteen to twenty miles out from the headquarter cities, the directors, managers and more prosperous professional people came to live in smart landscaped newly-built ghettos of their own. They too no longer took the part in local life that had previously been taken by the squire or the prosperous entre-preneur. Those who worked in the new offices and factories up-rooted themselves from the communities where they and their families had probably lived and made lively contributions for generations. From every centre of activity, out towards the newly made fences and patchwork gardens of the more prosperous and rapidly rising executive classes, sprawled new suburbs – ugly, clean and uniform, lifeless and leaderless. The rest of the country, the once prosperous cities of the north, for example, became drained of its balance and life and self-confidence. As the 60s and 70s came, one could see that these cities belonged to the taken-over or redundant.

The appearance of industrial and commercial Britain reflected the agreement of the classes to differ in living apart but other-wise to work together in unfriendly cooperation. What they had in common were negative things; no roots in their environment, no sense of belonging, no status or position, no authentic re-lationships with neighbour or nature, no participation in cultures or traditions, few opportunities to be fully themselves and a constant consciousness of being 'us' against any oppressive, anonymous and nowhere-to-be-found 'they'. Each family had its own loneliness and was not able to share its interests with any others. The rich were socially almost as functionless as the middle and upper working classes from whom they had come. Only the poor, the young and the exceptional had any fire left to love the liberty that had been so clear a vision at the beginning of the century.

At the end of the 1960s the cycle of liberal revolution to conservative counter-revolution was complete and had restored to power the privileged corporations and monopolies. Throughout the industrial world this was happening on a wide front. But this time they had at their disposal a massive revolution in techniques and means of communication which they themselves had pioneered and which now enabled them to bring under their control with bloodless administrative methods a very much greater proportion of the population than before – very nearly everybody. It is against these conditions that those who love freedom and justice must now rebel.

LIBERAL VERSUS UTILITARIAN AIMS

Counter-revolutions do not grow from circumstances unaided. Nor are they achieved solely by emotions. They grow in ground that is materially favourable to them and intellectually prepared – even if the intellect be only mediocre and timid. Surely this is the reflection which would cause most distress to the 1900–6 generation, were they to be brought back to life. They would be willing, no doubt, to admit to over-optimism. Some of them at least would be able to make spirited defences. But what they would most dislike facing would be the fact, now obvious, that in the hour of victory, when all their immediate goals had been won, there were at least two groups, one very large, in the great alliance they had and led who did not share their expectations of the future. These were the industrial working classes and the Utilitarians.

Of these two defections, that of the Utilitarians would have been, on grounds of loyalty, most keenly resented. Their practical methods and efficiency had been so telling in all the most permanent achievements of the nineteenth century. Indeed, it had

seemed that they would remain in permanent partnership with
Acton's 'sincere friends of freedom', Whigs, dissenters and others,
and with these continue to form the core of the Liberal party.
But Acton's friends, as he himself admitted, were innocent,
ingenuous men, easily deceived and robbed of their dues, whereas
the particular role of the Utilitarians since about 1860 had been
to reconcile the aims of the various factions of the alliance in a
practical and immediate outlook that would combine the demands of personal liberty with those of a growing social conscience. This they had done very efficiently. The truth was that
so long as the two sets of demands coincided – those of true
libertarians and those of the Utilitarians – so long as the masses
of men were poor and desperately needed improved material
conditions, the two groups could pursue exactly similar policies.
The one group saw that, before men could enjoy their liberty
fully or find any true happiness for themselves, they must first
be properly fed, clothed, housed and educated : 'Give them food,'
they might say, 'and only then would men be able to pursue
good ends of their choice.' The other, the Utilitarians, believed
that to be well fed, housed, educated and to enjoy the full satisfaction of the senses was to be both happy and good. This was the
basis of the political outlook to which they gave their support
and which has since engulfed the whole of society. So long as
industry and commerce could not provide enough to meet
minimal material needs, and so long as there was social hostility
to taxation and welfare measures that would ensure a fairer distribution of produced things, there was no practical difference
between these two attitudes. Not only could they be pursued
jointly, but there was ground for common optimism. With the
advent of improved means of production and with the introduction of welfare measures it became apparent, however, that to
give men food meant their being well-fed and nothing else. There
was no guarantee at all that they would be good or enjoy their
liberty or use it to improve the quality of life itself, or, indeed,
work towards any intrinsic good. On the contrary, the very
technological revolution and forms of production that provided
them with more food and so many other benefits gave rise to
techniques of work and organisations which undermined all their
faculties – physical, mental and moral – with which they might
have gained their good, their independence and their originality.

It is this conflict of thought that has bedevilled the twentieth century; the conflict between the view that productivity ensures consequences in terms of material benefit and pleasure that are good *per se*, and the view that produced things, such as food, housing, clothing, equipment and so on, are necessary before all but exceptional people can adequately pursue ends of their own choosing.[7] It is this conflict that underlies the dilemma and the loss of freedom and all the other phenomena of which modern literature speaks. Nevertheless it is a conflict which no political party of this century, least of all any nominally devoted to the advancement of liberty, has faced with determination or attempted to resolve with positive policies.

The defection of the working classes reflected another conflict that lay even deeper in Western society but which neither the working classes themselves nor their representatives expressed adequately. This arose out of the whole problem of freedom and other values in an industrial democracy; not simply the role of the working man, but the entire clash of values between those grounded in human personality on which the idea of 'liberty' from time beyond memory of men had been built, and those grounded on a mixture of materialism and puritanism out of which the modern utilitarian outlook – the midwife of the industrial structures of society – had developed. It was this second set of values that was responsible for the rapacity and brutality of the industrial process, the ugliness of almost every item touched or fabricated by it, its violence to nature and to human relations no less than its indifference towards the worker's claims to justice and the essential dignity of human life.

The profound conflicts reflected by this clash of values, until well after the Second World War, failed to make any impressive marks on the agenda of Western political discourse, let alone action. Marx, of course, displayed deep understanding of some aspects of it and so in quite different ways did the neo-Hegelians

7. Compare Karl Marx, 'The realm of freedom only begins where that labour which is determined by creed and external purposes ceases,' *Capital* ed. F. Engels, (London, 1887), Vol. 3 *ad fin.*; and J. M. Keynes, 'avarice and usury must be our Gods for a little longer still. For only they can lead us out of the tunnel of economic necessity into daylight,' 'Economic possibilities for our grandchildren', in *Essays in Persuasion* (London, 1931), p. 372.

and Idealists of Oxford. But neither advanced any really positive principles which would secure the first set of values as exemplified by freedom, justice, human creativity and dignity whilst at the same time preserving for industrialism its capacity to satisfy human need. Strange to acknowledge, writers in the first part of the nineteenth century were far more acutely aware of these problems than those in the first part of the twentieth; and men of literature, more than practical thinkers and activists. Ruskin, Coleridge and Morris began a critique of industrial society that was not wholeheartedly taken up again until the discussion of the Weber/Tawney thesis in the 20s and 30s and the 'human condition' writings of such people as Berdyaev, Simone Weil, Demant, Mumford, Camus and Simone de Beauvoir.

We turn once again to the disappointments of the partisans of freedom in this century. After the opening decade with its optimism and radicalism, the First War came, itself a revelation of the power of technology and of the many hidden forces in both society and history; and the society of each participant became organised as one vast, integrated, mass manufacturing colossus. There was the Russian Revolution too, and this was the decisive event in putting many zealous partisans of liberty on the defensive. But if this were so, there were others who appreciated the reasons for its excesses and hoped that, in Marx's thought as reformulated by Lenin, liberty might have found a new champion. But this hope proved to be an illusion. The dogmas of Marxist-Leninism became at least as ridiculous and arbitrary as those of the theology of the Church in its most despotic moods; and soviet economic and political organisations even more oppressive than those of capitalism at its most severe. Freedom during the rule of Stalin was not even nominal and Stalin himself was probably at least as ruthless and cruel as Hitler.

In such ways, the cult of liberty in man's public life, as a revolutionary interpretation of freedom, justice, conscience and compassion, was lost, and the very word 'liberty' was abused by demagogues and mediocrities alike. Nowhere was the rule of mediocrity more apparent than in Britain and the Low Countries, the twin cradles of the free institutions of the modern world.

At the end of the First World War, the true partisans of liberty were on one side, a tiny minority again; and facing them, opposed to them, were their former allies, the Utilitarians and the working class movement. The allies had drunk each other's wine and, still intoxicated by it, went on repeating each other's slogans. But they were empty slogans now. The minority had lost its powerful auxiliaries and all immediate chance of gaining its ends. It was, nevertheless, a minority that, through all the anxieties of the years since 1918, lost neither its faith nor its hope.

The idea of liberty itself did not die. Events of the contemporary world have shown it to be alive and to be capable of inspiring fresh policies and fresh courses of action in territories of human activity where its name was hardly spoken before. If we listen, can we not hear the ferment of fresh voices raised in rebellion against the impersonal forces and vast collectives of our age; voices, too, raised in protest against the hard, ugly, brutal, materialistic values of artificial utilitarian civilisation? And as we raise our eyes can we not see the banners of other minorities and new generations turning to join this truly radical minority in campaigns yet to come? From east to west, in southern and northern hemispheres, from lands of all races, from people of all generations, these voices are raised whilst the banners of these new causes are unfurled :

> Glorious was the aim that fired thee –
> But the goal was never won.
> Who doth win it? Question fearful!
> Fate withold the answering word,
> On this day of all most fearful
> When the nations bleed unheard.
> Yet take heart! Renew your singing,
> Stand no more with heads down-hung
> For from earth new songs are springing
> As they have for ever sprung.[8]

But do we not also hear the beat of other feet marching to join these forces – mercenaries and auxiliaries, as Acton called them – as false at heart today as any before?

8. Goethe, *Faust*, Act III, Second Part, trans. John Shawcross (London, 1959), p. 371.

PART I

THE ARTIFICIAL MODERN OUTLOOK

At the inquest our doctors absolutely and emphatically rejected all idea of insanity.

(Dostoievsky, *The Possessed*)

There was a man of double deed
Sowed his garden full of seed.
When the seed began to grow
'Twas like a garden full of snow.
(Old Nursery Rhyme)

Chapter 1

Dilemmas and Opportunities

One of the phenomena with which the literature of alienation
deals is the sense of dilemma experienced by sensitive men and
women in all industrialised countries. This sense of dilemma may
be expressed as a choice between two different appraisals of
progress. On the one hand people feel that they are riding on the
crest of a wave of almost unbelievable prosperity resulting from
scientists' knowledge of nature; on the other, they feel dwarfed,
awed and confused by the size and scale of both industrial and
political organisation, and by the complexity of machine production which has brought about this affluence. The good times
they enjoy, unparalleled in any other age of human existence,
are the undeniable result of modern techniques of production
and organisation. Yet these very techniques appear to modern
men as the symptoms of their alienation from the soil of existence.
They at once strike the individual with the awe ancient men felt
for the mammoth and the unexplained – the sun and moon and
the fertility of nature – and with the forebodings aroused by
strange forms in familiar places. Western values and aspirations
no longer appear to have roots, to have validity. All seems
chimerical. The human quest for knowledge has opened all
labyrinths save that vital one which explains to the ordinary
person his own role in this exceptionally complicated age.

What is so extraordinary is that Western man has lost his
confidence in himself at the time of what by any standard must
be counted as the attainment by him of the greatest achieve-

ments ever accomplished by mankind. Yet in spite of this, nowhere does civilisation any longer seem secure.

The techniques and modes of production of Western man have spread to other continents. His fractured traditions of thought and values are now taught in overseas universities and preached from distant pulpits. These traditions carry with them Western involvements and quarrels, Western obsessions and self-torturing doubts – and the Western world's uncertainty of the purpose of human existence. Thus, techniques of production are not neutral or autonomous; for, as they spread, they carry with them the dilemma of Western man. Moreover, in the countries of the Third World, those of Africa and South-East Asia in particular, the situation has become even more confused by the competition of other systems of thought – orthodox communism, Maoism, or the cults of Che and Castro – and sometimes, too, by the reactions of indigenous cultures and traditions. It is easier, therefore, to deal only with the dilemma of the typical man living in Western countries – his excited anticipation of a plethora of satisfactions at one extreme, and, at the other, his apparent loss of knowledge of the way he was so confidently treading at the beginning of the century. Nevertheless, in dealing with the problems of Western man, it will serve well to remember that as inhabitants of other parts of the world leave their agricultural economies and work in factories or dock-sides, they, too, become affected by the phenomenon of alienation born in the West.

The loss of way of Western man is readily exemplified by the fact that words which not so long ago helped him to discover his purpose in life have become blurred and vague. Good and bad, his most certain guides to conduct from the beginning of human existence; just and unjust, the ineffable standards of the Ancient Greeks; words such as charity, humility, mercy and compassion, which the Jewish and Christian religions gave to his vocabulary, and conscience – the 'discovery', as Acton called it, of the schoolmen of the thirteenth century; words, too, such as toleration, liberty, reason, and in personal aspiration, typical of the liberal tradition, proper names such as Christianity, socialism and humanism: all these words have become highly variable in meaning, and this variability reflects the lack of agreement as to the exact value they bear. Even 'God' has become for some a vague utilitarian word, a concept to denote something for them essentially unreal but nevertheless useful in their attempts to direct the lofty spiritual instincts of people towards more disciplined and practical social ends. One of the few words cherished by mankind to retain its pure meaning is beauty, which perhaps alone remains unchallenged and unblurred even by aesthetic relativists as the linguistic expression of one of the important values of human life. Yet even the survival of this word from a formerly generous, widely used and precise vocabulary may be due to little more than an awareness of the increasing lack of opportunity to employ it. For urban and industrial life, technical development and impersonal communities have robbed most men of occasions for wonderment and for recognising in the objective world that which has affinity with their own deeper feelings; and it was upon such that its daily use was once based.

No less deserving of notice is, therefore, the disappearance in urban industrial society of most experiences of the intrinsic. As more and more successful attempts are made not only to satisfy the material wants and sensations of the great masses of the people, but also to stimulate them artificially in order to extend the realm of the industrial process over all human life, so men cease to be able to recognise or to take pleasure in what is abiding in the universality of human experience, and transient events and items of personal relationships, knowledge and experience that begin at a particular time but the true significance of which, they instinctively feel, can only be fully recognised in a world outside time. This loss of the sense of the intrinsic, the eternal, being begun, being given birth, in earthbound time may much better account for the decline in religion than many other more sophisticated explanations.

What is lacking in the area of general ideas and values has become entrenched in specific fields of activity; within every such field, or subject, the terminology is as determined and clear as ever, but with an intentionally curtailed sense. Each subject tends to claim its own separate dictionary of what it calls 'norms', or recognised standards of excellence : for the economist, it is the maximum stable rate of productivity; for the industrialist, no longer maximum profitability, but stable oligopolistic conditions which optimise 'the trade-off' (horrible new word of the utilitarian vocabulary) between profitability, power and status;

B

for the sociologist, a balanced structure of society and efficient institutions, each possessing clear functions; for the social administrator, an efficient flow of minimum palliatives; for the psychologist, an adjusted personality; for one school of moralists, the degree of control which character can exercise over activity; for another, perhaps, a successful love-life; for the accountant, a 'healthy balance sheet'; for the personnel manager ('Human Engineer' is the latest title for this appalling new man of science), a superficially contented, albeit efficient and disciplined, staff responsive to the needs of the machinery employed. And so on, and so on. Yet there is no one standard acceptable to all – nor even sought. The student of each discipline is concerned to be exclusive, to emphasise this exclusiveness by an esoteric terminology, or by the naming of a goal which by implication he alone knows how to reach.

All this sophistry suddenly presented to the ordinary person (in an extremely simple form, and, sometimes, very ably through the media of television, radio and the popular press) was bound to upset his moral judgments. No longer is it true to claim, as F. H. Bradley did in the last century,[1] that the ordinary man, in pursuit of his ordinary concerns, has an instinctive knowledge of right and wrong conduct. He has not : or even when he has, he no longer has the confidence to apply it. The foundations of his moral confidence have suddenly subsided under the swift and confusing alterations in the course and character of his daily life. He tends to depend, *faute de mieux*, on experts and experts tend either to put the view of large collective bodies, or to latch on to large collectives in order to use their authority to mobilise opinion behind their own conceited views.

Never before in human history have entire populations of large geographical areas been confronted with the variety and magnitude of choice which face people living in Western countries and perhaps Russia too at the present time. Besides the more immediate question of how to use the industrial power that has been so suddenly discovered and organised, there is the even more central question that people know they must soon begin to answer; more central because it challenges the very idea of the value of their existence. The question is : 'How, in an age of

1. F. H. Bradley, *Ethical Studies* (Oxford, 1870).

increasing productivity and command over physical nature will men spend their waking hours?' Very soon, they fear, the machine will take over and then what will they do? – and not just what will they do, but what will they be justified in doing? Time, like everything else they touch, has now become guilt-ridden and the way in which they use it requires that an account be given.

A WAY TO RESOLVE THE DILEMMA?

The very prospect of further greatly increased productivity crystallises many of the problems underlying the present confusion and may, for the moment, take the issues out of the context of anxiety, commercial pace and bewilderment in which so far they have been set. How, looking ahead to this possibility, ought all the advantages of modern knowledge, of machine production and of automation be used? To what kind of social and industrial reorganisation ought they to lead? The crucial enquiry then becomes, not the role of the machine, but that of the individual human life itself. Is it to be part of the artificially created mechanism of production, tied as it is into the laws of men's enquiries into the physical universe? Or is human life to be the central point of value by which all proposals for the future shall be judged? That is to say, it becomes possible for mankind to seek a balance between production on the one hand, and the fulfilment of the aims of individuals' lives on the other; also to seek a balance in the tempo and in the process of deliberating between the two. Men can then ask each other whether there may not be many other ways open to them of using their know-ledge and of the individual 'spending the time' of his life span.

The significance of these questions can only be seen if we, the ordinary people, give ourselves long enough to ponder them. Suppose, instead of asking for a decision to be made and put into effect today, we say that it is one which can be taken and made effective over a period of time during which it can be postulated that the rate of productivity, excluding agriculture, in industria-lised countries will have at the very least doubled. Then we shall not be overwhelmed by the pace of our present activities and be caught up in new events before we have decided on the merits of the present ones. We shall instead, with some serenity, be able to contemplate many alternative series of future events and be able to argue their relative merits rationally and undisturbed. We shall also be able to use the conclusion at which we arrive so as to lay plans for many years; and some at least of us may be able to begin at once changing the direction of our lives.

A useful start to such an exercise would be to suppose that an opinion pollster were to put to us a questionnaire in this graphic form: 'Granted the very modest assumptions that the populations of Russia, America, Japan, Australia and western Europe will in the next twenty or thirty years be able, excluding agriculture, to produce at least double as much as they do today, how would you advocate that the various classes of workers, managers and organisers be employed? How indeed would you like to organise your own working day if you were alive then?'

No doubt an experienced pollster would have ready some simplified alternative approaches to put to us.

1. Would you favour (a) the achievement of such a prolific rate of production or (b) that the working day be shortened?

2. Supposing you prefer (b) to (a), then would you favour say, a four-hour working day for all, or a full eight-hour day for one half of the population and leisure or non-productive work for the other?

3. Or would you favour only a slightly reduced working day so as to be able to devote a substantial proportion of your country's productive output towards improving the living standards of the remaining two-thirds of the world's population who, today at any rate, survive precariously on the starvation line?

4. Finally, how would you employ your extra leisure, whether a matter of one hour or four hours, whether a day or the whole week; and, arising from this, what proportion of your country's total resources do you think ought to be devoted to the provision of entertainment, recreation and so on?

Such a questionnaire might seem convenient and helpful. But what we would ultimately realise is that its queries do not admit of responses that are equally so. There are broader assumptions underlying these questions, and these assumptions must be revealed and debated before the questions themselves can be meaningfully answered.

The ordinary human being has a need to do something positive and valuable with his life – by his own standards – and to feel that it has a significance in the larger scheme of things. He was once accustomed to look to work for this satisfaction and to believe that whatever object was worthwhile should be attained through effort, exertion or activity of some kind. On this point there has been little or no quarrel between Marx and other Western thinkers. They have all seen activity directed towards the achieving of a purpose as intrinsically work, whether accompanied by economic rewards or not. In this way they have assumed that formal work, besides satisfying material needs, should be something more – an outlet for purpose, skill, imagination and inventive idea. As far back as Aristotle, philosophers have conceived the products of work as the embodiment or extension of human personality. But in recent years many people have spent their working lives performing monotonous repetitive tasks in very large, elaborately organised offices and factories, making perhaps one small component of a much larger unit. This is simply not a man's life. However wonderful the machinery, or however much ordinary people have admired the superlative ingenuity of its inventor or designer, theirs has not been the creative role. It has in no way called forth their full human powers, so that they have felt detached from it and impersonal towards it. And such detachment is accentuated if they consider that nothing they have made belongs to them and it is not even theirs to sell, or for them to share in the proceeds of sale. Its future is of even less concern to them than its past. Psychologically impulsive industrial action and teenage revolt are most understandable. What must it be like for any but the specially gifted adolescent to leave school with its environment of values and hopefulness, then to face the prospects of a life of mechanised work in one of the giant impersonal organisations of the modern world?

These reflections are hardly put down on paper before other changes in the industrial process and in the economic realm take place. As detailed work is divided out into sub-detail work and within each sub-division further specialisations occur, so each specialised machine absorbs the personality of its worker and he becomes as impersonal or as brutal, as mindless or as lack-lustre and laconic as the particular machine to which he is attached. Strikes become so commonplace as to be accepted by many wise employers and students of labour relations as no more than the equivalent of two or three very necessary extra weeks of holiday a year. Even the industrious Germans begin to show signs of not wanting to work for any better reason than the prospects of increasing the monetary reward which it brings. Young people all over the industrial world come to regard working in an economic capacity as optional. They can almost as easily 'opt out', and the state with its generous welfare schemes is there to help them do so if that is their decision. As machinery and auto-mation take over what was once the universal human role, one begins to wonder whether we are not now experiencing the most terrible of all kinds of fragmentation of the human personality – the separation of man from his creative energy and skills, from his integrity as a worker and from the purposes which he had been accustomed to believe it was right for him to achieve with them.

But is not better organised leisure indeed the solution? One no sooner asks the question that one is deluged by the many problems attendant upon answering it. To give but one example, leisure is itself an industry, a separate department of life. Much would have to be done to make leisure more personal before it could be regarded as a fully satisfactory outlet for the expression of human passion and intellect. Indeed, what we seem to have achieved, as the result of all our busy inventive activity, is to improve but little on the Romans. Better wages; therefore super-markets instead of bread. More knowledge and diversity; therefore all the marvels of the mass-communication media and all the astonishing commercially organised ways of satisfying our sensations, instead of circuses. But the golden age of human ful-filment, which the prophets associated with the ideas of mach-inery and automation, when the machines would be slaves and men either skilled master-artisans or the living embodiment of a truly human life – this is as distant a prospect as ever.

And, to return for a moment to an issue raised by the pollsters' questionnaires, there is still the appalling contrast between the advanced industrial nations and the rest of the world. One quarter of the world, the posters published by the Society of

Friends tell us, employs two-thirds of the world's resources. This serves to remind us that, clever as we are at inventing machinery and producing things, we are still unable to find the means to produce enough food to satisfy the hunger of the world's rapidly increasing population. A food and energy crisis is said by many experts to be likely to prove a more direct and serious threat to human survival than any new weapon of war.

The purpose of existence is a question which people hardly ever now ask openly of each other but which nevertheless they worry about introspectively more than ever before. Life as it is is somehow inevitable and there is little that can be done to alter its main features. And to drive the point home, city magnates have suddenly become puppets of Marx even to the extent of being anxious to fulfil the most easily avoidable of all his prophecies – that of the inevitability of monopoly. Merger succeeds merger, and the prospect becomes real of the economies of the Western world being dominated by five hundred, or even one hundred, leading multi-national companies. Respect for one age-old institution after another is withdrawn and as this happens each institution becomes drawn into the unreal world made up of cynicism, mockery and fantasy. Even money itself, once the most concrete, tangible and neutral of all human institutions, begins to become unreal and void of stability. All the familiar boundaries of human life are challenged and one by one are seen to be capable of being broken down. Everyone accepts that what the experts say must be so, and that what they predict will inevitably come about.

The ordinary person in the USA, West Germany or Britain – and to a slightly lesser extent in any other Western economy – hardly feels himself permitted to examine the fundamental attitudes which underlie these tendencies and the hectic activities of both work and leisure which accompany them. He will admit to his own frustrations, to the monotony of his existence and to many similar, irksome causes of distress. But to any of the absurdities he will not admit. All his discomforts, whether due to frustration or other causes, have a price – his share in the growing heap of what is produced. It is very sad to observe that many Latins seem now to be on the point of being won over to similar calculations. Even the beauty of their cities and of their surroundings are under the threat of the ugly spirit of northern industrialism. They shrug their shoulders, climb into their motor cars and ask what they can do in the face of the inevitable, however absurd that may be.

This note of inevitability is struck because of the self-sustaining determinism of the logic of the modern industrial process itself. The labour it requires, the size of plant and of business undertakings, its enormous social cost, the roadways it tears through countryside, the densities and structures of its cities, the tower blocks and concrete cubes, even the character of the goods it yields and the forms of entertainment it generates: all are accepted as the consequence of an automated, mechanical fate. Accepted too, with no less fatalism, is the fact that only a capable few can invent techniques, take responsible decisions, and be independent or creative. For the rest, there are the fruits of their labour and organised cooperation to enjoy. And these fruits are indeed plentiful.

The ubiquitous mood of fatalism notwithstanding, much freedom remains in Western society. Modern industrialism has not yet eroded the freedom of the press, while personal life is less restricted by authority and taboo than it has ever been. On the other hand, two ideals of liberty – two focal points of its development – are being lost very quickly. One is that power should be decentralised into as many units of decision-making as are capable of acting responsibly and effectively. The other is that more and more civilised life and social institutions should be so arranged that an ever increasing number of people may acquire the means of achieving in reality and in materialised form the projects, the ideas and images which they have first conceived in their minds.

Most of those who mould attitudes and opinions in industrial society would have us believe that further progress in these directions is unlikely or impossible. We must admit, of course, that in the short term, since existing trends have already been set in motion, there is little of this to deny; but in the long term, there is very nearly everything. If we look back over the last four hundred years, we can see a development in Western Europe, telescoped into perhaps sixty years in Russia and possibly less in China, as a result of which the aim of man, the image of 'man' in the abstract, has become limited and restricted. Yet at the same time the limited image has been very much amplified into almost superhuman proportions. When we wish to hold this image steady in our minds for a minute or two, we have only to think of those elaborately produced books published say in the 1920s and 30s, and even today, on beautiful photogravure paper with double spaced type, describing the achievements of 'man'. Such a book will usually begin with photographs of the seven wonders of the ancient world; then will follow the spinning jenny and loom, the early steam locomotives and one of the paddle steamers – the 'Great Eastern' perhaps – off Southend Pier. Next will follow the dazzling achievements of the contemporary world – none perhaps so typical and definitive as a photograph of a very clean, modern, single-storey factory building extending over many acres of land. There will be an interior view of it, showing the light steel-frame, trussed roof dipping down in sections above overhead cam-shafts driving belts on to benches, by the side of which men and women in clinically white overalls will be standing. These, with many more photographs, accompanied by descriptive matter in confident prose, will lead up to a final photograph showing the blast-off of a moon rocket and to a final paragraph assuring us that man is only on the threshold of many marvellous developments.

We shall put down the book and many others like it feeling that 'man' is indeed a superb creature – if he is indeed a creature at all – of wonderful precision, skill and inventiveness for whom no material difficulty is too intricate to tackle. But we shall also inevitably reflect that man in the singular, and the reader in particular, is of no significance at all. It can all go on without him, as indeed it can. Not only is his role in life portrayed as totally insignificant, but almost nothing in the book corresponds with the person he knows himself to be. His abilities, needs, his searchings, his questionings, are not answered at all. It has very little to do with him, and he with it.

This image of 'man' is one we all, in some measure and at some time, have possessed. We are led to feel that our role in life is to be part of a whole and nothing more. Our only value lies in the value of our society, this medium of such marvellous achievement. Yet no sooner have we disciplined ourselves to resign our personal selves to this imagined 'whole' and to accept the loss of our own significance in that of the society to which we belong than we find ourselves in a state of considerable mental distress. Equally clearly we see another image of man, just as well authenticated as the other. This is the image of man in the singular, the image that gives validity to our own integrities, individualities and aspirations : the image that gives value to our moral standards and needs. It has been built up over centuries and is derived from the finest insights of religious thinkers, of philosophers, moralists and (in our time) psychologists, who have viewed each man as a whole person able to integrate himself into the world of things and people.

It is from the conflict of these two images that two words used in much contemporary discussion arise. The one is 'schizophrenia' and the other 'alienation'. Here we need not analyse their correct and incorrect usages, but simply observe that their increasing employment in the human vocabulary is one of the more significant features of these present days; the one referring to divisions in the self and the other to the separation of individuals from each other, from their purposes, from what they make and from the modes and institutions of society.

If we reject the solution that the individual can only achieve his self-fulfilment by surrendering his individuality to a vague, materialistic, impersonal concept of society, thereby achieving the satisfaction of playing a minute part in building the social whole – if we reject this solution – how then are we to overcome these feelings of internal division and external separation?

It is here that we must pause to see whether we have not said enough to make choice possible; or at least to lay down a proposition that will end this dilemma. Is not the following the situation in which we find ourselves?

First, we agree that our civilisation with all its knowledge and material equipment is indeed an astonishing and great human achievement and we are happy with what it has given us in terms of improved living standards. We cannot afford to return to the poverty we have forsaken. Second, we associate with this progress our present methods of work and organisation. And third, we are willing to recognise that the same artificial outlook which is the cause of our private unhappiness, our division and estrangement from each other, is also the outlook which has made this progress possible. However much, therefore, we may wish to jettison this outlook, together with the habits and institutions that accompany it, we dare not do so without the most patient examination of its composition – because we are afraid that at the same time we shall jettison material progress too. Is this indeed the situation? Or have we not just begun to doubt some of the priorities of this outlook? Have we not begun to question the value of everlasting progress and the spiritual cost this entails?

It is therefore our common outlook into which we need to enquire: the outlook that embodies all the assumptions and attitudes we share and accept without any due reflection. If this be so and we can find the causes of our divisions within it, and if also we wish to change it, or simply some features of it, then we can immediately set about making choices which we can begin to implement. The means are given to us in the assumption made by the opinion pollster at the start of his questions. If, indeed, at least a two-fold increase in productivity is possible within the next twenty or thirty years, we can choose to begin planning now the nature of the changes which we wish to take place in that period of time. We can say, clearly and decisively, in that period of time what items of our present system of production we either dislike or can do without; what methods of work we wish to reject regardless of their productivity, and what goods and services we do not really need. We can also say just as determinedly what we want in their place. We can declare now what we value, how we wish to spend our time and what the aim of our mortal lives should be in whatever situations we may find ourselves. We can patiently examine what in the past has most frustrated this aim and we can discuss with one another, as well as with inventors and experts, the means of securing our most important ends. We shall know the cost, in material terms, of obtaining the full and creative lives that we claim we need, and since these costs will be in terms of cakes not yet made, let alone ready for eating, we may count them as but trivial sacrifices. Moreover, once our ideas are clear and our plans made practicable, we can abandon the saws of the old outlook.

But do we really wish to do this? Or does the modern outlook so limit our vision and cripple our powers of resolution, that we do not know what we wish to do or how to wish consistently?

The heart of the ruler is sick, and the high priest covers his head:
For this is the song of the quick that is heard in the ears of the dead.
(Swinburne, 'A Song in Time of Revolution', 1860)

Chapter 2

The Modern Utilitarian Outlook I: Goodness, Truth and Pleasure

THE ARTIFICIAL FRAMEWORK

The artificial utilitarian outlook, the modern outlook, is derived from many sources; from the fields of thought, literature, politics, work and even ordinary daily living. One of the most important factors in its more systematic formation and widespread influence has been the defection of the Utilitarians, unhampered by any deeper beliefs in human purpose, from the alliance of liberty that was so decisive in the Liberal reforms of the nineteenth century. So pervasive has this outlook become that today it might seem to be an inevitable concomitant of factory and urban life. Nevertheless, it is important to see that neither towns, nor factories, nor offices would have come to be as they are without the existence of its priorities, its distinctive methods and its attitudes both to the living of human life and to the use of knowledge.

This outlook stems from the times when man first began to rationalise his 'predicament' and to compare it with his understanding of physical nature; when he contrasted the doubts and misgivings that he found in his own introspection with the certainties of the hard unyielding world of fact about him. Thus, the genesis of the modern outlook lies in a sense of human fallibility, of error, of history full of catastrophes and of events not working out in the ways that had been hoped – of sin, if that word is preferred. Those who have most influenced its formation have seen man suffering from his own and others' mistakes, miserable, filled with uncertainties and often close to destitution, yet living out his life under a sky behaving faultlessly, predictably, explicably and without apparently passing from crisis to crisis of misjudgment. Since the beginning of modern times, the dream has always been present that man is part of this universal order and, but for some hidden defect, could achieve the apparently faultless regularity of its other members.

Then from this dream arise questions and seemingly faithful answers. Is not man above all a maker of things – an artificer? Is it not possible for him to reproduce artificially in his own affairs the order that he sees in the faultless and predictable mechanism of the universe? Just as he has, with such advantageous consequences, improved upon his knowledge of the behaviour of much else in nature, so is it not true that nothing more is necessary to make his own lot faultless and predictable than for him to find in himself a comparable mechanism and then to improve upon his knowledge of the workings of that mechanism? In what else can such a mechanism consist than in the working of motive – motive considered in any of the ways that compel a man to start and continue a certain course of action?

For example, in a democratically organised society, or in a state ruled by a benevolent despot dependent upon the consent and goodwill of his subjects, the prospect of the pleasure and self-regarding happiness of the greatest number of its individual members would ensure that the ends of government were achieved. If a commercial corporation were constructed artificially purely for gain, the inducement of material rewards would make every member of the hierarchy of workers obedient to the management of the corporation. In both these instances the essential point is the connection between the individual member's motives (whether bare survival, economic gain or the experience of utmost happiness) and the actions required of him, which come to be directed automatically towards attaining the end set by the motive.

Actions in this way tend to be seen to be right by virtue of their fulfilling an express end, a precise motive. They are right because they are 'useful' in some exact and predetermined sense. Consequently, the principle of utility can be applied not only to the actions of individuals, but also to those of groups; and organisations themselves come to exist solely in order to satisfy those ends, to provide these satisfactions. Societies or states are thus conceived as artificial bodies existing solely as instruments for securing the satisfaction of individual human desires. This explains how the modern age, from its inception, turned its back upon any natural or organic conception of society, whether understood as all-embracing or merely as sub-groups of individuals between whom a continuum of personal communication might exist. It explains too why the modern age has been characterised by this obsession with artificiality, man's way of attempting to escape the consequences of the human condition and the fallibility and ambiguity of his own nature.

Anyone who has read some philosophy will have recognised in this description of the modern outlook a garbled and continuous account of up to a dozen works of intellectual distinction, and may think that the points should be argued at some length with reference to such writers as Hobbes, Paley, Helvetius, Bentham, Adam Smith, James and J. S. Mill, Comte and Chadwick. But it must be understood that it is not intended to imply that these men and their intellectual associates were a group of villains who propagated pernicious opinions. The account given would be, in fact, unjust to each one of them. It is not a description of what all or any of them said, but a collated abstraction of those few easily-understood features of their writings which have seeped through into popular thought and expression. This, together with a tradition derived from the most characteristic actions and words of certain typical men of affairs from each epoch, is the artificial modern outlook. Since the days of its formation, it has continuously attracted to itself other simplifications of thought and prejudice, so that it has always seemed contemporary and progressive; always seemed modern. So representative of the assumptions of the age has it always been that in each generation, the typical articulate modern man, especially he who has not been so familiar with the writers of intellectual distinction whose names have been mentioned, will have regarded it as a thoroughly relevant description of sensible, praiseworthy developments and aspirations. His is the outlook described; what for him is a 'common sense' attitude – the philosophy of the times: an amalgam of those distillations of philosophy, ethics, science and contemporary renderings of religion and theology, statecraft and

national politics, which have filtered down into the minds of
opinion makers, sophists, commentators, politicians and their
more active supporters.

It will now be clear that such an outlook has been essential
to the formation of the most conspicuous institutions and land-
marks of the modern age – its many new intellectual disciplines,
representative organisations, trade unions and limited liability
corporations, as well as the factory and urban development
which these corporations have spawned. But, even at this stage,
let a warning be added. In the history of each of these artificial
bodies, a time has come when it has seemed to breathe and acquire
a life of its own. Frankenstein's Monster, rather than Leviathan,
is its name.

SCIENCE AND THE UTILITARIAN OUTLOOK

The methods of this outlook are founded in the attempts of the
human and social sciences to achieve in their fields the prestige,
precision and certainty which it is believed the physical sciences
possess in theirs. However, when we look more closely we find
four separate aims concealed by these attempts. The first is to
restore to man some self-confidence in his existence, lost since
the Renaissance-image of himself was shattered by the first discoveries of modern science, perhaps especially, as Hannah Arendt
has suggested, those of astronomy demonstrating that the earth
was not the fixed centre of a revolving universe. The second is
to give to human beliefs, values and standards of moral conduct,
the same certainty, confidence and significance as it is believed
that the findings of science have; then to formulate them in terms
of 'laws' in the way that scientists describe their findings. This
involves overcoming the logical impasse, long since recognised,
that statements of belief and value cannot be deduced from
matters of fact: 'Tom is a good man' cannot be deduced from
the fact of Tom's existence, nor even the fact of his being well-
liked. The third aim is to introduce and use in the human and
social sciences the same empirical methods which, it is believed,
although not with complete justification, have been responsible
for the astonishing strides made by the natural sciences. The
fourth is to use the fabrications and possibilities of applied science
to human advantage: that is to say, not only to supply the world
with the goods and services it needs, but also to suggest the right

instruments, institutions and means of overcoming the distressing state of the human condition itself.

For the present there is no urgency to comment on these last two aims, which have indeed enabled some of the social sciences to make immense gains in knowledge. The first and second, however, have very little to do with science and to suppose they do rests upon a misunderstanding of its nature and purposes. The physical sciences made their breakthrough when they ceased to regard themselves as departments of philosophy. They are concerned only to explain the behaviour of the objects they study, and not to be able to say what these objects are or what values they may have in the totality of existence, or in any philosophy of existence. Moreover, as far as we know, physical objects do not have conscious aims and values which might cause them to vary their courses of action. If a meteorite and another heavenly body are set on a collision course, they will collide. But intelligent human beings who so wish and who have sufficient time to anticipate the probable outcome of their actions can, and frequently do, avoid seemingly inevitable collisions.

The progress of science, this illustration reminds us, rests upon an assumption that cannot be proved either logically or empirically, namely that the physical universe, observed and unobserved alike, is governed by laws of regularity. Every scientist practises this belief every second of his working day. His conjectures, his experiments, his 'laws' and his inventions rest upon it. These alleged laws are always inadequate, and sometimes blatantly so; but even when a particular 'law' is proved dramatically wrong, it does not discourage the scientist in his search for regularity, but rather impresses upon him all the more strongly the necessity of continuing this search for a better law which more truly explains the facts of his observation, giving even better opportunities for prediction. The future facts which, as a consequence, are discovered, support the initial act of faith and make it reasonable. Yet these discoveries cannot make the belief in regularity any less a belief, for they do not prove beyond the possibility of every intellectual doubt that the universe itself is a regularity.

Again, contrary to popular understanding, scientists do not only deal with objects they observe. The modern knowledge of physics, for example, has been reached through positing the existence of such things as electrons, positrons and electric waves, which have never been seen and almost certainly do not exist in the forms those who first posited them thought likely. Scientists, therefore, not only believe in a regularity which they cannot prove; they also assume the existence of things which they cannot see. It is the fact of discovery vindicating belief which gives science its confidence. And it is its confident assumptions which, although they need qualifying and revising from time to time, bring it such rich rewards.

On the other hand, such disciplines as moral philosophy, metaphysics, theology and politics suffer from a crisis of belief. They lack confidence. They do not trust their assumptions, and they crave for a certainty which even science does not have. Many of their practitioners have abandoned the attempt to find this in any objective criteria and have adopted contrived, subjective, inward-looking beliefs which, from generation to generation, have driven them to deeper despair and to greater absurdities. Others, as we shall see, cease to look for any fundamental tenet on which to base their conclusions; instead they have tried to imitate the physical sciences as they misconceive them and to join up with them by finding some part of the human constitution which either displays regularity already, or which they believe is capable of doing so and ought to do so. Yet it would seem that neither course will lead to what they desire. The lesson which the human studies can best learn from science is to act from the motive that the belief out of which the study itself springs is true. For science, this is regularity. For the human studies, this ought to be, but is no longer, the uniqueness and value of man. From this fact, if accepted, many other facts and convictions of value would flow : man's resourcefulness, his powers of conceptualisation, his capacity for response and creativity, his abilities as an all-rounder rather than as a narrow specialist, and many other qualities that belong to the category of the essentially, the distinctively and the fully human.

All human beings have, as a consequence of their common nature, needs and interests from which spring their sense of values, mutual dependence and obligation. From these assertions, reasoned generalisations are possible. But such generalisations can never be of the same kind or quality as those which the physical sciences call 'laws'. Although it is open to students of the humanities to assume the regularity of the physical universe; although they may legitimately assume the universality of many human needs and also of many aspects of human nature, and use the scientific method to enable correlations between many kinds of social behaviour to be established, their fundamental problems are not the same as those of scientists. The most important question for the humanities to ask is not whether these correlations can be regarded for practical purposes as immutable and as sound bases for predictions; but whether the correlations and the conditions of their continuation are right, just and good; then, if they are not, to seek effective ways of altering them.

One may also grant that a subject such as economics makes successful use of scientific assumptions; but this is a highly theoretical discipline resting upon highly factual but carefully selected assumptions, whilst most of the problems which lie at the root of human anxiety are not of this kind. These are real problems resting upon real spontaneous experiences of life. The questions which arise from such problems probe into the nature and quality of human existence, into the reality of mind and purpose, into the consistency of human evaluation and into the rationality of their extra-utilitarian assumptions. They ask whether such values as freedom, equality, right human conduct and respect for independent individual judgment are binding on all men, or whether they are aspirations of particular men in particular places at particular times.

Science is concerned with relating facts to explanations of the purpose of entities in the existing order of the universe : the humanities, with describing a disorderly human world – with stating how, and under what conditions, and making use of what assumptions, ideas and judgments of value may alter it; also whether or not it is a rightful part of men's purpose as viewed from a particular set of *a priori* assumptions to do this.

THE UTILITARIANISM OF THE MODERN OUTLOOK

The modern outlook must now be compared with more traditional outlooks. The latter assert that the human studies are properly based upon certain *a priori* assumptions which can be rationally defended by an appeal to human conduct and practice, just as science can defend its belief in regularity by an appeal to factual relationships. Marx, for example, says that work is the essential activity of man and adduces facts from the subsequent world of practice to support his assertion. Aristotle says that man is a social '*polis*-living' animal; accordingly, he describes the institutions and activities possible in this sort of society and discusses which are most appropriate in various circumstances. A religious teacher may say that man's spiritual life can dominate his animal nature : whatever successfully follows from this assertion in the realm of practice will give it confirmation. It may, in addition, demonstrate and exemplify, although not necessarily prove, the existence of a spiritual life distinct from an animal one, or that spiritual as well as bodily enjoyment is possible. Thus one might say loosely that, whereas in the popular view of science, seeing is believing, in matters of value and conduct, practice is believing, or at least confirmation of belief. This was the conclusion of many of the wisest men in the ancient world as well as the modern. A wise or prudent man, one fitted to give counsel, was one who had experienced and practised goodness. Marx's doctrine of practice, although very much wider, embraces the same assumption. The world of practice embodies the world of value. Social life is essentially *practical*. 'All mysteries which mislead theory to mysticism find their rational solution in human practice and in the comprehension of this practice.'[1]

The modern artificial utilitarian outlook does not take these points directly. It baulks at belief and strong convictions. It does, nevertheless, as we shall see below, make special use of the idea of practice. At the beginning it is faced by the same barriers dividing logical reasoning from fact, and fact from value, as are the more traditional outlooks; but it attempts to overcome them in another way. It seeks a solution which will be consistent with what, according to popular understanding, it considers science to be. In order to do this, it first reduces all moral criteria to the single standard of utility, judged in terms of the agent's self-interest. In this respect, it is no different from many other types of utilitarian doctrine, avoiding the dangerous

1. Karl Marx, *Theses on Feuerbach*, viii (1845), in T. B. Bottomore and M. Rubel (eds.), *Karl Marx: Selected Writings in Sociology and Political Philosophy* (London, 1956), p. 69.

territories of value judgments, belief and *a priori* assertions. Next, as we have already seen, it goes inside man and looks for a factual apparatus that will give sure and certain signs of what course of action on each and every occasion will be right, that is, yield the greatest utility. This apparatus, it hopes and indeed predicates, will be an automatic mechanism, requiring no intervention of reason or conscience. It will be of universal application, telling the individual what it is right and wrong to do in every particular circumstance, as well as telling politicians, moralists and legislators what are the right and wrong courses of action appropriate in both general and particular circumstances.

In the eighteenth century the discovery was made, or so it was thought, that such an apparatus did, in fact, exist. It was brought to light and applied to morals and politics with a promise that its use could be extended to any human study previously dependent upon human choice and caprice. The ordinary human sensations of pleasure and pain were the sovereign masters under the governance of which nature had placed mankind. 'It is for them alone to point out what we ought to do, as well as to determine what we shall do.'[2] The sensation of pleasure was the sign of utility, and pain the sign of dis-utility. The apparatus consisted in a balance weighing one against the other.

THE REDUCTION OF MORALS AND VALUES TO UTILITY

The subsequent intellectual history of this doctrine, its refinements and the philosophies derived from it, are not our present concern. What interests us is the way in which certain features of it have influenced and become formative parts of the modern outlook. Its setting was industrial, artificial and pseudo-scientific. Nevertheless, its appeal ever since has lain in its quasi-Old Testament, quasi-superstitious background. All our pleasures have to be paid for. The price is everywhere the same : pain. Work, the penalty of Adam's venality in the Garden of Eden, is in all

---

2. Jeremy Bentham, *An Introduction to the Principles of Morals and Legislation* (London, 1789). The Principle was, however, first enunciated by Locke in his *Essay Concerning Human Understanding*. It crossed the Channel to France, and came back to England, where it travelled around a good deal before finding systematic expression in Bentham.

minds associated with pain. All the goods of this life have to be purchased by shameful, degrading, painful work. The unpleasant fact of work itself cannot be altered.

The utilitarian view, with this puritanical background, recognises that pure pleasure is not within man's reach. There has to be pain. The best, it suggests, that man can do is to seek the greatest possible surplus of pleasure over pain. Seeking this is the basis of his moral life. In the experiences of his sensations of pleasure and pain he will know what it is right for him to do; and this assumes that the psychological mechanism helping him to sort out these experiences is a more complicated apparatus than it was first thought to be. It is not, as it were, a register which clearly and spontaneously displays to the owner-viewer whether the object of his contemplation is either right or wrong; or, in other circumstances, whether a particular act, already performed, was one or the other. True, it is an apparatus resembling a balanced weighing machine where pain is put on the one tray and pleasure on the other, but this does not always avoid its proprietor having to think and speculate; for the balance will only give a spontaneous weighing of pleasure and pain when the action performed is an immediate unpremeditated one. The balance then goes up one side and down the other simultaneously with the action. But if an agent wants to make up his mind about what he should do, if he has to decide between alternative courses of future action, an answer has to be found to this problem. The ideal is to say that he must calculate the quantities of pleasure and pain appropriate to every course of action. But since it is not feasible for him to do this spontaneously, another more practical answer has to be given; and it is this answer, when found, which simplifies the key doctrine of the modern utilitarian outlook and reaches down into all the most typical attitudes of the twentieth century. It is not the actual pleasure or pain caused by the action which determines what the agent will do. It is the pleasure or pain which he spontaneously, without any reflection at all, habitually associates with different kinds of actions and with choosing in particular kinds of ways, that will do so. What matters is the pleasure associated with the thought of one action that is put on the tray and measured against the pain associated with the thought of the action paying for it. The pleasurable and painful associations, rather than pleasure itself and pain itself, are weighed against each other. The operation is involuntary; the resulting measurement precise and immediate.

The individual, by the impulsion of his nature, seeks the greatest balance of pleasure over pain. This also may be described as the utility of an action; the greater the anticipated surplus pleasure, the more the utility. The combination of the two ideas is so precise and scientific, so happy in their coincidence, that objective usefulness and subjective pleasure become one. Each is the invariable measure of the other. In this way the human sensations do, in fact, become the sole determinants of human actions. Morals are taken away from the provinces of philosophy, conscience and religion – taken away from choice and responsibility altogether and given to the senses. In the end the individual is always justified in doing what he 'feels like doing'.

A consequence of this doctrine of motive-mechanism is that the utilitarianism of the modern outlook is not open to the same objections as other more academic forms of utilitarianism; for it does not judge the usefulness of action in terms of something else, such as advantage, when it would be forced to ask itself in what terms advantage is to be judged or defined. It entails no infinite regress. It simply looks upon the sensation of pleasure and the criterion of utility as inextricably interwoven, as associated qualities, the one not occurring without the other. In this way, it says, through the satisfaction of appetite and sensation by material things and bodily pleasures, nature has made man to be part of the material world. There is no argument. There is no mystery. It does not ask, therefore why anyone should recognise one act as right or good and another as wrong or bad. The 'why' question is abolished. It only asks how anyone is to recognise right and wrong; and the answer is, 'by the instantaneous, associative feelings of pleasure or pain that become preponderant as soon as the action is contemplated'. Pavlov's dog had all the mechanism needed :

Fantastic tricks enough man has played, in his times has fancied himself to be most things, down even to an animated heap of Glass : but to fancy himself a dead Iron-Balance for weighing Pains and Pleasures on, was reserved for this his latter years. There stands he, his Universe one huge Manger, filled with hay and thistle to be weighed against each other :

and looks long-eared enough . . . In Earth and in Heaven he can see nothing but Mechanism; has fear for nothing else, hope in nothing else; the world would indeed grind him to pieces; but cannot he fathom the Doctrine of Motives, and cunningly compute them, and mechanise them to grind the other way?[3]

GOODNESS, TRUTH AND PLEASURE

Usefulness, then, is the sole criterion of good. It is not that it leads to a good such as happiness, perfection or the will of God, as the different variants of utilitarian philosophy say. The quality of usefulness, according to this outlook, is itself good. It is the only good and the only standard of rightness. Moreover, in respect of a large area of human choice and action, it is a doubly enforced, a doubly confirmed, standard. First the individual, confronted by choice, if he is sensitive to his own feelings, will choose that action which, by image and name, he habitually associates with utility. His reflexes are conditioned to make this choice as soon as he accepts the equivalence of utility with good. From it, he is immediately aware of pleasure: 'instantaneously' might be the more accurate word; for the pleasure – or better, the good feeling – is contained in the operation of the reflex itself. Second, the choice will result in an action which will give him a tangible good, more often than not a useful object. Confronted by a pile of carrots in one corner of a field and a pile of stones in another, he has his first sensation of good feeling when he chooses to go in the direction of the carrots, and his second, if he has made the right choice, when he reaches them.

Pleasure, together with all necessary means of obtaining it, becomes a good in itself, apart altogether from the value of the consequences. If it transpires that the carrots in the first corner are imitation ones, the individual will still have had his first feeling of rightness and will still have made, in that sense, the right choice. What he will not obtain is the second wave of pleasure, because he will not have been able to eat the carrots. The second action will be wrong, but it does not thereby make the first one so. This disappointment may frequently be the lot of the modern

3. Thomas Carlyle, *Sartor Resartus* (London, 1871), Book III, p. 152.

unphilosophical utilitarian – the man with the artificial modern utilitarian outlook.

The modern outlook does its best to mitigate this disappointment. Not only does it appeal to experience and say that the sensations are so constructed that a given individual will not often make the same mistake twice (i.e. his sensations learn from his mistakes), but it appeals also to history, both as the collective experience of individuals and as a dimension of nature. History as well as the social studies, it claims, should be studied as sciences. This is a lesson the artificial modern utilitarian outlook adopts from the positivism of the nineteenth century. Both history and social studies yield facts and data which the social scientist may observe and use to form social and historical 'laws'.

One such law is, of course, the evolutionary law of progress. All our instruments, so the modern artificial utilitarian positivistic outlook (such is the full description) supposes, are given to us by history; the tools and machines in our factories, food from the fields, articles from the shops, our culture and our conceptions of cause and effect as applied through our techniques. Year by year, a greater quantity of such good things are revealed to us. History unfolds the provisions nature already has in store for us : history is but the time dimension of nature. This is the fundamental superstition of positivistic utilitarian man. The contemporary stage of this development is the experimental one. Man has ceased to live from plough and scythe to mouth. He is living through the age of history in which he is learning to control as well as to imitate nature. In fact, it is through imitation that he is learning to control it. He is in the process of turning the entire world into a factory which exactly, but artificially, reproduces the mechanism of nature. His mistakes are, therefore, an inevitable part of his training. One day soon this training will be complete and then this factory will work perfectly. Thus the disappointments of forecasting are also instruments of good : they are the instruments that teach him and will lead to perfect understanding, not so much of nature, but of man's use of nature – his own perfectible art of artificiality.

The view of human knowledge thus presented is based on more than half-truth. A great number of philosophical riddles which have tortured the minds of men since the Renaissance become open to solution once the premise is accepted that practice and experience are the necessary counterparts of speculation and expectation. Karl Popper, for example, has shown that the problem of whether or not we are born with innate ideas is soluble if we admit that :

> Every organ has inborn reactions or responses; and among them, responses adapted to impending events. These responses we may describe as 'expectations' without implying that the 'expectations' are conscious. The new-born baby 'expects', in this sense, to be fed (and, one would argue, to be protected and loved). In view of the close relationship between expectation and knowledge, we may even speak in quite a reasonable sense of 'in-born knowledge'. This knowledge is not valid *a priori* : an in-born expectation, no matter how strong, may be mistaken. (The new-born child may be abandoned and starved.)[4]

Marxists, with justification, also make a great deal of the fact that we only know anything to be true in so far as our practice has enabled us to know it to be so. We have to put in work upon the theory or expectation to verify its truth; for example, scientific theories become knowable to technicians through their practice of applied inventions. Facts which have taken the finest minds perhaps centuries to extract from nature become commonplaces of everyday experience in this way. Every time an electrical appliance such as a vacuum cleaner or a radio set is manufactured or even mended, a universal fact and a regularity is apprehended through practice as knowledge. Even more so, the Marxist theory would say, the first time a vacuum cleaner or radio set is made, a theory is verified by practice and a gain is made for human knowledge.

It is one thing, although not necessarily true, to say that human beliefs, values, theories and expectations are not grounded in certainty until they have been proved by some kind of experiment or practice; it is quite another to say that only those expectations are believable which, as it were, are daily handled in the processes of manufacture for use. This distinction is vital to the understanding of the differences between the more tradi-

4. Karl Popper, *Conjectures and Refutations* (London, 1963), p. 47.

tional outlooks and the artificial modern one. In the first, human values and beliefs hold the initiative. They originate the theories that are tested in experience. From their own conceptions of goodness and virtue, men act, make mistakes, learn prudence, develop better beliefs and eventually become fit to advise others. In the second, human values and beliefs come out of the factory-to-shop or factory-to-government store process. It would, for example, seem impossible for religious beliefs, for liberal values or for any convictions in human powers of self-determination to arise out of the second outlook.

The status of scientific objectivity and truth is similarly affected. Rutherford's experiment in proving that electrons and protons were the residual elements of atomic structure was 'only a theory', so modern outlook believes, until atom bombs were manufactured and exploded, or until atomic power was generated and used in factories. Thus the role of the mere scientist – his expectations, discoveries and testings – belong to the dimension of theory; they do not count as practice. In that capacity he only begins the process of unveiling nature. What he hopes to reveal only becomes a full part of human belief, a truth, when it has been practised, when it has been experienced, in the artificiality of mass-manufacturing itself. It is not fact which is ultimately valuable, but fact that can be experienced, that can be felt by one of the senses.

Are we to conclude, then, that truth itself is a factory-made product, and goodness merely the satisfaction of men's desires? These conclusions would appear to be warranted if we assume, as the artificial utilitarian outlook does, that the mechanism of the entire artefact of society – the muscles, gut and bowels of Frankenstein's Monster – consists of one vast manufacturing process, coordinated by the automatic mechanism of human psychology effortlessly assimilating the laws of human behaviour to those governing the operations of the universe. The grounds for this assumption we shall examine in the next chapter.

THE ARTIFICIALITY OF THE OUTLOOK

Not only do the facts of science, in order to be accepted as truths, have to go through the manufacturing process and to be experienced in it; so also do news items. An event is not newsworthy until it has been made into news by the processes of the mass-communication media. This provides the most telling of all illustrations of the artificiality of the modern utilitarian outlook. Not only is news-making an industry, just as any other form of manufacturing is; but in all probability it is more important than any other. It determines the ways in which other things are done, influencing political decisions as well as a large proportion of the cultural life of the community. Yet hardly any of us pause to reflect exactly how artificial the whole process is.

All news has to be artificialised before it can appear in print. Beginning with the reporter who extracts from the stories which he obtains only those items, only those bits and pieces of items, which his training tells him will interest his editor or appeal to his paper's readers, to the lead stories, front pages and banner headlines; the daily newspaper is not so much a record or evaluation of actual events as abstractions selected, magnified, reduced or given prominence and emphasis by the newspaper production staff itself. The newspaper has to be put together in such a way that its readers' senses are titillated, sensationally exploited or shocked. Every evening the news-makers gather together in clubs, pubs and private rooms deciding on the lead story, the punch line, on the biases to be given, the current affairs issues to be pursued and the sympathies or antipathies to be created. Higher up, the material is selected for campaigns to be mounted and circulation to be increased. Every night and morning after, the appropriate staffs from radio and television follow behind, nagging away at the personalities whose plights have been described in the morning and evening editions, thrashing threadbare the day's scandals or current affairs issues in ways which frequently bear little relationship to the reality of all that happened or to the deeper causes underlying it.

The most serious consequences of all this lies in the nature of mass-communication techniques themselves. The headlines and the front page stories and, even more important, the prominence and valuation given to them in their places of origin, spread across the world. An isolated act of violence committed by four or five depraved adolescents, or a hijacking of an aeroplane is likely to be repeated ten or twenty times around the world within the next few days. A small difference between two cabinet colleagues is magnified into a quarrel and becomes a national issue; an incident in a foreign country between people of different nationalities or of different religions, which previously diplomacy might have settled at its own pace, becomes the day's main head-lines all over the world and the chief topic for the extraordinarily efficient, well-informed but superficial and opinionated corps of pundits sitting in television studios around the world. The fault of all this, let it be repeated, is not that of the pundits nor of the initial reporters nor even of the mass media : it is of the modern outlook itself whose appetite for sensationalism and artificiality is cumulative and insatiable.

The mass-communication media are the most accurate and easily comprehended reflection of the modern outlook. The question of which feeds which is difficult to understand, let alone answer, until the view of truth underlying the outlook and the media alike has been explained.

To command nature is to obey her. (Bacon)

Chapter 3

The Modern Utilitarian Outlook II:
Its Laws

THE POSITIVISM OF THE MODERN OUTLOOK

More realistic inspection reveals a flaw in the value system of
the modern utilitarian outlook and this is to some extent dependent upon a confidence trick. The system attempts to marshal
a law (or laws) of behaviour in two different senses of the word
'law'. First, it advances 'laws' which are purely explanatory in
character, and which therefore fall back upon deterministic,
materialistic and psychological models to elucidate human behaviour. But next, it inserts into this explanatory law a normative
bias (the 'ought') which previously had been its entire purpose to
eliminate; for it is intended not only to suggest that men do
behave in a self-regarding way, but also that they are justified in
doing so. More than this, it is good for them to do so. Thus, where
the 'law' as fact does not obtain, its place is taken by the 'law'
as command or moral imperative. The transference from explanatory law to moral law is effected without any but the most astute
observer noticing it.

This flaw can, of course, be pointed out to the pundits of the
artificial utilitarian outlook, and they will be obliged to concede
that, according to their own principles, laws marshalled in the
second sense can only be regarded as applying to those consenting
to them : those who are conscious and approve of the fact that
their self-interest lies in the same direction as the laws of behaviour described in the first sense. How, then, is this need for
consent and approval to be overcome, so that everyone in a given
society can be included within the ambit of the laws uttered in

the second sense whilst the word 'ought' continues to be avoided? How is human behaviour to be tied into the artificial processes of society so that morals and politics and other social studies become positivist sciences without any doubt or possibility of counter assertion?

The answer, it can be seen intuitively, is to tie human behaviour into all that has previously been regarded as haphazard and the subject of chance or blindfolded fate, but which, by applying to it utilitarian methodology, can either be shown to be, or made to be, systematic, objective, regular and scientific. If such an answer can be argued rationally, or through the process of reasonable assumption, then the uses of the idea of law as a moral imperative and as a scientific statement with predictive powers can be shown to coincide. If this can be done, the word 'ought' can really be avoided and the predictive word 'will' can take its place.

The artificial utilitarian outlook had to contend in its later formative period with four other not entirely unrelated problems, which, when examined, contribute to an understanding of this central one.

1. The pure sciences could yield predictions, but the applied sciences were in an ambivalent position. The latter were equally bound by external physical laws, but they needed human cooperation in order to put their applications into effect. This cooperation might not be forthcoming, however, in at least the following ways : (a) humankind might not want the applications (i.e. the scientists might wrongly interpret human desire), (b) human labour might not be willing to work the processes of application and (c) there was no guarantee of consistent human behaviour in either of these respects, and therefore no certainty that the processes and inventions of applied science would become permanent and regular features of collective human life.

2. Other studies were also required to come within the same system, notably those within the ambit of public rather than personal behaviour, affecting the nature and development of institutions and the desirability of legislation. The artificial utilitarian outlook had to reconcile its adherence to democratic institutions with a seemingly passionate popular concern for individual liberty and free speech and comment. In all those

fields, therefore, in which choice, self-interest and value judgments were common features, it was essential to retain the appearance of volition, yet also to show that in certain specific fields, volition itself was dependent upon and determined by objective ascertainable facts; also that in these fields it was infallibly directed towards the public good in a specific recognisable sense.

3. Each subject of study and activity was to be pursued separately, and to be made into a positive science. Therefore, each norm had to be converted into a separate and independent good. Yet in order to be universally true and scientific, each of these *ad hoc* goods had to be reconciled to each other and to the general public good and to be 'scientifically' vouchsafed – that is to say, made capable of being pursued with consistency and permanence. The good of, say, mineralogy, of industrial psychology and explosive-making had to be reconciled with each other and the general good, and the general good had to be part of a science of social development which would subsume equally and indifferently social, as well as what we would now call technological development.

4. Last, the artificial utilitarian outlook had to show that all these many goods that were desired, these many preferences, were inevitable, and that their attainments were separate parts of a general scientific law consistent with their introduction by the applied sciences into artificial human society as they conceived it to be.

How was every subject studied to have its own standard of excellence and its own general law; at the same time, however much they appeared to conflict, how was one standard to be made consistent with each of the others and each set of general laws to be made to fit each other so that they were all included in an overall value-free law of social development, entailing indisputably the public good as a scientific non-emotive term? How was the volition of every individual to be included in these general laws and into the science of social development whilst the word 'ought' continued to be avoided and the appearance of human freedom maintained? In other words, how was it possible to reconcile moral laws in the form, 'this is good and therefore ought . . .' with law in the scientific form, 'if these

assumptions are true, then the following consequences . . .'? Or
was it possible to go even further and reduce one to the other?

It is, of course, impossible to do all these things in the ways
demanded and to produce a single good, a uniform standard and
universal law from all these disparities. Nevertheless, the artificial
utilitarian outlook is not aware that this is so and succeeds in
putting forward a very plausible series of arguments to produce
the answer which it has already intuitively felt to be necessary.

Now it can be agreed that the applied sciences do in fact
pursue a certain objectivity. Their role is to apply to human
needs the objective discoveries of the physical sciences. What is
true in the universe and in the world of physical nature they
attempt to introduce artificially into the human world. They
use the word 'law' exactly as the pure sciences do, to mean that
a statement with predictive powers is true. Their problem, as
we have seen, is to render human behaviour amenable to these
laws so that it too becomes reliable, consistent, predictable.

For the moment, we can take the first of the three stages by
which behaviour is rendered predictable by going back to the
example of the field with a pile of carrots in one corner and a
pile of stones in another. It was observed that the individual in
the field would experience two waves of pleasure; the first in
recognising the carrots and experiencing the pleasure the name
or idea of 'carrot' conveyed with it, and the second when he
verified his judgment by eating them. The possibility was also
mentioned that he would not be able to verify his judgment if the
pile proved to be one of artificial carrots or of stones.

This example provides the modern utilitarian with a double-
facing theory of truth. In the first instance, the man can say that
the statement based on the universal pleasure attached to the
name 'carrot', or 'that particular pile of carrots will give me
pleasure', was true. It did indeed give him pleasure the moment
he believed it to be true and this pleasure was greatly increased
when he verified his belief. Suppose, however, his first perception was wrong and he had mistaken the pile of stones for one
of carrots, he would, if he discovered the truth in time, still
experience pleasure – the pleasure associated with the relief of
discovering his mistake before he had attempted to bite a stone.
But if he did not discover the mistake in time, he would have
been practising a falsehood and the consequence would be pain.

Whichever course he took, he can now say that truth is always associated with pleasure and falsehood with pain. Because of this, because pleasure is good, and because also, as we have already seen, the applied sciences and the normative studies pursue a certain objectivity which yields truth, these objective truths or 'laws' are good and should be pursued.

The idea of 'ought' is still there. But it is already becoming a little more objective. In the second stage it becomes still more so and in the third it disappears altogether. The second stage consists in creating an identity between the social good and the greatest pleasure or happiness of the members of the society and then in showing that any activity undertaken by society or by a corporate body has its own in-built standard of utility giving pleasure to its members. The third is to relate that utility to a scientific 'bait' which the individual will mechanically follow.

The second stage, then, is to pursue the idea that social or corporate good promotes the greatest pleasure of those belonging to the society or corporate unit with which it is concerned. This presents no difficulties at all to the modern outlook; for it is implied in its very first assumptions, namely that society and every sub-entity of it is a man-made artefact operated by its relationship to the human motive mechanism. In the artificial society of the utilitarian outlook, the motive selected is self-interest, and it is this by which the individual can be induced always to seek the means of maximising his pleasures. Each individual's good is the satisfaction he obtains from this happening, i.e. his getting what he wants – his 'interests'. Thus society is an artefact which can only exist, and continue to exist, if each of its members gets as much of what he wants out of its existence as is possible. Each part of the system is man-made by experts who have very much in mind the problems raised and who are concerned that it will finally reproduce the orderliness of universal nature.

In order to perform these functions, the experts have to borrow such terms as 'good', 'right' and 'duty' from the ordinary moral vocabulary and use them in an artificial sense. The good of society, therefore, is the sum of its advantages to its members and this good is identical with its function. The good, the utility, of any subsidiary organised unit within society, any corporation, is part of that good. And similarly, the good or utility of any

c

particular activity or study is the same. All intermediate and interconnecting stages of reasoning can mercifully be neglected. The principle of utility is universal and mechanical in application. One has, therefore, only to discover the function of any body, corporation, institution, activity or study, and one has named its built-in utility. The duty of any individual pursuing that activity or belonging to that body is to 'maximise its utility', namely to secure its excellence, or its optimum efficiency, as far as possible. This is what is meant by seeking to reduce morals and politics to a single science. Good becomes an artificial concept and one that is transparently easy to follow.

To the applied sciences and to the normative studies aiming at a degree of objectivity, this is a double-edged boon. It justifies their work and converts their norms into objective standards. It also places the ordinary person under an obligation to accept these standards and, if he be a worker, in a place where they apply, to be obedient to them. The world at large will, therefore, treat the inventions of applied science or the finding of normative studies as inevitable, in the same way that it does the workings of nature revealed to it through the lenses of the microscope or telescope. If a motor car can be made to travel along motorways at 150 miles per hour, then it will be right to sell it, right to buy it and right to use it. If the processes of manufacture can be made more efficient by the introduction of 'management methods', it will be right to call these methods 'laws' and to apply these 'laws' irrespective of the dissatisfaction of the workers governed by them. (The pain of workers is outweighed by larger human advantages.) It is not only right to develop the napalm or atom bomb, given the discovery of knowledge which makes it possible to make napalm or to split an atom, but it is also right to manufacture and use, in appropriate circumstances, both kinds of bomb.

The discussion of this second stage has shown the determinism that is implied in the artificial utilitarian outlook, and invites again the question of how such determinism is to be reconciled with liberty and free institutions. The short answer, which is developed in Part II, is that according to the philosophers of this outlook, there are two spheres of freedom, one private and one public. The invention of this distinction makes it possible to suppose that free men with independent wills of their own can invariably be induced (or with such rare exceptions as can be looked after by the law of large numbers) in the public sphere to behave consistently with the operation of the laws of science and the applied sciences.

THE LAW OF INCENTIVES

It might appear that some confusion would result from the norms of many applied sciences and studies conflicting with each other (the third problem on the hands of the modern outlook in its formative stages). This, however, is also sorted out artificially and 'scientifically' by the same principle of utility which assimilates human behaviour and values to the applied sciences. Utility is intimately associated with another 'law' of universal consequence. This is the law of incentives which, crudely stated, says that every man has his price. By describing it in this way it is not intended to decry the price or market mechanism, which is indeed a characteristic feature of any free society (each price paid is the equivalent of a vote), but to point to the way in which the price mechanism of itself supports the claims of objectivity advanced by the more successful applied sciences and their associated normative studies. It is another piece of the machinery of the artificial utilitarian's moral science.

Human cooperation, as we have already seen, is the weak link in the attempt to make the applied sciences completely objective, and the still more fragile link between the desire to make, and the achievement of making, a normative study into a social science. The prophecy that a given scientific discovery can be applied through a particular invention to meet a particular human need is likely to be of little effect unless human behaviour can be adjusted to its use. Hence the 'laws' of business management which show managers exactly how to do this. Yet in spite of the fact that the individual worker ought to obey these laws because, properly conceived and formulated, it must be assumed that they will give pleasure and happiness to the maximum number of his fellow men, he may not be willing to do so. His own self-interest may not be sufficiently involved. His and his fellow workers' cooperation can, however, be assured by the 'law of incentive'. This could be stated as follows : for each quantity of pain suffered at work there is a corresponding wage per function which will give the worker that fractional margin of extra pleasure sufficient to induce him to perform the task. This being at any particula short period of time very nearly an accurate statement (subjec to the normal frustrations of industrial 'detail-work' causin sudden strikes), such laws will be effective – and will be believec by the earnest modern utilitarian student of the social sciences.

This does not entirely solve the problem of different disciplines different subjects of activity and study, having conflicting utilities But only one step more is required. The utility of architectura study to retain buildings of a particular period, because it i generally agreed that they give pleasure, may be at variance witl the utilities of the study of town planning and of propert development, the aims of which happen to coincide in demandin; that buildings should be so designed and arranged in relation t each other that they provide the community with the maximun usefulness. There is thus a conflict of utilities – visual pleasur against other pleasures. The moral 'science' of the moderi utilitarian outlook avoids the necessity of a human arbiter. I simply asks which utility will yield the greatest surplus of profit A town with a large overseas tourist trade will thus be able t save its beautiful buildings. A town without will have to yielc to the argument that redevelopment will 'provide a living fo more people'. If the dispute is pressed it can be resolved factually that is, by a method which modern utilitarians think is of th essence of the scientific spirit. Which state of affairs will yielc the best return on the net expenditure? Market rents based o the value in the market of the town's existing assets plus the cos of bringing them up to date, or the rental yield of new building calculated as a percentage of the cost of acquiring the town' existing assets, demolishing them and building new ones?

In a similar way, it is possible to settle conflicts arising betweer the norms of different social studies and of different appliec sciences used in industry. Each norm has to be related to a corresponding incentive. But only those norms will survive tha are related eventually to consumer goods which will sell in th shops, or to the rewards posited by the law of incentives. Thus the market mechanism is the determining factor in converting hopes and 'norms' and 'oughts' into 'laws'. There is not space to show how the system spreads out through statistical laws sampling methods, advertising and 'consumer persuasion' so tha a 'law' once made may be sustained. It is sufficient to say, as can easily be imagined, that the system is a circular one and lies entirely within the area of artificiality already described.

There is, however, one technique which, because of the way in which it makes use of the price mechanism as an abstract notion, deserves singling out from all the other techniques associated with the 'laws' of the social sciences. This is the cost-benefit analysis, which its inventors claim 'operationalises Bentham's felicity calculus', and which they might describe as an analysis of the total cost of an exercise including social costs and what economists call 'externalities'. What this analysis does, in fact, is to make a list of all the advantages and disadvantages of a proposed course of action irrespective of whether the advantages will produce tangible revenue or the disadvantages have to be paid for: then to give monetary weightings to those items which do not normally have a monetary price as well as to those that do. For example, at a public enquiry into the desirability of a noisy jet aeroplane, a weighted price could be put on a calculated number of businessmen who would benefit from the increased speed of the new plane and this would be put against another weighted price of the suffering which the noise would cause to an actual number of people living along its proposed flight path.

The role of the price mechanism in most aspects of social choice is exactly the same as the role of the pleasure-pain mechanism in private choice. Private conduct is determined by the weighings of pleasure is gain, of the other, loss. There are, of course, and experience has taught the agent to regard as pleasurable or painful: this is private utility. Nearly all social conduct is also determined by a pair of scales: the name of the one evocative of pleasure is gain, of the other, loss. There are, of course, and it is important to note this, some actions and policies which cannot be determined in this way. These are, in fact, related to standards surviving outside the system of artificiality. A discussion of them belongs to a later chapter. They certainly form no part of the modern outlook.

This description of the role of market evaluation in the artificial utilitarian system must not, however, give the impression that money is the crucial item in utilitarian society. On the contrary, in common with all the key concepts in the outlook, that of money is artificial too. Money is merely notional. It is no more real than the symbols in the equations of cost-benefit analysis. The money price of anything is not its real value in the market imagined by the classical economists; but its artificial prices when other conditions have been specified or certain features of the flow of supply and demand have been artificially manoeuvred. The amount of money available over a period of time bears no fixed relationship to the sum total of real wealth in that period. It is an artificial amount regulated by the fashion or the theory in vogue at the time adjusted to employed and unemployed resources, to the quantity of goods on offer, or to the capital needed for future production. Nor does it matter greatly how it is created or by whom it is created; central banks, joint-stock banks, the mint, discount houses or the printers. So artificial indeed has money become that in the United States, for example, it is one of the forms of currency least preferred by shopkeepers, hoteliers, petrol stations or travel agencies : better to have the credit card, the banker's card, the loan account, the budget account or plain credit supported by acceptable references. Each of these creates unreal money situations that bear little relationship to the individual's wealth or the actual state of his affairs. Each contributes towards an ever increasing rate of inflation and, since inflation can easily be proved to be a more decisive underminer of the established order than threats of outright revolution, it can be shown that in a country such as the United States or Britain, the joint-stock banks and credit institutions are far more important saboteurs of the conventional capitalist system than the communist party in those countries.

THE LAW OF SCALE

Positivism teaches us, as we have already seen, that besides the recognised sciences, history and society have laws which may be discovered. Similarly, institutions and corporate bodies have laws which may be discovered. The law which especially concerns us is the 'law of scale'. It has evolutionary overtones. Only the fittest organisations survive. Small organisations are destined either to go under or grow larger. (The modern artificial utilitarians have heard of Leviathan and possibly of Frankenstein's Monster; but none appears to have thought about the dinosaur.)

This is clearly good positivistic doctrine in a popular sense. All around can be observed small organisations collapsing, takeover bids bringing about amalgamations with larger and larger units. These must surely be positive facts and fitting foundations for a 'law' of the history of our times. It is but a short step to predict that tomorrow belongs exclusively to the large organisations. This is precisely the doctrine which the upholders of the 'human sciences', especially in industry, wish to be popularly accepted. There is nothing like introducing the word 'history' to sound a note of inevitability. It is an interesting fact that the larger the typical unit which dominates the economy, the more successful are the predictive powers of the 'sciences' required by the modern outlook, and, as a result, the more solidly do they become entrenched. A robust competitive economy is far more sensitive to the non-material needs of the worker and is apt to upset the predictions of the spurious sciences. But the 'command organisation' of large-scale firms not only eliminates the human element much more successfully; it is also the customer with huge spending power who can assure that things go its way. In the short term the commandant organisation is almost a source of inevitability on its own.

The latest of all sciences to incorporate all these 'laws', prejudices and shallow estimates of human behaviour into a single concept of infallible predictive and prescriptive power is that of business management as currently taught in the business schools. The concept is that of corporate planning, which is a bag full of ruthless ready-reckoner formulae produced for the ambitious (but not above averagely intelligent or able) executive. By virtue of corporate planning with its motto of 'either expand or go under' it becomes certain that, except for the intervention of a revolution or some other expression of the popular will, nearly all business enterprise within a comparatively short period of time will be concentrated in, say, Britain or the United States into 500 mammoth firms then in only a little longer period into 100. A final stage is not difficult to imagine when a few hundred corporations will own the entire productive equipment of the Western world.

Once the fact of large-scale organisation has become accepted as an inevitable consequence of history and science and has become part of the laws of the modern outlook, then the work of management sciences, 'human engineering', industrial psychology or marketing studies, and many branches of applied economics, as well as the work of designing machinery itself, is made easy.

Most of the imponderables normally facing them have been removed. They no longer have to provide for innumerable contingencies or for many customers with different characteristics; they can address all their studies to the single postulate of a firm of a given minimum size dominating an industry and setting the pace of its activities. In brief, this sized firm is their customer. All their 'laws', applications, inventions and researches then posit its existence and its preferences. It will of course already have been noted that the words 'law' and 'science' are throughout misused more or less deliberately, first by the advocates of positivism, second by the applied and social sciences and last by those who have personal power in the system so that they may sustain and increase it with all the appearance of detached objectivity. Because it relates these three aspirations to historical 'laws',[1] the artificial system has itself become very nearly foolproof. It would, indeed, seem that human choice and intervention cannot upset it from outside.

It is not only commercial corporations that become subject to these laws. All organisations do: in particular, organisations of government. Small local government units become out of date as quickly as small firms do. Independent political and quasi-legal bodies disappear or become incorporated in central government

1. Of course, once relatively few 'laws' of the artificial outlook are established, a host of others may be adduced from them; thus making up a kind of special literature of the artificial utilitarian absurd. For example, from the laws of large numbers and the 'laws of scale' and the 'laws of management' and in any particular market dominated by a few large firms (large according to a law of scale), other laws are constructed so as to reduce to a minimum the hazards of a market economy. 'Marketing' then becomes a highly efficient science in its own right. More laws are then introduced so as to classify both products and consumers into categories. Any quantity under say 1.05% of any given market can be discussed as statistically insignificant. Thus a great number of commodities not falling into one of these categories ceased to be offered for sale (one's favourite blend of china tea, for example) and then to be produced. One particular casualty of such a 'law' is the educated general reader. All readers – except the statistically insignificant – having been exhaustively divided into one market class or another, and almost all privately conducted booksellers – except those in university cities – having been absorbed into a chainstore catering either for the mass sensationally orientated reader or for general stationery, gramophone records, party games and those books likely to have mass circulation sales, there can be no educated general readers left. There is no class left into which he can fall and very few bookshops left to cater for him, even if he did perchance still exist.

machinery. Centralism replaces decentralism everywhere. Self-styled efficient administration takes the places previously occupied by thousands of centres of discussion and decision. Local cultures, local traditions, local pride and self-determination go. In the same way, individual opinion and choice cease to be heard. Instead they are 'forecast' in statistical sheets which administrators find easy to read and amenable to their decision-making processes.

The truth which must be faced is that the modern artificial outlook does not need any of the standard features of texbooks on democracy. They are old-fashioned concepts that belong to an era that is past. The idea of checks on power, of personal aspiration, of individual responsibility for acts of administration, of local community, of personal opinion and value, are as out of date as the Gladstone bag. This outlook has sprung in reality from one wish, one value, one aspiration alone. This is the pursuit of individual material advantage. Out of it has grown the artificial system described. We must concede that it is an efficient system, with the minimum of mistakes that all machines must make.

This, then, is the modern artificial utilitarian outlook and this is its positivism. It is the outlook which determines a larger part of our lives. Yet it does not determine all of them. Outside the realm of its influences we can and do have our different beliefs, our personal values, our political alignments, our loyalties, our friendships, our preserves of private activities. We also have our common beliefs – and although they may be few, our common traditions are many. The predicament we share is the inability to draw on either our personal values or the common values of our tradition in order to make this outlook more representatively human. Nor can we prevent its vulgarity and coarseness from debasing the currency of our personal relationships. Should we then abandon it? We turn to do so and see at once that for the present we cannot. It is not only that our particular well-being is at stake; but that of the whole world. In less than two centuries, from material conditions which were hardly more prosperous than those of the ancient world under the Romans, it has taken us to the standards of living and the expectations we enjoy today. Nevertheless, two-thirds of the world is hungry and perhaps a fifth very near starvation.

So long as we admit the absolute priority of material standards, the modern artificial utilitarian positivistic system seems almost certain to remain in its entirety in capitalist, communist and socialist systems alike. It has been built up with immense skill and ingenuity so that each part is indispensable to the working of the whole. It is a closed circuit, a self-adjusting system, having its sole contact with human value at the point where it is related to the satisfaction of daily recurring appetites and sensations. On the other hand, the human race is drawn into this circuit at many thousands of points. It affects us very much more greatly than we affect it. It disturbs our existences to their depths. Yet until we have thought out a practical alternative, we dare not reject it. But even then, even if we were suddenly confronted with such an alternative and, in addition, were shown convincingly how we might exist enjoyably on lower material standards, are we not apprehensive that the marketing men, the advertising agencies together with all the subtle pressures of the mass media and the seductive demoralisation of mass-culture, would mesmerise us into doing nothing? For it is these influences which have finally made nearly every one of us a utilitarian man — mentally, imaginatively and voluntarily as well as physically, an ordered, measured part of the artificial utilitarian system's rhythmical process-cycle. It is not, therefore, merely a practical alternative that we need; prior to that we must have an alternative outlook, with convincing roots in our political and spiritual tradition, which is capable both of giving birth to new policies and of sustaining them in their application and development.

And so the Britons were gradually led on to the amenities that make vice agreeable — arcades, baths and sumptuous banquets. They spoke of such novelties as civilisation when really they were only a feature of their enslavement.

(Tacitus, *Agricola* 21)

Chapter 4

The Modern Utilitarian Man

THE MODERN ARTIFICIAL UTILITARIAN POSITIVISTIC MASS-MAN

There is no man in the street who corresponds to the monstrous assemblage of words with which this section is headed. If such a representative person exists in contemporary society, he does so as an image — as a schizophrenic hallucination.

> There was an old Colonel of Kenya
> Who suffered from slight schizophrenia
> It wasn't his double
> Who caused him the trouble
> But which of the two was the senior.

Which of the two in the modern world is senior? The older image of man of the Western tradition, now exemplified separately in Christian, liberal and Marxist thought — the image to which all the best thought in the West has addressed itself — or the image of the man at the head of this section? To which of the two should the man in the street go for his values and his guidance in the personal decisions he has to make? This is the conflict which, almost undetectable in his external actions, at times threatens to destroy the core of his personality by the divisions it creates within it. Although the artificial utilitarian outlook constitutes the concrete standards of his everyday choices, traditional beliefs still give him uneasy feelings of 'ought' and 'ought not', and raise images of intentions which he would like to follow, but because of his superficial commitment to the other outlook, cannot. They are also in one form or another the basis of his political and legal institutions and of much else he values in his common life.

He certainly needs objective standards; for the more the individual is conscripted into the artificial processes dictated by modern positivism and utilitarianism, the more isolated and estranged from the human and material environment he becomes. The more too he becomes isolated from his society and its traditions. Thus, he experiences the need for beliefs that are founded in something more real, enduring and significant than the artificial processes to which his life is apparently devoted, yet also something more profound and understanding of his bewilderment than the philosophies and theologies of other generations. Because the world is now made up of the consequences of artificial processes, he senses the absence of God in the same way that he senses the absence of every other reality. Either he has abandoned God or God has abandoned him. It makes little difference, yet he yearns most passionately, secretly and muddle-headedly to awaken from the Cartesian dream and to find neither true.

If God has abandoned the world, left the individual subject in a state of atheism, or if God is dead, then there is no human nature, 'because there is no God to have a conception of it'.[1] Or the individual, although still believing in his existence, can no longer experience him as an objective external God. In either condition he is driven, because of his inherently moral nature, to seek subjective standards of conduct. These standards are at sixes and sevens with each other and present no harmony, nor even a pattern. They are gathered from totally different sources, arrived at through different theorems, or are the result of higgledy-piggledy passions justified by different sincerities. They may even come about as a result of his attempts to introduce into his private world human imitations of the motions and rhythms of the industrial world.

The corrective offered by the modern outlook against all this introspection and moral loneliness is the solace provided by mem-

1. Jean-Paul Sartre, *Existentialism and Humanism* (London, 1948), p. 29.

bership of the masses. This is nothing like as unpleasant as it sounds. Today the masses are not separated on one side of the class barrier as they were in the nineteenth century. All who look at television, use telephones or motor cars, travel on public transport, shop in supermarkets and multiple stores, buy brand-name commodities and submit to advertising slogans, are members of the masses. It is an abstract term that is employed as much for the sake of our convenience and for the sake of marketing men with their test questionnaires, as it is to denigrate us.

It will be seen how easily the contemporary idea of the mass man fits into the modern outlook. The mass man became conceptually possible as soon as the assumption was accepted that all men are governed by the same pleasure/pain mechanism. They were thus motivationally identical and functionally interchangeable. Men valued objects in terms of the amount of pleasure they gave, and men were themselves valued in terms of the number of pleasurable objects they produced. The value of a man was thus equivalent to that of a series of objects. These 'discoveries' put all men on a basis of sameness, rather than of equality with each other. They also put men in general on a basis of comparability with any collection of identical physical objects employed in a mass – bales of cotton or hundred weights of pig iron, for example. As soon as manufacture became organised on a relatively large scale with employers, technicians and managers on the one side, and workers on the other, the use of the idea in practice became well nigh inescapable. It was the crude assumption of all industrial and commercial processes of the late nineteenth century that labouring men, for production purposes, were identical quantities with similar predictable qualities. In the twentieth century, refinements have been made that allow for a difference between one individual's performance and another's, but have rendered the idea of the mass of mankind an indispensable assumption to many social sciences as well as to the policies of most large political and commercial organisations. Statistical laws state that whatever variations there may be in individual choices and actions, the behaviour of large numbers in the mass can be accurately determined. The certainty is no less than that of the behaviour of atoms *en masse*, however free may be the movements of the particles composing each one of them.

The discovery that the structure of the human cell is in some respects similar to both the structure of the atom and to that of the most distant observable galaxy of stars merely reveals that man is not entirely unique; but it does not and should not detract from man's own dignity. Pascal, one of the most sensitive minds of the seventeenth century, expressed much the same idea in his Pensées when he wrote: *'L'homme borné dans sa matière, infini dans ses voeux, l'homme est un dieu tombé qui se souvient des cieux'*. T. S. Eliot, a sensitive mind of this century, wrote:

> The trilling wire in the blood . . .
> The dance along the artery
> The circulation of the lymph
> Are figured in the drift of stars . . .
> ('Burnt Norton')

The artificial utilitarian mass-man does not experience this thrill. Or does he, and is he too inhibited to express it?

HIS KNOWLEDGE

The utilitarian man is certain only of that which he himself makes. His knowledge of reality is thus restricted by the artificial processes his civilisation has contrived from its limited and selective understanding of the ways in which universal nature behaves. This knowledge is no more than abstractions from nature of what is likely to be useful according to the utilitarian judgment of usefulness. It is merely the abstract utility of a limited knowledge with which he is familiar. And this limited knowledge is not true knowledge or understanding. It is 'know-how', and out of this know-how his society has been artificially constructed. Although he lives in an age that is fortunate to possess more knowledge than the Victorians would have dreamed possible, the modern outlook has taught the modern man to regard it almost solely through the narrow two-dimensional mask of sensation and utility. Thus his collective ambitions have become those of technical know-how, effortless mechanical labour and satisfied sensations. So accustomed have most men become to wearing this mask that they no longer think of the possibilities that knowledge has for them in terms of the older ideals of human independence and wholeness of personality. Instead they have come to regard their own roles in life as no less inevitable than those of the particles of energy on which those roles have been artificially modelled.

They too are parts of a process and the essence of process is its regularity – the fact that each particular pulse-beat of its articulation and rhythm is identical to the rest; hence, when the individual life is identified with a process, it merely appears to be a succession of moments of equal value. The now is the only reality he knows for certain. Tomorrow it may be forgotten, or doubted perhaps, in tomorrow's succession of moments. Thus the fullness, the relevance and excitement of contemporary knowledge is not understood as such, but as a series of moments, each separately grasped by a series of individuals, each isolated from the others.

In all this, the individual has lost his sense of wonder and sense of individual identity to stand alone and wonder. His ability to respond to the discoveries of scholarship and the inventions of science no longer has the edge it had. In this respect, it is not that his appetite for knowledge and wonder is surfeited; rather that, in accepting the part assigned to him in the mass by the modern outlook in its artificial processes, his only appreciation of the relevance of knowledge to him personally, and to his own interpretation of his own role in existence, is as the explainer and governor of processes. As a result his palate and his vision have been spoiled; he can only taste and see the artificial. As a result, too, he sees his role in the universal process and his role in society as corresponding: in the one as the equivalent of a particle; in the other as the equivalent of an item or quantity in a table of statistics on an administrator's desk. It is hard for him to believe these things and not see himself as part of a universal law of process, or one of numbers, and not also to think of them as true laws of nature in which his part and the parts of other men are utterly determined, and his own, because of its statistical insignificance, as irrelevant. It is hard for him also not to be affected in his private life – however intellectually independent it may still be said to be from his public role – by the values of this artificial utilitarian positivism. For man is a value-discerning creature and, however much it may be claimed that the structure and workings of his society are objective and valueless, he is bound by his nature to discern a hierarchy of value in it. It is inevitable, as we have seen, that the moral coinage of the industrial, economic and social mechanisms, with their emphasis upon the human sensations as reliable determinants of conduct, will also be used in his private life.

HIS PRIVATE LIFE AND MORALS

The activities of the artificial utilitarian man in private life – and what was stated at the beginning of this chapter must be stressed: there is no-one who is one hundred per cent artificial utilitarian man – are governed by the obsession that actions are only valuable if they are useful, and this instrumentality is somehow cocooned around the action itself. Similarly, time is well spent if it is spent usefully, which has three meanings: it can be productive in the way that working or digging the garden is productive; it can be pleasurable as entertainment or in the way that anything which satisfies the senses is pleasurable; or it can mean 'making use' of time as compared with the lady who sometimes sits and thinks and sometimes, reprehensibly, just sits. No one activity, no one way of spending time, is intrinsically better than another. Each has a name and each name has equal recognition. Objectively, each chunk of time usefully employed is the same as another. But privately it is permitted to make backward valuations and to say in retrospect that one such chunk was more enjoyable, therefore better, than another. To repeat this experience, therefore, is better than any other way of spending time.

The best evidence of well-spent time is something tangible, a useful thing: the modern house and garage is crammed full of evidence of a well-spent utilitarian life. Appearance, the most tangible sense-evidence of all, counts most in the utilitarian man's hierarchy of values. This is not because things are of intrinsic worth. On the contrary, it is because having particular things is proof of good utilitarian behaviour. They show that the owner has been obedient to the utilitarian 'scientific norm' in his work and in his private morals. He has played his part well in whatever particular process he has participated in, and has acquired the appropriate material symbols. What substantial and enduring items of mahogany were to the Victorians, 'consumer durables' such as motor cars, refrigerators and washing machines, with their much shorter lives, their built-in obsolescence, are to the modern utilitarians. Their ultimate importance, however, is to the industrial processes rather than to the home or to the individual: so also the host of proprietary articles and preparations without which no good man's home, however poor, would be complete; things for the bath, the sink, the dressing table, for the garage or for sitting next to somebody else in an underground train.

Nowhere is this materialism – the manufacturer's outlook – as blatant as when its values creep into the writings of some of its critics. When, for example, Simone de Beauvoir says, 'when a man deliberately sets about to debase man into thing, he lets loose a scandal upon earth that nothing can make amends for', or when she says, 'if I oppress only one man, all humanity appears to me as a mere thing',[2] she accepts the manufacturer's assessment of what he produces. She would much better have stuck to the text of Kant and said that the irredeemable sin is for the individual to treat other men as means for his own ends.[3] Although all things are instruments of man's purposes, they can also have intrinsic merit. The degradation of the value of things is as much a sign of the utilitarian outlook as its degradation of man. This is because for the manufacturer and technician, things are only the by-products of process. Neither the design nor the quality of things, nor the worker's feelings and values put into them – his workmanship – are of any real concern to them at all.[4] Everything instrumental has developed from the needs of the 'process' of which nominally man is master, but, in the ultimate Baconian sense, is servant and is expendable. Indeed,

2. Simone de Beauvoir, *Pyrrhus et Cinéas* (Paris, 1944), p. 140.
3. Kant's imperative is better understood as 'act only on maxims in adopting which you can at the same time wish that they should become universal laws.' To this he adds, 'So act as to treat humanity, whether in your own person or in that of another, in every case as an end, never as a means only.' See W. D. Ross, *Kant's Ethical Theory* (Oxford, 1954).
4. The very opposite of the existentialist view of things is taken by Jung, who sees a created thing, at least in part, as a reification of the collective subconscious and, in all respects, superior to the personal:
    The personal orientation that is demanded by the problem of personal causality is out of place in the presence of the work of art, just because the work of art is not a human being, but essentially suprapersonal. It is a thing and not a personality; hence the personal is no criterion for it. Indeed the especial significance of the genuine artwork lies in the fact that it has successfully rid itself of the restraints and blind alleys of the personal and breathes an air infinitely remote from the transitoriness and short-winded excursions of the merely personal.

everything, including the worker himself, has to become expendable in order that another phase of that process may be begun. In all this, the two theoretically independent spheres of the individual's private life and of his public working life have ceased to be separate. No sacred barrier lies any longer immutably fixed between the two. Every year the individual's private freedom is increasingly invaded by industrial and commercial forces. Once the priority of the latter has been granted, the more demanding do these invasions of private life become.

These circumstances make it easy to understand why it is that another mark of the utilitarian man is his utter faith in legislation. There is no wrong, no evil that it cannot remedy : no right, no good that it cannot promote. The result is a parliament

---

(From *Psychological Reflections: An Anthology of the writings of C. G. Jung*, selected and edited by Jolande Jacobi (London, 1928), p. 177.)

On the etymology of the word *Thing*, I am greatly indebted to Felicity Baker of University College, London, for the following note, which reinforces what I have said about man-made things belonging to a moral, aesthetic, feeling and interpersonal order. Marcel Mauss, *Essai sur le don* (1925), first published in England in 1954 as *The Gift*, reprinted London, 1970, is all relevant, but the Roman etymology mentioned here may be a sufficiently suggestive illustration of the point (Chapter III, p. 50ff):

The *res* cannot originally have been the brute and tangible thing, the simple and passive object of transaction that it has become. The best etymology seems to be that which compares the word with the Sanskrit *rah*, *ratih*, meaning a gift or pleasant thing.[16] The *res* must originally have meant that which gives a person pleasure.[17]

Mauss appends two footnotes to the above lines:

16. On this etymology see Walde. Cf. *rayih,* property, valuable thing, talisman, cf. Avestic *rae, rayyi,* same meanings; cf. old Irish *rath,* gracious gift.

17. The Oscan word for *res* is *egmo*. Walde connects *egmo* with *egere,* 'the thing one lacks'. Possibly ancient Italic languages had two corresponding and antithetical words meaning a thing which one gives and which gives pleasure (*res*) and the thing lacked and which one expects (*egmo*).

The 1970 edition has an Introduction by E. E. Evans-Pritchard, who remarks:

Mauss is telling us . . . how much we have lost, whatever we may have otherwise gained, by the substitution of a rational economic system for a system which exchange of goods was not a mechanical but a moral transaction, bringing about and maintaining human, personal, relationships between individuals and groups. We take our social conventions for granted and we seldom think how recent many of them are and how ephemeral they will perhaps prove to be.

that has little or no time for the consideration of the major issues and tendencies of the age and a statute book so full that no single person or body of persons can know or even comprehend its contents. Indeed acts of parliament become like so many terriers, worrying the public to distraction by their barking but very rarely biting.

All these pressures make the external world, even the conventions and personnel of the society surrounding him, seem to the individual to be independent of him, and he to be meaningless, totally dispensable, to them. His private wants, his need of other people and desire for objective standards become items in a world of private introspection. They dissolve into his fantasies, whilst he is forced to justify his private actions and aspirations purely subjectively. Until he comes up against an experience that is more real than any of his anxieties, he finds himself doing all this solely in terms of the artificial and utilitarian standards by which the rest of his life is governed. Thus, for example, he interprets rightness by its 'feel' and by nothing more. The pleasure/pain calculus associated with his working life has, of course, conditioned him to do this; and for so long has he been conditioned by it that it is no longer necessary for him to be aware that he is actually ruled by such a calculus. All that he needs to remember from this artificial point of view is that in his feelings is to be found his own sense of right and wrong. But, of course, this standard of private feeling places too great a burden on him. No part of life in the artificial society where he works, makes his purchases, is entertained and relaxes, equips him for so great a responsibility and state of independence. There are times, therefore, when his need to make decisions leads him down a private *cul-de-sac*, and he will find Descartes' Demon waiting for him there to tempt him to doubt not only the reality of his own feelings but even the genuineness of himself in having them.

Modern novelists and short story writers are often fascinated by this theme. It is variously treated as a problem of loneliness, individual freedom, individualism and even anarchism. The Marxist regards it as a problem of alienation; the existentialist, as one of *angst*, faith and commitment which leads into the arbitrary need to create a self-willed order out of the chaotic wilderness which surrounds the individual. Sometimes the predicament is purposely represented as absurd and sometimes as one that is essentially to be resolved by the relief of sexual tension in a manner appropriate to the particular individual. The least complicated and most faithful portrait writer of modern utilitarian man and woman in this respect is probably Alberto Moravia. In *Bitter Honeymoon*, for example, his men and women are simply and honestly worried by the difficulty of discovering truth in sexual relationships. They then face the problem of artificial utilitarianism at the most intimate level of personal life. How can one use the intensity of sexual experience as a means of knowing the truth between two individuals? Men and women desire a union that will not only last but be truthful in itself, and being modern utilitarians they expect the initial pleasure of physical attraction to yield this truth. Appearances, they must tell themselves, are true in themselves – the taste of the pie can be told by the look of the crust. But when they proceed to the stage of confirming their predictions in the experiment of the sexual act itself, they are disappointed – on one level – to observe that the standards of the greatest physical attraction and of the most excellent sexual performance do not necessarily correspond. They are disappointed – on a deeper level – to discover that the excellence of sexual performance is not necessarily related to mutually responsive love and to the personal truth for which Moravia's men and women, in common with all other men and women, are seeking.

To sustain this emphasis upon feeling and sensations is nervously exhausting and emotionally exacting. There are all kinds of aids: the cinema, speed, television series, as well as motor cycling, gang warfare and the urban guerrilla movement for adolescents. Yet in the end it becomes too much without more powerful stimulants. Drug addiction and alcoholism become common-place illnesses that beset and baffle doctors and social workers, none of them able to get behind the disease and cut out the causes in the artificial utilitarian way of life itself.

The modern outlook, however, can look after itself. It can, at this point, call out the principle of utility to mount a rescue operation. Feelings and sensations, it can say, are not always the best guides in private judgment. They have to be considered in relation to the principle of utility, which is impersonal, scientific and universal in its applications. This principle, therefore, steps onto the scene and puts these private cul-de-sacs out of bounds.

If Alberto Moravia's characters had adhered to the utility principle, they would not have been searching for any such mystique as that of permanence in human relationships. Pleasure is a utility and the matter need not be made more complicated than that, except to stress that the artificial utilitarian is not required to seek ends. He is guaranteed that, if he chooses actions which are useful, they will give him pleasure and lead to happy results and, conversely, pleasurable actions will lead to useful consequences. Pleasure and usefulness are the causes of their own consequences which go on being useful and pleasurable in an unending sequence. Moravia's characters should have been happy with these reflections and not have looked beyond the fact of the pleasure in their actions.

Because of the confusion between ends and means, between different grades of priorities and between different depths of meaning to the same words, because also of the absence of a commonly accepted scale of standards, conversations between modern utilitarians and non-utilitarians are restricted to the superficial. In conversations between artificial utilitarians themselves, communication is hardly more meaningful. The billiard ball never goes into a pocket; the technique is to bounce it back off the cushions of artificiality and to let it continue in another direction. Real topics can only be discussed in artificial terms; so that if the analogy of the billiard table is continued, one can say that it is one constructed without pockets. The modern outlook has successfully removed the *real* behind appearances, sensations, immediate utilities and tangible advantages. It gives only one standard of value : utility. It does not offer any criteria by which the more and the less valuable may be judged. One thing, one action, one thought is as good as another; or, looked at from the other way, as bad as another. The inadequate film or the Shakespeare play are on a par; they are good or bad, pleasant or unpleasant, ways of spending two and a half hours being entertained. The burning alive of people in a church, be they Greek or negro, is conversationally on a par with the failure of a football manager with his star player. They have made the same sized headlines in the morning newspaper or 'on the news'. Indeed, topics of conversation are much like the furniture of a room :

My room is furnished with people,
My carpet is threadbare with talk,
His church is as high as its steeple;
The doorstopper, ash tray and cork.

'Surely', one is bound to reflect, 'if this is a faithful description of modern man and his wife, then it is not relevant to attribute it either to the death of God or to his abandoning the world'. Rather, if it is true, it must be stated straightforwardly as evidence of the dying of man and of his abandonment of all the values of his humanity and deeper happiness. It must be seen as man who has abandoned the real for :

Carnival coloured dreams that die like confetti
Stained into dirty sidewalks wet with the rain
Of unjust desires.

The real and unreal alike have to be reduced to phantasm and epigram.

THE OTHER PORTRAIT

The above is not, however, the only possible portrait of modern man. Turn the canvas round and there on the other side is one that is equally faithful to another interpretation of him. Indeed a totally objective observer from another planet or from a distant age of the past might hardly notice the existence of the other, so impressed would he be by the attitudes of fair-mindedness and justice, compassion and kindness, and by all the other evidence of immense respect for the values emanating from the importance attached to personality. It is, moreover, these values and attitudes that prevail in all the important public institutions of Western society, and especially British society, as it exists in Australia, New Zealand, Canada and some former colonies as well as in the United Kingdom itself.

But it would not only be the reign of law, parliament, free speech and other freedoms that would impress such an objective visitor : so too would all the associations and organisations for generosity and good in different parts of the world, concern for prisoners and old people's welfare and all the efforts made in parliament, in local authorities and elsewhere for the unfortunate, the homeless, the unjustly treated and those handicapped in many different ways. Everywhere he would notice moral concern – true, on many occasions, very muddled – for issues of peace and war, for the unjustly and badly treated. Similarly he would be immensely impressed by all the many signs of revolt against the artificial utilitarian system, especially amongst the young. Even more impressive would be the fact that the demonstrations, revolts and strikes were permitted by the authorities and that those taking part did not lose their national assistance payments, unemployment benefits and grants. He might well marvel that the welfare state actually continued to pay the protesters and rebels their statutory entitlements and so provide them with the means to live out their rebellion.

All these facts stem from widely shared beliefs in the values and precepts of the traditional Western outlook and its immense respect for human personality. This outlook is fundamentally Christian, drawing on Judaic and Greek sources. It reached the height of its political influence in what is loosely termed the Western liberal tradition and this tradition can now be considered, again very loosely, as consisting of Christian and liberal with Marxist and social democrat sub-divisions. Yet however and why ever divided, they, at any rate as evinced by their best representatives, share the basic concerns the last two paragraphs have noted – concern for the values of human personality, concern for people and, although interpreted with great differences of application, for freedom and justice. In this connection one would have to think of Marx and Engels as representatives of Marxism, rather than of Lenin or Stalin.

Although they would probably be astonished to learn it, it is this traditional outlook of Western values – not in the form of any specific doctrine, but in terms of its priorities – that influences and justifies the rebellion of a great many people. Possibly there has not been a generation since the 1830s or 40s in Anglo-Saxon countries when so many individuals have been actively and seriously concerned to apply its priorities, however confused, to the actual conditions and circumstances of the years immediately facing it. What privilege, poverty and political corruption were to the Whigs and Liberals of the Reform Act generation, so materialism, false values, artificial utilitarianism and hypocrisy are to many of the rebels of the 70s. Their rebellion takes, of course, a variety of forms, many of which, such as hard-drug taking and violent weapons in the street, are totally objectionable. Nevertheless, much of the rebellion is constructive – even those who withdraw from society and live simple lives in communes intending to harm no-one. At their core is a body of people who have given up artificial, utilitarian and materialistic standards for good. The excessive and foolishly exaggerated gestures are not struck by them but by those surrounding them, who, in re-acting against the artificial standards of the society of their birth, have become even more imbued with its attitudes than their parents whom they affect to despise. Most of these, it is not surprising to find, are the very earnest children – and their voluble accomplices – of those most typical utilitarian and generous of all modern men and women – the inhabitants of the large industrial guilt-ridden cities of the USA. That they have reacted at all, or have seen the need to react, is, however, cause for hope.

PART II

UNSOLVED PROBLEMS OF LIBERTY

Do you know Dante? Really? Well, I'll be damned! Then you know that Dante accepts the idea of neutral angels in the quarrel between God and Satan. And he puts them in Limbo, a sort of vestibule of his Hell. We are in the vestibule, *cher ami*.

Patience? You are probably right. It would take patience to wait for the Last Judgment. But there you are, we're in a hurry. So much in a hurry, indeed, that I was obliged to make myself a judge-penitent. First, however, I had to make shift with my discoveries and put myself right with my contemporaries' laughter.

(Albert Camus, *The Fall*)

At this, Petro Bembo replied: 'It seems to me that, if God has given us the supreme gift of Freedom, it is wrong that it should be taken from us or that one man's share should be greater than another's.'

(Castiglione, *The Courtier*)

Chapter 5

Back- and Front-garden Liberty

Part I has described the dilemma of people living in the West and the two images of human purpose confronting them, between which they cannot choose. It has also described the composition of the outlook sustaining one of those images, the artificial modern utilitarian outlook; but it has not explained why the more traditional outlooks built on the values of human personality have failed. This chapter and the next will attempt to show that liberal thought has never with any real sense of commitment attempted to tackle the problems implicit in applying the principles of freedom and personality to industrial society; nor has it ever really solved those problems of freedom bequeathed to it by Europe's experience of the French Revolution.

The divisions in the liberal tradition itself can best be illustrated by pointing to the different moral and intellectual assumptions underlying two different sets of institutions and attitudes typical of all Western society, but especially of Britain. The first are its legal and political institutions together with its humane attitudes; represented respectively by the law courts, parliament or the 'individual freedoms', and the great number of voluntary societies or national welfare organisations. These are all founded on values of personality. The second set are its economic institutions, industrial structures and practices of commercial exploitation; these are all founded on the principles of the modern utilitarian outlook.

Part of the crisis we now face is due to the fact that the liberal thought on which Western society is based has never adequately confronted the problem of freedom in industrialised societies: how can people enjoy the vitality, creativity, sense of independence and freedom in their working lives that they experience, theoretically at least, in their private lives? This is no longer a problem that concerns the working class alone. Economic institutions have been created that, in spite of glaring defects in the machinery of the distribution of the wealth produced, go a very long way towards satisfying basic material needs; yet these very institutions have rendered self-subsistence impossible and have crippled the workers' capacities to achieve the realisations of the very values that the political systems of the liberal West promise. Moreover, the time has now come when the momentum generated by the success of economic activity not only threatens the political institutions but begins to transform them into creatures of its own will. Political activity and governments are fast becoming – in many instances have already become – little more than instruments and agencies of utilitarian economic planning.

THE CONFLICT BETWEEN TWO CONCEPTS OF LIBERTY

Side by side with the conflict between Western political and economic institutions goes that between two Western concepts of liberty. The philosophical form which this conflict first assumed – over a hundred years ago – was a belief that there were two separable spheres of public and individual activity and that the individual could be free only within the second. According to this view, which is most popularly associated with the name of John Stuart Mill, the individual sphere is at once extremely precious and extremely vulnerable, constituting the special preserve of genius and eccentricity, of the inventive and the novel – each of which is seriously endangered by the encroachment of public power, as well as by the expanding intolerance of public opinion. Public power – which meant the liberty of the state or the people collectively to act – was inevitable, and thus needed primarily to be bridled. But private power – which was the liberty of the individual to grow, create and put his abilities to good uses – primarily needed to be encouraged. Thus, typical of mid-nineteenth-century British liberalism was the view that public and private powers – and hence public and private liberty – were opposed.

From this position, and from the need to reconcile liberty with the independence of the applied sciences and of the economic and technological development generally, there grew up what might be termed the back-garden and front-garden view of liberty. In his back garden (there might be a gap in the hedge or fence – and probably was – but it made no difference) the individual was free to do as he wished, to cultivate his native abilities and characteristic inclinations, to take himself seriously or to behave as eccentrically as he wished. But in the front garden the individual faced the public highway and had to conform to the rules of public necessity. Here he was not free : he was a member of society, itself determined by the laws of technological and economic development; the laws of progress by which social evils would be overcome, poverty abolished and by which all would eventually be well. It was, therefore, only in the back garden that rights of individual liberty might be claimed; in the front, the individual had to be obedient to 'objective laws of development' and his claims of personal fulfilment had to be subordinated to the techniques and processes that his experts and betters deemed best, or which presented themselves as most fitting in the circumstances.

The case for the front-garden view of liberty rests upon the supposition that economic institutions contain a potential that, if left alone to develop unimpeded by extraneous human value judgments, will bring about the optimum satisfaction of material needs and, therefore, the greatest possible degree of human happiness. These institutions belong to the natural material, or physical, order rather than to the human order, so that man's role with regard to them is to learn those secrets of nature that are relevant to his purposes and to apply them, together with a sound knowledge of how his own natural desires are fitted to cooperate with such learning and application. Both liberty and economic development, according to this view, are pursued for the same end, and to separate their realms of effectiveness is merely a procedural distinction made for the sake of achieving the maximum human happiness. The economic mechanism, if left alone, will therefore bring about an utopian condition of plenty, and human interference or the intrusion of irrelevant ambitions, such as trying to incorporate the aim of enjoyment or of creative satisfaction in work, will slow down or hinder altogether the realisation of this possibility.[1]

This doctrine, if pursued logically or historically over a period of time, tends to the same position as that adopted by other forms of economic determinism, such as that of Augustus Comte or Marx or of evolutionary socialists. The house dividing the back from the front garden has to be rebuilt on a series of new sites, always moving towards the back boundary of the plot until there remains barely enough space for the clothes-line.

A more modern version of the doctrine of the private and public spheres of liberty places primary stress upon negative – formal or procedural – liberty, with which it contrasts positive liberty. This distinction, today primarily associated with the name of Isaiah Berlin, is based upon the difference between the freedom of the individual from outside interference so that he can live as he desires and the freedom to develop the best in himself and according to a single rationally understandable motive; the difference between doing what he wants to do and doing what he morally ought to do. Given this distinction, it is possible to maintain, on the one hand, that the term 'liberty' should only be applied descriptively to the doing of those things one wants to do, and on the other, to the doing of those things one ought to do. A writer like Berlin, following Mill's direction, holds or argues that there is considerable value, within certain limits, in merely doing what one wishes to do, whether one 'ought' to do it or not. Hegel, on the other hand, argues that one is only free when doing those things one ought to do; realising one's true self or some other form of rational self-direction; therefore, that the term 'liberty' should only be applied in those instances where one does those things.

The connection between the older 'public and private sphere' distinction and the more modern 'positive and negative liberty' distinction is that emphasis upon the importance of the private

1. There were exceptions to this view, as in the case of Malthus. But Malthus was in this important sense not a Utilitarian, for he believed that the maximisation of human happiness was not a possibility in practice. This he thought despite the blind operations of the market, and despite also all deliberate human efforts to ameliorate the disastrous consequences of these operations for the poor.

readily leads to a negative view of the state – whose purpose becomes that of defending the private sphere, with its originality and wealth of independent personality, against further public emasculation. Accordingly, it becomes right to legislate *against* the invasion of certain well-defined and recognisable liberties, but wrong to do so to further the individual's self-development or the realisation of his conscious purposes.

The reason for the aversion to positive liberty is, however, a practical one, namely that negative liberty can be asserted without dogmatism and ensuing violence, whereas positive liberty, before it can be pursued as an aim of social policy, entails the statement of a commonly accepted dogma of what are good purposes, of what is good. Such statements of good in the past have become ideologies, the altars on which millions of human lives have been sacrificed; in particular the detractors of positive liberty have in mind, of course, the ideologies of fascism and communism, and national socialism.

However these distinctions are formulated, the effects are very similar. The liberty of self-determination, of self-fulfilment, of doing with one's life as one judges best, is to be esteemed, but it is a liberty that is restricted to private life and free expression; individuals cannot challenge the underlying assumptions of the activities of public life in such ways as to effect changes in public structures that will enable them to be the fuller persons, or to make the fuller contributions, that in their consciences they think they ought. There is not simply a tension between the private and public, between the negative and positive spheres of liberty, but a barrier. Liberty of personal thought and expression is preserved, but liberty of action is denied at the point at which Acton's 'sincere friends of freedom' deemed it most valuable; that is, at the point where there is the possibility of individual thought, conscience and project being materialised in effective forms of public action. Moreover, and this is an additional cause of frustration, this barrier is not the clear, easily definable stationary line that exponents of negative liberty claim it to be. It is a shifting barrier; one that is always moving towards the position where it constricts the individual and walls him up inside his own solitary thoughts, sensations and private judgments.

TRADITIONAL BRITISH LIBERTY

There is one particular objection to both these accounts of liberty, which when developed becomes crucial. It is that neither half of the dichotomy, negative liberty and positive liberty, back- and front-garden freedom or public and individual freedom, coincides with the most precious forms of liberty originating in the Low Countries and Britain and now valued throughout the Western world. If this be so, then why emphasise these particular divisions of liberty – divisions, moreover, which exclude on either side much that we mean by liberty? This objection can be developed independently of Berlin's special definition, if three rather more conventional attempts than his, to distinguish negative from positive liberty in general terms, are examined.

The first states that, apart from any narrower meanings belonging to special theories, negative liberty means free from (a constraint or interference) and positive liberty means free to (do something) or free and able to act according to 'the determination of the will', as, for example, Hume defined liberty.[2] Assuming this distinction to be formally valid, it would not in practical terms add up to very much. Generally it is true that if someone is free from a given constraint, he is thereby free to do a great number of things corresponding to the class of the absent constraint. For example, if a man's legs are not tied, he is free to walk, run, hop, skip, and jump, or, of course, to stay still. It ought to be possible to think of a set of positive and good activities to correspond to each 'freedom from' acknowledged to be virtuous. In ordinary speech and also in oratory, such a correspondence is in fact assumed. Most renowned eulogies of freedom – for example, that of Pericles – have been made up of what its exponents would call negative freedoms – freedom of the individual from many constraints by the state. Yet to recall the celebrated funeral oration is to be reminded that the free life which Pericles praised had a very vital content. Indeed, this is what the speech is about. Similarly, if many other memorable panegyrics of freedom made at the time of resistance to aggressors or to tyrants are examined, it will be seen that what originally concerned the speaker was the quality of the active

2. David Hume, *Inquiry Concerning Human Understanding*, Essay 39.

life which aggression, revolt or tyranny put into jeopardy.

The individual's freedom from constraint without lawful cause is, of course, the basic freedom; but it is understandable that this should be associated, mentally at any rate, with the need to have the power to act according to the reasonable determination of the will. A man in prison does not only want to get out; he also wants, when out, to be able to enjoy his liberty at least as completely as anyone else.

The second familiar way of distinguishing negative from positive liberty is to say that its practice is concerned solely with the kinds of activity which enter into any normal definition of freedom (i.e. both free from and free to); whereas positive liberty is concerned in addition with justice. However, if what it is intended to mean by negative liberty is illustrated by the particular freedoms enjoyed in Britain, then plainly this basis of distinction is wrong. The concept of justice is at the root of every single freedom cherished in Britain. The most basic of all is the right to a fair and open trial before a person can be constrained for any wrongful act alleged against him. It is for this reason that we place such importance upon separating the judiciary from the government, the civil service and police forces. The normal liberal's hatred of the regimes of Hitler and Stalin is founded upon his detestation of the police state – arbitrary arrests, concentration camps and judicial murders – and not in the first place upon intense disappointment at the absence of equivalents to Hyde Park Corner, *The Times* and *Sun* newspapers and the Houses of Parliament. Eventually, of course, free speech, free comment and the freedom to criticise proposed legislation are all of a piece with a non-police state.

The third way of distinguishing positive from negative liberty is probably the most informative. This is to say that it is especially concerned with freeing the individual in accordance with principles of distributive justice, that is, with the distribution of what it is within the power and competence of the state to distribute according to the needs of the person to act characteristically of his free will. Thus, Hume's definition of liberty would be extended to include the material means so far as available – the institutions, the knowledge and the opportunities – for the individual to act according to the determination of his will : the faculty, the power, the means and the opportunities. This is

D

probably as sound a description of the ideal and ultimate aim of positive liberty as any other; yet in a minimum sense the recognition of distributive justice is the distinctive feature of every democratic state, because, although treating of wealth and honour, it implies also equal treatment of every citizen with regard to all material rights and liberties. In this third instance, therefore, as in the other two, the isolation of negative liberty is no help in identifying the kind of freedom, or the quality of life especially valued in 'the highly civilised societies of the West'.

The Dutch and British are probably the two countries in Europe since the Reformation whose liberties have been envied and copied most. It is easy, in the case of Britain at any rate, to see why they have been called negative in spite of the fact that conceptually they are both negative and positive and include at least as much justice as freedom. This is because many of the values and practices with which they are associated – especially those embedded in the common law system – go back 'beyond the memory of man'. People have grown up accustomed and secure in them. They have become traditions. It is natural to think they have come about without any special effort; also that they exist together and imply each other in a well defined and easily recognised area of non-interference. They are rights already enjoyed; they assert nothing beyond that to which the ordinary individual thinks he is already entitled. They do not have to be striven for. They come to be called negative, understandably, in contrast to those fresh rights which agitators and radicals wish to obtain for their own generation from complacent governments : liberties, perhaps, to act in ways or to acquire the means to act in ways which existing conventions, institutions or forms of property distribution prevent. To keep the traditional involves no interference with established rights and expected practice : to assert and establish new liberties does.

But let our governors beware in time, lest their hard measure to liberty of conscience be found the rock whereon they shipwreck themselves, as others have done before them in the course wherein God was directing their steerage to a free Commonwealth. (Milton, *The Ready and Easy Way to Establish a Full Commonwealth*)

Chapter 6

Liberty and its Sponsors

Freedom is a very much wider concept than the doctrines discussed in the last chapter imply. Except when speaking or writing of moral freedom itself – the freedom of choice between good and evil, right and wrong – to be free is a morally neutral expression. It is given colour according to the context in which it is used. A particular freedom or cause of freedom may be good for one man and bad for another; a given piece of wealth, for example, may enable one man to do many of the things he wants to do whilst being the cause of almost enslaving others to him.

Defined as the absence of all constraints, obligations and ties, freedom raised for Aristotle a picture of meanness and for Milton one of license. In fact, it is almost impossible for human freedom to be anywhere as total as this. People are born with physical needs and all their lives long have different needs of varying complexity, the satisfying of which ties them to means of various kinds. They can, for example, only live where there is water. Sharing the society of other men creates needs of another kind : these are satisfied in the first place by morals, laws, institutions and conventions and imply a state with at least minimal authority over life and limb. No reflective person, political theorist or ordinary man has maintained for long that it is possible for men and women in society to be completely free. Rousseau came close to doing so, and the soldiers of the French Revolution were responsible during a brief period for carrying the idea into one country of Europe after another. However, the subsequent histories of these countries showed that, when the concept was thus left in a void, it very quickly attracted the notion lying in the void next to it; in these circumstances, that other creation of Rousseau 'the general will'. Soon after that, millions of innocent people came to believe that the only proper subject for freedom was the entire collective that could be identified by the use of a common language. Thus began liberalism's, and later socialism's fatal association with nationalism.

Freedom tends to be employed as an emotive word which different people use differently according to what they want to be free to do or to the particular class of constraints from which they want to be free. Seen in this way, it is possible to select, from amongst many more, eight motives for large groups of people wanting freedom and two particularly important attempts to justify it. These form eight separate schools of freedom and two schools of justification. These schools are not mutually exclusive, and only the eighth claims to represent a commitment to a belief in the value of freedom as such. Not only is there competition and tension between some of the different schools; some also give rise to conflict between their own members. The freedom given to the expression in speech, writing and action of any particular belief or body of opinion is often a threat to other beliefs and opinions. Hence freedom in society can never be absolute. There has to be order and both conventions and laws to support it. A thorough and active policy of freedom implies a consistent and patient attitude of toleration to implement it.

Very briefly, the eight different motives for wanting freedoms of different kinds are as follows :

1. *From motives of self-interest.* This group consists of those, for example, who struggle against established authority, conditions and customs in order to better their own positions or to gain freedom in order to express their self-interestedness. This school comprises not only those with economic interests to further, such as those who cry 'no taxation without representation', or who call for the lifting of restraints on trade, but also those who are held in subordinate social and political positions by the existence of superior classes; indeed, any who are constrained by law,

authority, custom or superior power from seeking what they consider to be legitimate self-dictated ends.

2. *From religious motives.* This comprises those who seek freedom of worship and toleration of their religious views, rites and customs. Locke puts the case of this school :

> I regard it as necessary above all to distinguish between the business of civil government and that of religion and to mark the true bounds between the church and the commonwealth.[1]

Because of the particular emphasis this school places upon personal conscience, it is closely linked with the eighth, but it differs from it in that its members are prompted not merely by the voice of conscience and 'attraction of ideal right' but also by such group-interested concerns as the desire of a sect to claim the same legal status as the established religion and to pursue its own ways in freedom; thus to claim specific exemptions from more general laws.

A species of freedom sought from religious motives, but in reality a separate class altogether, is that freedom which the religious individual attempts to experience who tries to obey 'the perfect will of God'. When this motive is secularised and comes to be understood as obedience to necessity – or a necessary law of history or nature – it is the basis of both schools of justification discussed below.

3. *From the desire for intellectual freedom.* This may be conceived as a general demand for the right of everyone to freedom of thought and expression or as a particular demand made on behalf of a given class of intellectuals for their freedom as a class. Their case may be that society requires an intellectual elite for the promotion of its values, or the narrower utilitarian one of, for example, the physicists in Stalinist Russia who could realistically claim 'No freedom of experiment and discussion, no bomb'. Hence, contrary to general opinion – in the short term at any rate – the satisfaction of the demands of this school does not necessarily lead to the establishment of more widespread freedom. It may well lead, and in practice often does, to the limited freedom of a narrow class and no further.

1. John Locke, *A Letter Concerning Toleration*, Raymond Klibanski and S. W. Gough (eds.), (Oxford, 1968), pp. 65ff.

4. *From the motive to participate.* This is the demand to be free, to be an effective member of an effective group, to be a strong link 'in a chain of larger purpose'. It is not necessarily a desire to be included in democratic procedures as they are experienced in Western countries. It is often something more intimate and continuing than that – a demand both to be consulted and to play a recognised, responsible and full part not simply at election times but all the time; a demand, too, for the individual's role to be recognised as a significant one in a project of greater significance. On the basis of this last formulation, many authoritarian political movements have been founded. However, not only do black sheep belong to this school, but so also do many white sheep such as social reformers, social democrats, syndicalists and advocates of co-partnership in industry.

5. *From motives to remove the stigma of second-class citizenship from a group of people.* This is not the same as the first school. Other men can and do support the claims of minorities. This is the demand of human justice for members of minorities and under-privileged classes to receive political recognition, the same rights and treatment as majority groups and other classes. It is a demand made by members of offended groups themselves as well as by others on their behalf.

6. *From the desire to remove a specific category of constraint.*

. . . The liberty of the man . . . consisteth in this, that he finds no stop in doing what he has the will, desire or inclination to do.[2]

Members of this school select one particular 'stop' or hindrance which in their opinion is responsible for man's lack of freedom, and then claim that he should be exempt from its effects. Hence such slogans as 'freedom from want', 'freedom from fear', 'freedom from state interference', 'freedom from male domination'. The most celebrated is, of course, the plea for freedom from necessity. This interpretation of freedom meaning 'exemption from' is customarily contrasted with other more specific usages of freedom, such as 'freedom of speech and expression', or more precise and negative ones such as 'freedom from arbitrary

2. Thomas Hobbes, *Leviathan* (Oxford, 1960), p. 137.

arrest'. Members of this school are interspersed throughout most of the others.

7. *From the desire for collective liberty.* This is not the same as the motives of the fourth or fifth schools. It springs from individuals recognising that they belong to a group (nation, race, sect or class) which they believe to have a mission of some kind to fulfil, a purpose or function that can only be performed in independence – perhaps to throw off an oppressor, to achieve a collective ideal of some kind, or perhaps just to conquer weaker groups. Then from their identifying themselves with such purposes, these individuals do not so much want freedom for themselves as for the group with which they have identified themselves; they want to be governed by people of their own kind, who speak their own language, share their beliefs or ideals and who will perhaps conquer in their name or at least vicariously add to their prestige.

8. *From the claim that freedom is a self-evident value of human life.* This is a school whose commitment to freedom is total. They regard it as 'not only a value in itself; but the condition for the realisation of all other values'. It is believed by them to be far and away the most important value of society,[3] because it is needed for men and women to make their moral choices effective. For the modern era it has assumed ever-increasing importance because of what Acton calls 'the discovery of conscience in the thirteenth century'.[4] Moral duty for members of this school means everything dictated by their consciences for them to do : to be good and to do good; to put all their qualities of person and skills of body and mind to the right use. It means continually making demands for the fresh means and conditions of the individual using his freedom positively and constructively for the good of others as well as for his own. It means, as Socrates taught, using one's freedom to fight the injustices done to others even before thinking of the injustices under which one may oneself suffer. Milton has heroicised this vision of liberty of the eighth school :

I cannot praise a fugitive and cloistered virtue, unexercised and unbreathed, that never sallies out and seeks her adversary,

3. Acton, HF, pp. 3, 4, 288; FR, p. 107, and elsewhere.
4. Acton, LMH, pp. 31–2.

but slinks out of the race, wherein that immortal garland is to be run for, not without dust and heat.[5]

The fact has to be faced that this conception of liberty goes far beyond any normal definition of freedom. It claims not only the freedom, but also the effective means, the institutions and the resources for the individual to carry out whatever he may think is right or whatever he believes the mission of his life to be. It speaks of 'the attraction of ideal right',[6] 'the conscience of mankind',[7] the 'doctrine of clear ideas',[8] that in time become self-evident maxims of revolutionary advancement towards 'new constitutions of liberty'.[9] It sees liberty as a positive complex of ideas always stirring society to achieve fresh objectives and regards it in retrospect as 'a series of violent shocks by which the nations have struggled to shake off the past and to rescue the world from the reign of the dead'.[10] Clearly it is of such stuff that Berlin's objections to positive liberty are made. 'In them [those of this eighth school],' Acton again gives Berlin his ammunition, 'is a principle of revolution, if not aggression'. The passion for power over others is always a threat. The method of modern progress was, therefore revolution.[11]

Here then is the crux of the problem to which the theories of back-garden and negative liberty draw attention. The partisans of the eighth school have made some of the most valuable and original contributions to human history, and the same dynamic positive spirit is needed at the present time in order to recover for the working population the freedom and significance which utilitarian industrialism has denied it. Yet it is the fear of this type of dynamic liberty and of the positive methods used by its partisans that has arrested the development of all liberty in the twentieth century and thus prevented its going beyond its nineteenth-century political and legal achievements. Now even these liberties are in danger. Can, therefore, a vision of liberty such as

5. John Milton, *Areopagitica* (London, 1927), p. 13.
6. These are all expressions used by Acton.
7. Acton, LMH, p. 32.
8. Acton, quoted in G. E. Fasnacht, *Acton's Political Philosophy* (London, 1952), pp. 140–8.
9. Acton, Inaugural Lecture to Cambridge University, LMH, pp. 4ff.
10. Acton, LMH, pp. 31–2.
11. *ibid.*

Acton's and Milton's descriptions of the eighth school be rescued from the implications that Berlin pins to all forms of positive liberty?

Before it is possible to develop an answer to this question, it is necessary to examine in some detail the two intellectual attempts to justify freedom which characterised the most influential philosophies of the nineteenth century. It is in reaction to the second of these – those that have tried to justify freedom as a form of self-realisation identical with that of an historical identity – that most negative theories of liberty owe their allegiance.

These two schools of justification may be regarded as additional to the eight already described.

THE JUSTIFICATION OF LIBERTY

From the beginning of the nineteenth century onwards, there was an increasing desire to intellectualise and account for the concept of freedom. This was partly due to the inconsistencies, the violence and consequences of the French Revolution and partly, as already noted, to the success and prestige of the physical sciences. Liberty, equality and fraternity needed a fourth sister – reason; moreover, reason as understood by science.

Acton regarded freedom as a self-evident value of human life, which was itself valuable chiefly for the opportunities it gave the individual to achieve his moral purposes. His fellow members of the eighth school of liberty either shared this conviction or at the very least considered that the desirability of liberty could be assumed and fought for without question. But the more sophisticated thinkers of the nineteenth century were not able to accept either of these positions; they had already rejected the concept of self-evident truths as well as the method of deducing general moral principles from them. Natural law theories could no longer be used, as Acton wished, as the basis for a political science, an ethical science, or indeed for any social science at all. On the other hand, these thinkers were anxious that certain of the general principles vouchsafed by natural law should be founded on at least as firm ground as the laws of the physical sciences.

In the same way they wished the humanities and social sciences to have the same intellectual status as the physical sciences. Their situation was, therefore, in many ways anomalous. They liked many of the principles that Acton and the eighth school of liberty considered self-evident and wished to make them pillars of their own scientific theories and policies; but they could not do this without first justifying them in reason as they understood reason to be.

In order to extricate themselves from this situation, they were obliged to face the formidable problem of converting what for them were no more than moral preferences and personal value judgments into facts of the same solidity as the data of the experimental sciences. This could not be done directly. But they discovered a way round the problem and achieved what seemed to them equally satisfying solutions. The methods of the physical sciences, so it was fashionable to assert, were inductive in formulation and deductive in application : that is, from specific instances of observable data, it was thought that scientists first constructed laws of explaining the ways in which particular entities of physical nature behaved; then, having framed such laws in universal terms, they were able to apply them to particular practical problems as they arose. The more sophisticated thinkers of the nineteenth century sought, therefore, to use such a method in order to discover social and historical laws which would enable them to apply them to specific social, political and moral problems, and at the same time to justify such principles and values as they cherished. They recognised that in order to do this they were faced with more complex problems than the physical scientists. Society and history presented a great number of facts and tendencies. What they had first to do was to distinguish between the significant and the irrelevant; then from the significant not only to formulate universal laws, but also to explain how the constitution or mechanism of individual human nature was related to the historically inevitable and therefore why it was that individuals were willing to cooperate in bringing it about.

If the problem could be seen in this way, it would become possible to justify freedom as the necessary condition for men lending their entire support and good will to the realisation of these historical laws. As men were free to give or to withhold this support, their 'right' use of freedom must make all the difference between the slow and more rapid fulfilment of such laws. Indeed, behind the desire to discover them lay the belief that mankind had reached a stage of development where not only men's acts, but also their motives, could be rendered entirely amenable to reason, and that they could be induced to forgo the temptation of following the more obvious courses of irrational action.

Thus were formed the two modern schools of justification; each using its own form of reasoning, its own special theory of truth, in order to justify freedom, and besides freedom, a great many other values and judgments of value; the first school argued that the rationality of history could be explained by a law of inevitable progress, an evolutionary law relating material progress, human happiness and individual development; the second, by a law showing how the historical absolute realised its will through certain chosen concrete entities, such as a particular nation, church, state, class or race, and how the individual's own potentiality could only be realised through his devoting himself to these entities.

Both schools of justification assumed, however, in formulating their laws, something far more fundamental than the reality of self-evident truths or of values such as freedom. They took over from 'natural law' theory, without any questioning at all, the very basis of all the convictions it yielded, namely the certainty that 'all things worked together for the good'; the belief that history moved to a desirable end, to discover which was both to be able to name 'the good' and to explain the *modus operandi* of an historical law.

The first school was utilitarian; therefore it had to justify freedom first by an historical law of progress and next by making use of its own special theory of truth. This theory of truth is described in Chapter 2 above. It was a double-facing theory which provided for objective truth and also for a utilitarian standard by which to judge it. Objective or scientific truth, for utilitarians, was always associated with, and could invariably be verified by, the pleasure principle, or utility; that is to say, it assumed that any increase in knowledge would be made useful through the applied sciences and this application would give pleasure. That theory or explanation was true, therefore, which at one and the same time yielded objective knowledge and also yielded useful results in terms of satisfied appetites and heightened sensations. Thus, if increases in knowledge eventually meant, through this application to industry, an increase in material goods, and an increase in these entailed greater happiness, then progress became inevitable; for men were bound to do what would make them happy and be forever goaded on by the prospect of increased doses of happiness.

With its theory thus established, the first school was able to justify its particular version of liberty. It took as its starting point a definition of liberty similar to that borrowed by Acton from Abbé Sieyès: 'liberty is that which makes men completely master of their faculties in the largest sphere of independent activity.'[12] Liberty, by setting men free and by ensuring the best development of their powers, created the only conditions possible for the fullest and most varied discoveries of (scientific) truth (third school), and enabled them to apply that knowledge to yield their own greatest satisfaction in terms of appetite and sensation. Only through developed individualities and by free thought, free expression, free discussion and by trial, error and experiment could the truths of physical nature be maximally knowable. Secondly, only so could methods and means be found of applying such truths to the human situation and obtaining the maximum benefits – the applied sciences and industry (first school). From this point it turned its attention to the social sciences free of any ethical considerations and of the unpredictable variety of human behaviour and choice. The development of the social sciences, too, had to be conceded the widest sphere of independence; only so might objective truth be pressed to yield the highest satisfaction of human wants. In the end, this theory of truth led to the compromise doctrine that complete liberty inevitably entailed the best independent development of its two separate concerns, of the individual on the one hand, and of the applied sciences and technologies, on the other. The 'back-garden area' of liberty and the 'front-garden area' were both self-contained and isolated from each other. Each must be allowed its separate liberty.

The second school of justification, in contrast, drew on the motives of the fourth, fifth and sixth schools and associated them with some of those of the eighth. It was historicist but denied the assumption of utility. Reality, it said, presented itself to the individual consciousness as the unfolding of potentiality. The

12. Acton, FR, p. 169.

natural or physical order, through time, revealed this unfolding
of potentiality which was directed towards a rational preordained
end and was realised by the combination of exceedingly minute
parts into larger and more intelligible wholes. Similarly, the
socio-political order revealed through time a potentiality trying
to reveal itself through individuals and through their combination
into more significant entities – societies, states, nations, races, and
so on. This process of realisation would only be complete when
it reached its purposed end – the perfection of civilised mankind,
which was to be recognised not only as moral perfection, but also
as a concrete reality, the perfect social entity in which the
rational will would finally declare and embody itself. History,
was, therefore, moving stage by stage towards the materialisation
of the purpose contained in all things and in man as the supreme
collective species of history. Thus, the truth and the rational
good for the individual were synonymous terms. His truth was
his realising his own best nature, not as an end in itself but as a
part of a process of combination; he was a social being and his
own potentiality could only find goodness and significance in the
reality of a social entity, a good higher than himself, which in time
would become combined with others into a yet more perfect
entity.

The second modern school, therefore, united something very
similar to Acton's doctrine of conscience to its special theory
of truth, as it proclaimed it. 'Conscience is the highest and best in
man', and it is justified (not provoked, as Acton said) in its
pursuit of liberty 'by the attraction of the ideal right' and which
seeks to 'establish its own conscious purposes'. But, said this
school, the highest and best in any individual man is but one
single, one very small portion of ideal right and his conscious
purposes are only infinitesimal parts of the rational good, a very
much larger reality which is only fully expressed in such concrete entities as states, nations, classes and races.

This same theory may be expressed in a less mystical way :
freedom lies in the individual's self-determination or self-realisation; the essence of the self is rational will; the truly free person,
therefore, will only want what is rational. Since the rational is
embodied in a process that is broader and more inclusive than
an individual's life, the appropriate good at which the individual
must aim is a good external to himself. Thus the rational will is

only fully embodied in – or fully achievable through – the institutions of concrete entities such as the nation, class or race. Each branch of this school, according to its particular philosophy and interpretation of the facts of contemporary and historic society, has selected one of these entities – a particular class, race or nation – as the only true expression of the rational will and of the ideal right with which the individual should identify the highest and best in himself. Moreover, this entity, because it was the rational good, had an historic mission to embrace all humanity and its triumph was a necessary truth. The rational individual, therefore, being aware of this ideal right, and of its identity with the best in his conscience, would only be free if it were achieved; its achievement would accordingly be his own self-realisation. Moreover, being vouchsafed this knowledge of the rational good and knowing that it was latent in all men of good-will, he would not wish to keep its secrets from them. It was indeed his duty to share it and to see that his less intelligent fellow-men understood it. As the history of this century has shown, there have been no limits to what he would do in order to ensure that this end was achieved: he has not shirked at bludgeoning or shooting it into the brains of the more obtuse or resolutely opposed of his contemporaries.

There is another point. Although the rational individual was able to see plainly the connection between his own self-realisation and the good of the higher entity with which he had chosen to identify himself (the choice is offered by a number of higher entities competing for his loyalty – for example a German in the early 1930s could choose between a communist class-loyalty and national socialist, Aryan-race or German-nation loyalty), he must also be wise and humble enough to recognise his own inability to interpret how that good should be brought about. Instead he would trust implicitly the judgment of the men chosen by party-voting procedure or by destiny itself to rule that entity. He would submit himself to their authority. Their judgments were infallible and he was only truly free and self-realised when he obeyed them.

The principle of these branches of the second school of justification are the principles of the inquisition at its worst: truth is the prerogative of a select body of men with a message of salvation that justifies every human obscenity. Thus have been born all modern movements of violence and the uniqueness of human life rejected as the ultimate principle of liberty.

POSITIVE AND NEGATIVE LIBERTY

If these examples of the second school of justification are to be taken as representative of the desire for positive liberty, it is easy to sympathise with the sentiments of advocates of negative liberty. All attempts, they say, to achieve positive liberty have led either to wholesale violence or to despotic or to arbitrary government; therefore the more modest, more easily controllable aims of negative liberty (even if it has to be admitted that this is a name none too accurately given to a conservative theory of liberty) are to be preferred : they at least enable us to keep the precious civil liberties we have and perhaps occasionally even give us some bonuses in the shape of well-constructed schemes of social reform.

The argument is easy to follow, but ought we accept it? There are two fairly obvious flaws in it. For one, it assumes there to be an unbreakable connection between all theories of positive liberty and either historicism or authoritarianism. It reaches this conclusion because of a faulty starting point, that the good at which the individual's self-realisation should aim must be a more extensive good than the individual's alone *and* that, because it is more extensive than himself, it must be located or defined by an agency above or more important than himself. This agency in the case of historicism is an impersonal law of history, and in the case of authoritarianism an individual or group of individuals wiser than the ordinary person : for in practice, authoritarianism tends to need an authoritarian leader to render its 'laws' into explicit positive terms.

The second ground of criticism arises from the first. The argument assumes that there is only one form of positive liberty, namely the claim to self-realisation made on the supposition that men have necessarily only one purpose in them to realise and that this is a rational self-direction. The philosophical notion of the rational will is a strict one, and was doubtless adopted in the nineteenth century to bridge the distinction between fact and value; for, if men can rationally discover their purpose in life and freely accept it as good, then their freedom becomes related to a verifiable fact. But this single-choice concept of freedom is not what the ordinary man understands freedom to mean. For him the essence of the free life in practice is that it offers a variety of choices and sometimes even a conflict of good ones; and the essence of positive liberty is the idea that society, to the degree that can be afforded, should enable the ordinary individual to make his well-balanced and realistically considered choices effective by there being available to him an equitable share of resources that he can transform into the means of carrying them out. If there is conflict, it need not be tragic; there are law courts to iron it out.

There is a third objection, this time to be made against the utilitarian upholders of negative liberty; and this is not so much against their interpretation of positive liberty as a *tu-quoque* argument against their basic position. As we saw above, the utilitarian justification of liberty with its emphasis on a separate private and public sphere is historicist. It relies upon a law of inevitable progress related to material determinism. It does not regard the individual in any significant sense as free at all. He is not free to change material or historical tendency: nor free to name something as evil and stalk it down; nor to shake off the chains of unthinking routine which artificial utilitarianism has allowed mechanistic progress to impose on him. Where artificial utilitarianism is kinder to him than the second school of justification is that it does permit him a private house where he can relax from the severe and often heroic disciplines imposed upon him by the necessities of the public sphere, and a back garden in which he may be as eccentric or odd as he wishes. But if wars and revolutions can be shown to be the result of the second school of justification, it is easy to demonstrate that mankind's present spiritual plight and dilemma has been caused directly by the utilitarian school's uncritical support of the mechanistic law of progress and by linking it, freedom and happiness to the capacity of men's appetites and sensations to exploit that law to the full.

If these indeed are the flaws in the argument of upholders of negative liberty as the only rightful interpretation of freedom and if the connection between positive liberty and historicism and absolutism is not a necessary one, a more widely and liberally conceived concept of positive liberty will be worth thinking out afresh in independence either of any kind of historicism, absolutism or authoritarianism. True, it would still be difficult to ascribe any virtue to the demands of self-realisation, self-determination or self-fulfilment if it could not be shown that they lead to a recognisable good or goods. But why must this good be defined and called 'The Good'? Still more, why should it be selected by someone different from the agent himself? Then, we may enquire, how can an individual be morally free, unless it is he alone who decides how to dispose of his person and his actions and it is he alone who asks himself to what ends both his person and his actions should be devoted? But we must also ask how, if such decisions are required of the individual, he may face up to making them in some kind of solidarity with other men, so that the cause of freedom loses the loneliness and anxiety that many thinkers now associate with it.

Freedom, understood as something positive and joined with creative-ness, becomes creative energy. Freedom means not only freedom of choice, but choice itself. Freedom cannot be simply a formal self-defence; it must lead to creative activity. The transition is inevit-able. . . . (and it is) by means of this that human society itself is creatively transformed. (Berdyaev)

Chapter 7

Freedom and the Human Condition

FREEDOM AS INDIVIDUAL NEED AND LIBERTY AS PUBLIC POLICY

It is now possible to return to the problem left unresolved in the middle of the last chapter – that of developing a workable concept of positive freedom without the blemishes attributed to it by the exponents of negative liberty. A solution to this problem is sorely needed in the contemporary world, if, on the one hand, the precious and long-established rights of freedom and justice are to be preserved; and, on the other, the mechanistic materialism and positivism of the modern utilitarian outlook are to be challenged effectively.

When the last two chapters are looked at again, in particular the account given of the two schools attempting to justify freedom, it will be found that two distinct subjects have been discussed.

One subject is freedom, especially the individual's own need of freedom to follow the good or goods chosen by him; the freedom due to him as a person both to make effective moral choices and to turn the qualities of his life to creative uses in accordance with those choices. In the present century, this kind of personal freedom has to be put in the context of the urgency of the individual's search for his significance in a mostly alien world of de-humanised practices and synthetic objects from which often all values, except the useful and commercial, have been extracted. Also the fact has to be faced that, although much richer than those living at the beginning of the nineteenth century, most individuals today have been obliged to surrender a very considerable portion of this kind of freedom to large collectives of one kind or another and to a great number of mindless pressures derived from them.

The other subject of positive freedom is really quite different. Here the word 'Liberty' is employed more often than 'Freedom' and stands for more than 'Freedom' does; it is associated with other concepts, especially justice, that make up the social ideals of Western Christian civilisation. It thus becomes a broad umbrella name for a great number of separate public policies directed against the inevitable constraints of human life. Under the shelter of this umbrella first one condition of man's servitude to man or of his bondage to necessity and authority is attacked, then another and then another. Often the umbrella name is misused; people try, and often succeed, to put policies under it which have no right to be there; many of the first seven schools noted in the last chapter press their own claims for their particular *ex parte* interpretation of liberty to be the sole basis of public policy.

Liberty in this second sense has been a particular concern of those who write about the human condition. Developed by them in an atmosphere free from certain academic constraints, it has become a word to express a great many of intelligent mankind's yearnings for a fuller human life. It has, as it were, been taken out of its more normal context as a strict term of political thought and employed by a number of other disciplines concerned with human behaviour, history, psychology and anthropology; even by disciplines concerned primarily with other species. Sometimes it has been given its most suggestive meanings in imaginative general literature; for example, in the writings of French and Italian existentialists.

It is worth noticing that the reconciling of these two ways in which the words freedom and liberty have come to be used is another aspect of the problem of human significance summarised at the end of Part I. How can these two sets of ideas be reconciled: one, human freedom and the search of the individual for a full, creative and significant role for himself in industrial society; the other, liberty as a public policy and the search for at least a minimum objectivity to the personal values that must underlie the articulation of such a policy?

The human-condition understanding of freedom attempts to place these two sets of ideas in the same model of thought. How the reconciliation must proceed can best be seen by studying some of the suggestions of the nineteenth-century precursor of this view – Acton. Although he often used the words almost interchangeably, he is one of the first writers who are made easier to understand if one thinks of the word 'freedom' as meaning either 'free from constraint' or 'free to carry out the determination of the will', and the word liberty as meaning the public policy implied in rendering freedom fully effective in both of these two senses.

THE ACTONIAN VIEW: LIBERTY CONSIDERED AS FREEDOM, JUSTICE AND OTHER VALUES COMBINED IN A POLICY OF DEVELOPMENT

Acton's approach was, of course, that of an historian who believed that all that was finest in history could be written as the study of mankind's progressive struggle for conditions of greater liberty. He also wrote as a political philosopher, although not always with the consistency and regard for rigorous thought nowadays expected of a philosopher. It was the human condition acted out by and seen through the eyes of those men whom he called 'sincere friends of freedom' that he used his immense knowledge of human history to describe. For him it was the consciences of these men and the concrete, practical ideas developed by the curiosity and good will that an active conscience stimulates, which were responsible for the liberal attitudes and finest achievements of Europe in the modern age. This was the theme of his celebrated essay, 'Freedom and the Modern State'.

The notion [of Conscience] was restrained, on its appearance, by the practice of regarding opposition to church power as specific heresy. . . . With the decline of coercion the claim of Conscience rose and the ground abandoned by the inquisitor was gained by the individual. There was less reason for men to be cast of the same type; there was a more vigorous growth of independent character, and a conscious control over its formation. The knowledge of good and evil was not an exclusive and sublime prerogative assigned to states, or nations, or majorities. . . . its action was to limit power by causing the sovereign voice within to be heard above the expressed will and settled custom of surrounding men.[1]

First and foremost, the concerns of conscience were moral and it was the expression of these in speech, in writing, in activity and in material achievements that needed the growth of conditions of liberty[2] and made liberty itself the chief end of human social life.[3] Choice was itself a concern with moral implications. The individual had a duty to identify his life with a moral purpose or a number of moral purposes. He had to stand for values and objectives outside the range of his own self-centred desires. As the notion of freedom of conscience gradually became accepted as an essential Christian principle, so it demanded a greater corresponding measure of personal liberty. When its domain was extended from that of belief to action, it set in motion great political, religious, intellectual and pioneering movements – and sometimes, much to Acton's resentment, movements of unrestrained nationalism.[4] It enabled individuals to be 'masters of their own faculties, in the largest sphere of independent action'.[5] Also it awoke in them awareness of the plight of those worse treated than themselves, compelling the better off in society to recognise the injustices done to others as well as to condemn broader categories of social evil. When any of these were overcome or reduced, Acton saw the actions done as 'triumphs of liberty' or as 'the victories of its minorities'. Acton concluded his eulogy of conscience with words that reflected the developing social concern of the nineteenth century and that were prophetic of the welfare legislation of the twentieth. This he did by singling out as a special triumph

1. Acton, LMH, pp. 31–2. See also HF, p. 3; 'By Liberty I mean the assurance that every man shall be protected in doing what he believes to be his duty against the influence of majorities, customs and opinions.'
2. 'The growth of Liberty is to be identified with the cause of morality, and is the condition of the reign of conscience.'
3. Acton, HF, pp. 22, 298.
4. HF, Chapter 9 passim, especially p. 288; 'Nationalism overruled the rights and wishes of the inhabitants absorbing their divergent interests in a fictitious unity.'
5. FR, p. 161, quoting the Abbé Sieyès.

of liberty 'the domain of disinterested motive; this growing concern for the weak in social life'.[6]

Acton was neither an analytical thinker, nor a systematic writer, so that one has to search his many lectures and essays in order to find consistent meanings for the concepts he uses most frequently. Liberty for him is in one sense the condition or 'the security', as he frequently expressed it, for conscience to pursue its positive aims; in a second sense it is the positive activity itself; in a third, it is a state – liberty is the highest and best in man; in a fourth, it is a value in its own right. Because he saw the whole experience of human life to be the reflection of man's striving for moral value, he regarded the institutions of society as no more than a flexible framework to be improved upon whenever possible by enlightened generations for the sake of their moral struggles and eventual triumphs. Hence liberty for the realisation of moral duty is 'the end of civil society'.[7]

The concerns of liberty and conscience were different, but the territory they covered was identical. Once, therefore, it had been established that the growth and development of each worthwhile value and policy in Christian civilisation had its roots in 'the psychology of conscience', the jump from liberty to its objects could easily be made. He more than once quoted Sieyès approvingly : 'They fancy that they can be free and yet not be just';[8] and on the basis of this and similar assertions, he wrote as though the growth of justice and freedom as practical working concepts in the world were irreversibly intertwined and the practice of one was the necessary condition for the fuller realisation of the other. To these he added 'the cause of morality'. The growth of these three not only depended upon each other, but were for the sake of each other.

Of course, Acton knew that freedom, justice and morality were independent concepts and independent values. As an historian he was only too well aware that one could be practised without the other : indeed, in the course of any epoch, the concentration on one to the exclusion of the other produced great instability and imbalance in society, usually resulting in social upheavals

6. LMH, p. 33.
7. Compare 'The Christian notion of conscience imperatively demands a corresponding measure of personal liberty', HF, p. 203.
8. FR, p. 102.

or discontent on a wide scale. His point was different. He was not writing of absolute or conceptual justice and freedom but of the very limited degree to which their realisation in history was made possible by their being measured against each other; by their achievements meeting in each other, balancing each other, and by improvements in institution and by other means which affected both equally. Freedom, as he understood it, was the supreme value of individual life. In this respect his language was not far away from that of some twentieth-century existentialists : the individual is always confronted by moral choice and to be himself he must choose for himself. But it is not only the essential value of the individual's life (essential because an individual is still free to make moral choices even under a dictatorship or tyranny, as the stories of Sartre's character Matthieu, and Camus' Rieux show); freedom is also a category of law and politics, the condition for the full realisation of all other values. Only in an environment of freedom can the human personality flower and justice really be done. He had in mind not only the justice of the law courts but, even more, social justice. Here again Camus makes the point for him :

There is no justice in society without natural or civil rights as its basis. There are no rights without expression of those rights. If the rights are expressed without hesitation it is more than probable that, sooner or later, the justice which they postulate will come to the world.[9]

THE EIGHTH SCHOOL OF FREEDOM AGAIN

The association of freedom and justice, as well as of morality and all the other values thrown into prominence by conscience, was the habit of political expression shared in reality by a very much greater number of people than Acton implied when he referred to them as 'sincere friends of freedom' who 'have at all times been rare'. It was this large class of people who in the nineteenth century was responsible for the achievements of free-dom and justice on a considerable scale, and who in this century has wished that similar achievements could be made in the economic realm, both so as to give the worker his just dues and

9. Albert Camus, *The Rebel* (London, 1953), p. 254.

to make the typical place of work an intimate environment for the exercise of skills. It is indeed a class made up of all those who, across the span of history and the spectrum of politics, have wished and do wish themselves to be regarded as liberal or Christian. The prime assumption of their approach to political issues has been admirably described by Sabine : 'at the core of this mode of thought was a fundamental postulate about the nature of value, viz., that all values inhere ultimately in the satisfactions and realisations of human personality'.[10]

Liberty is the name which has been given by the leaders of this body of thought to the policy which, whatever the circumstances, attempts to maximise these satisfactions for the greatest number of people, and also links as far as in practice is possible the applications of freedom, justice and a moral view of life. This school of thought has tended sometimes to use abstract words loosely and thus freedom or liberty has come to stand for all the virtues which it has valued in public life when they have found a state of balance in each other in conditions of general political liberty.

In effect, the concept of freedom in Christian civilisation, at any rate since the Renaissance and especially in Anglo-Saxon countries, has occupied the position of preeminence that justice occupied in classical Greece. This becomes increasingly apparent if we accept Aristotle's two definitions of justice; general justice as that justice 'which answers to the whole of goodness . . . being the exercise of goodness as a whole towards one's neighbour',[11] and particular justice as 'that part of the general which consists in behaving fairly'; and more apparent still, if we add to these two definitions the idea of distributive justice – social fairness. As Ross observed, 'justice in this sense . . . is thus co-extensive with virtue, but the terms are not identical in meaning; the term "justice" refers to the social character which is implied in all moral virtue but to which the term "virtue" does not call attention'.[12]

For Acton, liberty was the social conscience permeating the whole of active life which, given free rein, obtained social fairness, and it was the individual's conscience in action in conditions

10. G. H. Sabine, *History of Political Theory* (London, 1951), p. 562.
11. Aristotle, *Ethics*, Book 5, Chapter 2, para. 10, Baker ed. 1946.
12. W. D. Ross, *Aristotle* (London, 1937), p. 209.

of free choice which made actions virtuous or not. But claims made by Acton in the name of liberty go far beyond those the Greeks could possibly have made for justice. Liberty, for the whole of the wide class whom Acton and Sabine described, is not just one simple idea, the motive for following which is to be free from one particular constraint, or to be free, or even empowered, to do one class of thing. Nor is it a demand to be free of all constraints imposed, or sanctioned, by human authority : nor even simply, although it does include it, a demand to be free and empowered to do a great number of things. Instead, it is a complex of ideas. It is concerned with what is implied by freedom as well as with the formal and procedural freedoms themselves. It is concerned with the policy of liberating men and women from all that hinders them from doing what they think they ought to do and also, on its positive side, a policy which encourages the flowering of personality in activity. In the early days of the rediscovery of the idea of liberty in modern Europe, it could be seen as, for example, Montesquieu described it – the goal of just laws. But after Rousseau, the true liberal understood that it was liberty, in its guise as the moulder of radical policy, which created the laws;[13] and for this purpose it needed the authority of the state to be on its side.

None of those in Britain who formed the eighth school of freedom, certainly not Acton, believed that the objects of either freedom or justice could be won solely by taking away privileges, rights and possessions from establishments, elites and those with authority. True, such people, and such bodies, it could be seen, greatly constricted the power of lesser privileged people to act purposively and to carry out 'the determination of their wills'. But so also did the necessity imposed upon human life by nature. Thus knowledge and discovery – ideas – were as liberating as political revolutions; were, indeed, the causes of them. 'It is truth which sets men free'. Acton even saw the growth of medical knowledge with its promises of a longer mean life span and greater freedom from disease as conspicuous evidence of the revolutionary power of liberty itself. Thus, it was right to speak of the 'Scientific Revolution' and the 'Industrial Revolution' in the same way as the 'Glorious Revolution' or the 'French Revolu-

13. Acton, LMH, p. 32. See also Appendix to his Inaugural Lecture, 'The Study of History', note 43.

tion'. Only radical changes derived from ideas aimed at creating conditions for men to use their freedom creatively, and to be more fully and effectively themselves, could properly be called revolutions.[14] This is a point we shall be at pains to elaborate in a later chapter.

Closely associated with men's struggle against the constraints imposed by physical necessity was the whole problem of the economic realm and the redistribution of property rights, without which men would not have the means to make constructive use of their liberty. 'A man's most sacred property is his labour'.[15] In Acton's view it followed, although perhaps not obviously, that all who contributed to the creation of wealth through work or services should have rights at least as strong, but not necessarily the same, as those of ownership. The type of British middle-class liberalism represented in the nineteenth century by Mill and Gladstone and expressed vividly in the doctrine of back- and front-garden liberty never understood that industrialism created conditions in which the working man was denied these rights, indeed, any positive use of his freedom at all. Especially in his letters to Gladstone's daughter, Mary, Acton looked forward to 'the new Socialism' achieving an immense redistribution of wealth.[16] One of the tragedies of the twentieth century is that it has not done so.

Acton was really a philosopher of liberal revolution, and his 'sincere friends of freedom', that rare minority, were really liberal revolutionaries. Liberty, for him, was, substantively, a spirit that hovered above society, ready, if invoked, to move it forwards towards morally, politically, and intellectually better conditions; and, formally, a policy that must constantly be reformulated in order to give men the means, mental and moral as well as material, to reach towards the just, the free, the good, the

14. LMH, p. 3, See also F. Engels, *Anti-Dühring* (1877), Part I.
15. Acton, FR, p. 11. It is, according to this passage, a right prior to that of property. A man 'must be free to make the best use of it he can'. Free labour is one of the first two conditions of legitimate government. The power of government must intervene to guard the individual (having this right) from oppression.
16. Acton, LMG, p. 72. If Adam Smith were right that labour was the only source of wealth, 'it was difficult to resist the conclusion that the class on which national prosperity depends ought to control the wealth it supplies . . . ought to govern instead of the useless productive class, and that the class which earns the increment ought to enjoy.'

true. Thus it was that the old notions of formal liberty, of text-book liberty, dear to the philosophy schools, made no appeal to Acton.

The old notions of civil liberty and of social order did not benefit the masses of the people. Wealth increased, without relieving their wants. The progress of knowledge left them in abject ignorance. Religion flourished, but failed to reach them. Society, whose laws were made by the upper class alone, announced that the best thing for the poor is not to be born, and the next best, to die in childhood, and suffered them to live in misery and crime and pain.[17]

Liberty was man's perennial revolt against the limitations of the human condition, a continuing state of revolution against all the restrictions which limited human life – the constraints imposed by nature and ignorance just as much as those imposed by inept political constitutions. Thus, of the many definitions of liberty which he quoted from French and German writers in the appendix to his Inaugural Lecture delivered to Cambridge University, the two which probably best represent his powerful insight into the nature of liberty as public policy were the one which described it as a continuous pressure, 'the motor and regulator of society moving it and shaping it to its own image', and the other which asserted that liberal and constitutional government 'was and ought to be a state of perpetual battle'.[18]

LIBERTY AND VIOLENCE
This heady rhetoric revives rather than allays the fear of Jacobinism. How may it be possible to preserve from invasion and violence the back garden of private liberty and 'the easily recognisable territory of negative liberty' or all those liberties and rights of justice that have come to be considered as 'individual freedom'? This is a question we must ask again. Acton had three replies available to him. First, he could say that man is a rational creature and just as his freedom is given to him to work

17. HF, p. 94.
18. Brisson, *Revue Nationale* 23, p. 214, quoted in Appendix to LMH, p. 327; and de Serre-Broglie, *Nouvelles études*, p. 243.

out his salvation by use of his reason in conjunction with his creative energies, so his reason is given to him to use his freedom responsibly and justly. History shows that as events become more complex, so ideas and principles tend to become more clear, and as they become so, they become more manifestly right. This is the 'doctrine of clear ideas' which he attributed to Leibnitz. The individual had to measure the ideas and projects of his own conscience against the more enlightening general ideas of common reason and to adjust them to axioms of general meaning. Second, he could say that there is a limit which must be put on all campaigns for greater liberty or even greater justice. This limit is prescribed by the ultimate principle of liberty – the sanctity of human life. The same point was made by Camus more than sixty years later in response to almost the same dilemma :

> Every rebel, by the movement which sets him in opposition to the oppressor, therefore pleads for life, undertakes to struggle against servitude, falsehood and terror, and affirms, in a flash, that these three afflictions are the cause of silence between men . . .

> In a flash – but that is time enough to say, provisionally, that the most extreme form of freedom, the freedom to kill, is not compatible with the motives of rebellion . . .

> The true partisan of Liberty rebels in the name of life, so that its conditions may be more just for all.[19]

All values under condition of the fullest liberty must find their common limit in each other, this limit being 'precisely (the) human being's power to rebel'. The principles of freedom and justice, of compassion and a fully moral view of life, act as checks and balances to each other. Pursued together they produce balance and proportion.

Third, Acton valued the principles of both constitution and authority, as the means of sustaining liberty. The revolutionary and constitutional principles were complementary. The enemy of liberty was oppression, not authority. The enemy of authority was anarchy and self-will, not liberty.

19. Camus, *The Rebel*, p. 248.

British thought has never been obsessed, as French thought has been before or after Acton's time, with the spectre of authority as the sole and permanent enemy of liberty. Nor has authority, or the state itself, been posed against the individual so starkly and deliberately as it has been in France. Many continental thinkers and those who might now be called anarchists have conceived of liberty very simply as either the absence of an heredity or of any authoritative power, human, natural or supernatural, over them – what the England of Milton would have considered to be licence, and of Burke, anarchy. In Britain, majesty has been the endowment of that set of prerogatives in which church, state and law separately meet; not of the state separately. The British liberal may mistrust authority, dislike the conventions of the establishment and be determined to control the use of power by qualifying the rights it gives to office holders so that these are never greater than is appropriate to its functions. But he does not deny the need of authority in society nor see it as 'the enemy'. Indeed, he needs it for his own special purposes.

Similarly, British thought has never been obsessed, as German thought has been, with the absolute regarded sometimes as history and sometimes as necessity. In guaranteeing order and giving sanction to general, particular and distributive justice, the state, according to British thought, is necessary both to the rule of law and the reign of liberty. Moreover, from the time of the beginnings of the Scientific Revolution in the seventeenth century, it became clear to the politically conscious in Britain, especially to the Whigs, Dissenters and others whom we now call liberals, that liberty had many other enemies besides authority – above all, ignorance, anarchistic moral standards and material scarcity. The severity of these three restrictions could be greatly reduced and, whenever this happened, men would be much more able to carry out their chosen ends and therefore, be more free. Only in a secondary sense, that is, simply in so far as they were conservative, did establishments and privileged classes oppose the expansion of freedom in relation to men's common bondage to the human condition. The Scientific Revolution and the Industrial Revolution provided material advantages which all classes could share and be at least partly liberated from the age-old chains of necessity and ignorance – the chains could be greatly lengthened and to that extent greater freedom would be possible.

FREEDOM AND THE HUMAN CONDITION

The human-condition view of freedom may now be stated. All human activity, seen either from the standpoint of the individual or of the human race collectively, it suggests, is bound by limitations of two kinds; those which arise from the necessity of nature and those which arise from the defects of human nature, psychological, political or moral or whatever it is they are. Throughout their lives men collectively have to deal with both types of restrictions in four typical ways; and these ways can also be represented as four typical pursuits of different kinds of good. The first is through seeking knowledge; in this way they hope to learn about both types of restriction, that is to say, about the constitution of human nature and of physical nature. The second is through economic activity and productive installations; the third through institutional, political and legal means – enlightened and just authority enforcing cooperation, interpreting justice and so on; the fourth, by moral and personal means. Each of these typical activities, therefore, seeks greater freedom for humanity from a typical constraint in a distinctively different direction of good. Each direction points to a goal or standard regarded as good in its own right : truth, abundance (or enough-and-enough-to-spare), perfect cooperation, human integrity.

The problem to be faced now is how these four different concepts of freedom and of good may be related in the same model or illustration of thought; and how, thereby, the different aims of various militant interpretations of freedom may be reconciled to each other whilst at the same time giving validity to the individual's own search for his activities to have significance. An analogy can be used to illustrate this problem and to show how eventually it may be solved.

We can say that ignorance, scarcity, defective cooperation and human ambiguity are the names of the four boundaries of the human condition itself – the field of limitations. Over against each of these boundaries, undefined but intelligible as points outside and infinitely beyond, are the four typical ideals of human ambition; truth, abundance (or enough-and-enough-to-spare), perfect institutions and human integrity – the ideal of the 'fully human man'. Living in this field is the typical individual human being with his needs of balanced personality and balanced values requiring to be reflected by a balance between the forces in his environment. For these needs to be met, the sides of the field have to be in proportion to each other; the moral and material have to meet, match and parallel each other; so too do the intellectual and the institutional.

The desired proportion which this analogy illustrates must not be thought of as quantitive proportions as though human values were commensurable; but rather as the balance of constitution and character and aspiration, so that each of these typical human values can be given equal emphasis, equal importance and consideration. If any single one should be regarded with more attention than the others, then the human condition gets out of harmony and man's development loses the equilibrium and sense of fairness it needs. There could, of course, be a fifth or sixth or seventh or eighth class of flexible limitation. If so, this would not affect the illustration. If it were an exhaustive class, the same rules of proportion would need to be applied to whatever quality it represented.

Reflection will in fact show, if we think hard enough, that in all probability, all the problems of political and social thought which we ourselves encounter, for example, all theories of freedom or of liberty that legitimately compete with each other, are covered by this analogy.[20] Not only can all eight schools of freedom as described in the last chapter be included under one of the four headings; but so also can Marx's freedom achieved through the understanding of necessity and Engels' freedom from material necessity, Berlin's negative freedom, the socialist's ideal of freedom sought through institutions, the moralist's freedom found in obedience to the moral law and, of course, constitutional freedom, the quintessence of the third limitation itself.

20. Maurice Cranston, in his succinct *Freedom* (London, 1953), quoted R. S. Peters, for the suggestion that the terminology of freedom and constraint can be employed in discussing all our major social and political problems in terms of philosophy. He believes that all the most important questions in political theory can be discussed under the headings of Peters' proposed programme, viz.:

the limitations on freedom imposed in nature;
constraints of law, morality and convention;
freedom and constraint in education;
the role of the state in constraining the individual.

There are many limitations upon human abilities to act and carry through desires outside the range of the four discussed here; but they do not present either political problems or aspirations of liberty to satisfy. Men are not magicians, cannot stay still for long, cannot swim through the air or jump into the clouds at will. But more important than these examples is the fact of no certainty in almost every single aspect of human life. Men are born, live and die : there are no other certainties. More tantalising and, in some senses, more fascinating, challenges to the creative artist especially are the two absolute unalterable limitations which have a prominent place in classical philosophy: 'Out of nothing is nothing made', and 'everything perishes'. These do not form boundaries in the illustration.[21] Because they are unalterable, men can do nothing about them. However it adds a certain tension to the field of limitations as an illustration of the human condition, to say that these two absolute conditions

21. The boundaries of the field can also be reached by a process of logical division as follows: by comparing man as a species with the rest of nature, it is possible to distinguish six broad categories of imperfections; the first two absolute and the remaining four relative and contingent. These imperfections limit all that he does or attempts to do. Man is part of the world, needing to draw upon its resources for his sustenance and survival. Also, like everything else in it, he perishes. In these respects, he shares with the rest of the universe two limitations which he is unable to alter in any way: first, that of being unable to provide for any of his needs or projects out of nothingness and second, that of perishability.

Third, he shares with all animate things a limitation that he strives to lessen. This is the restriction imposed by the scarcity of the world's materials to satisfy the needs of his own nature. Seen from another aspect man is separated from the world and from everything else in it. This is by virtue of his awareness of it as an entity external to his own self-consciousness; also by virtue of his desire to impress upon it, and thereby to change it with, his constructive projects. Unlike the rest of nature known to him, he is dissatisfied with his condition and his aims that make use of concepts of perfection. These concepts arise from his lack of knowledge of the universe by which he is surrounded and from his own consciousness of the more perfect person he would like to be. Fourth and fifth, therefore, he is unable to see himself to be limited by his ignorance and by his divided nature, part rooted in the world and part seeking the perfection set by these standards of truth and integrity he cannot attain his ambiguity. Finally, each man is part of mankind with common needs and common human nature and sharing many aims with other men; yet also he is an original identity, different from other men with aims and methods of his own that conflict with theirs. Perfect human cooperation is impossible to achieve and therefore constitutes the final limitation upon men's aspirations and activities.

underlie all the activities, all the aspirations and all the yearnings of those living in it. Similarly, and closely related to these two absolute conditions, are those of space and time.

Within the framework of this illustration, many questions concerning human significance, human activity and aspiration and a full policy of liberty will be discussed. This is the task of Part III.

E

PART III

THE CREATIVE OUTLOOK

Long time hath Man's unhappiness and guilt
Detain'd us : with what dismal sights beset
For the outward view, and inwardly oppress'd
With sorrow, disappointment, vexing thoughts
Confusion of opinion, zeal decay'd
And lastly utter loss or hope itself
And things hoped for. Not with these began
Our Song, and not with these our Song must end.
                    (Wordsworth, *The Prelude,* Book 12)

It may seem strange to you that man should concern himself with Utopians? Utopians in an epoch of proletarian dictatorship! Where's the inner logic of it? Admit that you are surprised!
(Alexei Tolstoy, *The Road to Calvary*, translated by Edith Bone)

Chapter 8

The Field of Limitations I

Part II has shown how liberty is often regarded in two ways; one, as the individual's need for freedom in order to fulfil himself in a distinctively personal form, and the other, as a public policy illustrated by the concept of men collectively living out their days in the field of limitations. This illustration can now be developed to show how these two very different ways of considering liberty may be reconciled to each other.

UTOPIA AND FALLIBILITY

How feasible are the aims of self-realisation or self-fulfilment? This is not a purely abstract question. There is a prevalent view according to which fulfilment is impractical and irrelevant to the complex character of society. Progress, according to this view, is what matters; and progress is the outcome of social movements devoid of all personal aspects. It is not, therefore, to be accomplished by aiming at fulfilment or even by considering it. Even those who do not believe that progress is so important, or so impersonal, may join in disclaiming all personal aspirations, simply because they disclaim the excessive nature of all aspirations. Violence and bitter disappointments, they claim as we have seen earlier, are the outcomes of any attempt to change society by asking it to follow any positive or consciously formulated aim.

Those who take this last stand are joined by others who urge the more sober view according to which progress should be achieved

evenly and with sufficient guarantees. It cannot be carried out
they suggest, by a forward surge, nor even in a manner that i
aesthetically or otherwise pleasing. On the contrary, it car
only be the outcome of men patiently eradicating well-recognised
evils – one at a time – not in any set direction, but first in one smal
area and then in another. The correct analogy for social reform
of this opinion is to the clearing of the jungle surrounding a
secure and orderly base rather than to a line of march. This
is the approach offered by advocates of piecemeal engineering
notably by Karl Popper.[1]

At the other end of the scale of political argument are the
utopians, each of whom has described a vision of perfect human
happiness, achievable on reaching a particular ultimate o
human ambition. By naming these ultimates, four types o
utopia can be distinguished. With the first, perfect knowledge
can be associated Simone Weil's interpretation of Descartes
dream of pure knowledge descending on to the earth in term.
of geometrical axioms relevant to every human problem, o:
the eighteenth-century philosophers' dream of a heavenly city a
described in Carl Becker's work of that name. With the second
abundance, Marx's state of ideal communism defined as freedom
from necessity, or Bacon's New Atlantis, the paradise of the
applied sciences. With the third, perfect institutions, Plato's
Republic of perfect institutions or Thomas More's Utopia o
common sense customs and conventions. With the fourth, the
perfectibility of human nature, there are the visions of Godwin,
Shelley and Bakunin of a paradise of human integrity.[2]

Each of these utopias does not simply describe the imaginary
conquest of a particular human limitation, but invites the reader
to believe that in conquering this particular boundary the fortunate utopians will cease to be restricted by the others as well
However impractical or unrealisable these utopias may be, they
have in common one undeniable merit. They all reflect a yearning to achieve a particular good that men from the beginning of
life have experienced; yet, at the same time, each somehow be-
trays an awareness that in the constitution of human life these

1. Compare Popper's objections to utopian engineering, *The Open Society
   and its Enemies*, (Princeton, 1963), p. 159.
2. For Popper's views in detail on the helpfulness of standards, see the
   Addendum to Vol. 2 of *The Open Society*, pp. 369, 381–93.

goods lie beyond the boundaries of achievement. Even the most
cynical audience is sensitive to this tension.

The various handlings of the Faustian legend are perhaps
literature's acknowledgement of the almost magical nature of
these boundaries that separate the articulation of men's goals
from their realisation. For man to cross them would involve
him surrendering all kinship with other men; but for him not to
wish either to cross them or speculate upon the nature of the
goals that lie on the other side of them would involve him in
renouncing even more – the human soul. Then again, one is
somehow intuitively aware that to break the boundaries or to
tear them asunder where they join one another would be an
obscenity which neither fate nor prudence would forgive.

> I have smelt them, the death bringers, senses are quickened
> By subtle forebodings . . .
> (T.S. Eliot, 'Murder in the Cathedral')

Utopias have this undeniable dramatic quality. Do they not
also have something practical to offer the piecemeal engineer?
For him surely the values of utopias is to be considered as
residing in the recognition of these four particular and typical
ultimates of human ambition rather than in precise prescriptions
for realisable forms of society. Is there not a sense in which
piecemeal engineers cannot afford to neglect the intuitive
recognition of certain categories of human aspiration, certain
descriptions of good, that utopias provide? How else than by
the objective standards they set up – truth, sufficient materials
to meet all human needs, perfect cooperation and human integrity – can the piecemeal engineer himself name the areas
around the base camp that are evil, and step by step go about
eradicating them? Moreover, would his activities not be far more
intelligible and capable of being followed, if he were not only to
clear the jungle around the camp but also to cut paths through
it towards these recognisable goals, thereby creating arrowheads
into the gap between us and them? Is this not what in fact he
tries to do? After all, it is the conviction that better human
conditions are the result of institutionalising individual ideas and
actions which is at the bottom of the philosophy of piecemeal
engineering: surely we need some understanding of how institu-

tions come about in this transition from the personal to the social? Popper would probably be the last to be deaf to the plea that the piecemeal social engineer should select his target with reference to the criteria offered by these objectives, provided, of course, he would say, that the social engineer were conscious of his own limitations and were critically aware that his interpretation of the standards he used needed correction and adjustment in the light of new moral and practical experience : for example, of any unintended consequence his well-meant actions did not foresee.

There is another point in this approach which might appeal to piecemeal engineers, and would almost certainly appeal to Popper; namely, that by introducing these ultimate standards of human ambition while admitting that they lie beyond the capacity of human definition, let alone of achievement, the idea of fallibility is introduced; whereas to eliminate them, thanks to this admission, is to fall prey to the idea of infallibility here and now. Man can never define his standards clearly and, even if he could, because of his moral ambiguity he would never seek them wholeheartedly. For moral as well as intellectual reasons, therefore, he never reaches any of his ultimate goals; but he would make very little progress at all if he did not work on his imperfect images of them and set out on his way towards them. They are directional points for all the activities he would describe as good.

The contemporary reader may well be prepared to accept the fact that in pursuing truth or human integrity, men will always fall short of perfection, but will be impatient with the assertion that an age of world-wide abundance is as unlikely as a state of perfect knowledge or perfect human behaviour. He may admit that at present one quarter of the world's population enjoy two-thirds of its resources, and that the population itself may be doubled within the next forty years, yet may still claim that technology developing at its present pace and combined with adequate and fair institutions of distribution will ensure all having their material needs supplied. Even if these claims were optimistically conceded, and it were conceded too that modern man is as yet nowhere near as zealous to produce food for other societies as he is to produce luxury and semi-luxury goods for his own, it is incontrovertible that men's appetites and their conception of what is necessary to them for a normal life can be almost infinitely expanded. In the *Republic*, Plato makes the same point.[3] In primitive agricultural societies men thrive on a simple diet of barley-meal and wheatcakes, salt, olives, cheeses, fruits and vegetables and live very heartily; but, 'if you wish to see a state of fever heat', you will have to add sofas, tables and many other sophistications of civilised living. And two thousand years later Marx echoed the same theme : 'the number and extent of man's so-called necessary wants are themselves the products of historical development and depend to a great extent on the degree of civilisation of a country'.[4] New knowledge and new applications create new necessities. Medical discoveries give rise to demands for adequate sanitation and water supplies in one generation and to sophisticated drugs and apparatus in the next. As brooms and brushes and kitchen sinks become plentiful, so refrigerators and dishwashers become the next objects of universal demand.

If men were to live by bread alone, needed only a staple diet and a minimal standard of clothing and shelter, the problems of scarcity might conceivably be soluble. But men's natures are not like this. They need literally 'all that they can put their hands on' to express their different projects and purposes. The more civilisation expands, and the more men's greed for practical knowledge and what we now call technology grow, the more complicated and varied do all these demands on material production become. Far from appearing closer, the day of total satisfaction seems to recede, and, instead, the day of catastrophe comes closer.

EXCESS

The rule of proportion is the measure of a healthy, civilised life. This, the golden mean, which must not be confused with the English idea of the middle way or compromise, was the rule cherished by classical Greece, and it is also seen by many modern writers as the only direction for contemporary society to take, if it is to extricate itself from excess, violence and tyranny. 'Absolute Freedom mocks at Justice. Absolute Justice denies Freedom', says Camus in *The Rebel* :

3. Plato, *The Republic*, Book 2, Jowett's translation (Oxford, 1892), Vol. 3, p. 53.
4. Karl Marx, *Capital*, ed. F. Engels (London, 1887), Vol. 1, p. 150.

To be fruitful, the two ideas must find their limits in one another. No man considers that his condition is free if it is not at the same time just, nor just unless it is free. Freedom, precisely, cannot even be imagined without the power of saying clearly what is just and what is unjust, of claiming all existence in the name of a small part of existence which refuses to die. Finally there is a justice, although a very different kind of justice, in restoring freedom, which is the only imperishable value of history.[5]

When the boundaries of the field are in proportion to each other, activities within it are varied and compounded of features drawn freely from the well-developed characteristics of each boundary, and the total of activities represent a balanced entity. When they are hideously out of shape, as they are now, the activities within them are distorted, unbalanced, ugly and overspecialised. The initiatives to correct this shape and to restore balance to the human situation must come from the human base-line by means of which men are able to make personal and true of themselves what otherwise would be entirely utilitarian and materialistic activities.

The many other excesses of contemporary industrial society have become so well-known that, in order to argue that the field of contemporary human existence is excessively distorted, one need only name some of the headings under which they, or their consequences, are discussed. There are the tensions caused by the proletariat attempting to start their working lives enjoying standards previously only attained by the bourgeoisie after years of hard work and thrift; industrial alienation, pollution, overcrowded centres of production and administration; the giddy isolation of families in tower blocks and the solitariness of the bed-sitter; the threatening crises of food and energy shortages, and the billions of items of wasted materials and millions of wasted labour hours spent on replacing consumer durables and capital equipment with built-in obsolescence or in producing shoddy gimmickry. There are also the grotesque facts of uneven distribution; the poorer countries send away to the richest the raw materials of utilitarian production yet receive in

5. Albert Camus, *The Rebel*, (London, 1953), p. 255.

return comparatively few of the manufactured goods and food-stuffs into which they are made. Yet, if this situation were to be suddenly changed and, for example, the populations of India and China, perhaps together as many as 1,500 million, decided to acquire the productive techniques of the West and of the USSR and of Japan – if these people become mesmerised by the spell of the artificial utilitarian process too – then scarcely any power on earth or any inventiveness could save mankind from coming to the end of many of the earth's resources or save the environment from an intolerable degree of poison.

These speculations point to the fact that the greed, materialism and selfishness created by the modern outlook's emphasis upon appetite and sensation, no less than the ways in which it has taught men to look upon the objects of the natural world – the animal, vegetable and mineral kingdoms – have created a distance between man and nature that is not compatible with his dependence upon it for his existence. It has also created a void in the average man's spiritual values and an insensitivity to any preoccupation other than his own. So excessive indeed is the spirit of materialism and the cult of individualism that the height of fashion for the intellectual surrounded by a plethora of manu-factured goods is to denigrate what he calls 'the world of things' – his comfortable chair, his desk, his stereo, his radio, his lighting system and his books. Utilitarian man has alienated himself on the one side from the natural order and, on the other, from that very world of making and enjoying things which was once re-garded as an extension of his creative nature and the tangible evidence of his concern for aesthetic values.

But it is important not to be pessimistic to the point of despair about all of these items. Once standards are changed deter-minedly and individuals are willing to alter their priorities, decisive actions can be taken by governments to reinforce these standards. Moreover, the mass communication media are able to bring home each new crisis or peril to human life as it emerges. As this happens, public opinion has shown itself quick to react – sometimes possibly too hastily – to demand fresh policies, pro-vided these policies do not immediately affect the pockets or material standards of its own broad masses. It is possible, there-fore, that the fear of men not being able to bring under control items such as industrial pollution – or at least of their not being able to bring them into proportion with the rest of mankind's problems – have sometimes been stated too uncritically.

THE TWO ABSOLUTE RESTRICTIONS

Besides the four limits of ignorance, scarcity, defective coopera-tion and human ambiguity, human existence is beset by two other limitations which fascinate and challenge the noblest of men; but, unlike the other four, which are relative to social develop-ment, these two are absolute and unalterable. They underlie the entire field of existence. One of these is the condition of perish-ability. Everything fabricated or living in the field has defects of structure and either wears out or dies. This condition may be resisted for many centuries, but in time all gives way before it. The other, which is complementary to it, is expressed by the old philosophical maxim, '*ex nihilo nihil fit*'. Out of nothing is nothing made. Against these two conditions human life perennially strives, but it is impossible to overcome them. Nevertheless, the attempts to do so characterise some of the most cherished activi-ties of all. Man is therefore driven on the one hand to recognise the impermanence of his fabrications, and, on the other, to search for ideas that are free of these physical limitations. But although this search may sometimes yield what may seem a time-less idea or form, even the most abstract kinds of communication, such as music and the plastic arts, break down under the demands of expressing such ideas perfectly and lastingly. Moreover, all the forms in which they can be embodied are perishable – scores, metal, stones, plans, canvas, plaster paper – and human beings themselves. Leonardo is dead. One day Mona Lisa will die too.

Despite these inevitable facts, those who believe in the power of ideas remain. There are some, they would point out, which if destroyed and forgotten could be rediscovered – a pythagorean theorem or a particular invention. There are others, they would say, which, perhaps because of the very impossibility of men ever expressing them completely and perfectly, and because they arise from their most intimate experiences, will continue to undergo attempts at expression whilst human life itself endures. As long as there is human tradition to value and discuss them, to try to capture and express them, they will remain. If Mona Lisa were to perish, there would yet be living artists – painters, poets, sculptors and even musicians – to try to express the idea of the enigma of the human face. According to this view, even if concepts such as freedom and justice were to be deleted from every political constitution of every country in the world and if every book containing their names were to be destroyed, philosophers, poets, artists and less talented men and women too would yet strive to express them and to find for them fresh formulations.

The medium then which expresses these ideas, these distillations of human experience, are only the packing cases; and the meaning of words, as well as the niceties of art-styles and conventions and even political constitutions have not the same significance for one generation as for another. The original medium helps to express and pass them on; it is the cocoon of the grub. The fullness of the meaning hovers above both and is never completely materialised :

> If all the pens that ever poets held,
> Had fed the feeling of their masters' thoughts,
> And every sweetness that inspir'd their hearts,
> Their minds, and muses on admired themes :
> If all the heavenly quintessence they still
> From their immortal flowers of Poesy,
> Wherein as in a mirror we perceive
> The highest reaches of a human wit.
> If these had made one poem's period,
> And all combined in beauty's worthiness,
> Yet should there hover in their restless heads,
> One thought, one grace, one wonder, at the least,
> Which into words no virtue can digest.
>   (Marlowe, *Tamburlaine the Great*)

But if men were to desist continuously attempting to realise it through the mediation of their experiences, this thought, this grace, this wonder, would cease to be.

THE SIGNIFICANCE OF ACTIVITIES WITHIN THE FIELD

The thoughts of men free-range far beyond and above the limitations imposed by the boundaries of their public lives; also, on their own and in their intimate relationships, they are very much more free to behave in accordance with their highest standards than in their public activities. Then the problem arises, how apart from pioneering the boundaries, can men achieve original purposes characteristic of their own natures and at the same time carry out activities that are relevant to and share the limiting characteristics of all four boundaries of the field? How in such a frame are the aims of the free man to be illustrated?

This undertaking is not as difficult or as paradoxical as it sounds, especially if, for the moment, one forgets the irregularities and excesses that mis-shape the field at the present time and instead think of one that is well-proportioned. Seen by a remote super-human observer who is only concerned with measuring and recording the collective achievements of humanity the field would be described as an area bound by four limiting lines, each one of which had behind it one fixed star – an ultimate standard of human ambition on to which the great numbers of men appeared to march – total knowledge, abundance, perfect institutions, and human perfectibility. He might even describe these fixed stars as 'directional goods', or give them more traditional moral names such as truth, enough-and-enough-to-spare, perfect freedom and holiness. But for human viewers, standing on the baseline, the descriptions are very different. They too see the fixed stars, as men from the beginning of time have watched the night and have found their ways by picking out the Plough or the Southern Cross. But they also see the whole sky above them filled with stars – the constructive aims, the plausible projects of their millions of ordinary lives, and, in following some of the course of this vast host of stars, the feet of each person makes patterns on the ground.

In calling these patterns, these activities, good, they do not regard them as ultimates in the same way that they think of truth, or of an existence free from evil of any kind, but rather as immediate activities complete in themselves and not requiring any external justification for their merit. Each such activity produces some new quality and something fresh in the human situation, an end in itself, in the bringing about of which the doer transcends his own egotism and immerses, involves, commits himself. Thus, although close to the doer and understandable by him in every aspect and detail, they do also share some of the qualitative character of the ultimate goods that are beyond both his understanding and powers of attainment. They are consistent with the direction in which ultimate standards lie; they do not conflict either with them or each other, yet they do have consequences that may be judged meritorious by other standards.

Just as virtues such as courage and charity are both good in themselves and also means to other goods, such as someone else's life or someone else's happiness, so also are the aims of human fulfilment. What is truth? What is justice? What is freedom? The questions are perennially asked but can never be satisfactorily answered. Nevertheless, we can all point to examples of statements that are true statements; conduct that is good, actions that are very much more free than others. We can detect lies and malice and condemn states of injustice and tyranny. We know when our values and standards are dishonoured or denied, but we cannot define any of them exclusively. In the same way, we can recognise activities that are done by the agent for the sake of their own excellence; and it reflects no demerit on them that we can at the same time say that many of them also give great satisfaction to their doers; nor that besides being intrinsically good, beautiful or valuable, and besides satisfying its agent's own motives of fulfilment, the same activity may also be called useful.

Most objects of antiquity that we admire today for their intrinsic qualities were designed and made in their own day for a useful purpose as well as to give delight, please the eye, or to be magnificent and express majesty – the Ducal Palace in Urbino, the Acropolis in Athens, the countless vases and pieces of pottery in museums all over the world. Even adornment was designed to be appropriate to the particular object, building or room on which, or in which, it was placed as an ornament. The paintings and pieces of sculpture that we now regard solely for the aesthetic pleasure they give were conceived and executed for particular purposes, this one to communicate a thought or practical emotion, that to fit a particular place and that other to record for perpetuity some transient moment of experience. Above all, in the greatest ages of Christian civilisation, beauty was expressed with such confidence and joy because only through its medium, it was believed, could the individual's mind be lifted up to meet the splendour of God. Thus the purpose of the work of the creative artist – the painter, the mason, the sculptor, the musician – was to enable the human spirit to overcome its need of verbal understanding and so to pierce the limitations of its own flesh as to direct itself towards the uncreated.

The most certain definition of decadence is an art form which appears to have beauty but neither content nor purpose nor relevance. In this connection, modern utilitarianism is condemned, not because it draws attention to the usefulness of objects and to the necessity of producing them, but because it preaches that usefulness and satiated appetite alone should be the criterion of worthwhile effort. The notion, for example, that form follows function in architecture, that producing a building can be done simply by concentrating on its uses, that this, done rightly, will produce the right building, is not mistaken because it emphasises function or utility, but because it assumes that beauty or good design will result without effort or thought or addition.

Purposeful activity has its own self-contained merit : it brings about something new or enhances an existing situation. It improves the quality of life – both that of the doer and of his society. Any piece of work that is the product of its maker's intention, values and skill, stands to be judged by itself as an intrinsic object, independently of its usefulness, just as much as a sculptor's figure or a potter's vase. In a similar way, new thought, new traditions and new institutions that embody human intentions in a fresh and relevant way and meet human needs, or relate the human outlook to objective knowledge or materiality, stand to be judged on their intrinsic merits and as instruments of purpose.

The most devastating crime of all is excess and the cause of excess is greed. It is as possible to conceive of greed for knowledge and greed for what the Puritan Divines called 'filthy righteousness' or to have an insatiable appetite for believing in the efficiency of institutions to deal with human problems as it is to think, write and speak of greed for material things. Any excess, any attempt to satisfy the demands of one side of human life at the expense of the others, any distortion of man and his environment is bad. The present shape of the field of human existence, the field of limitations, is hideously irregular – very wide at the end of material productivity; very narrow and constricted at the end of human value and aspiration. It is essential to reshape it. In all industrial countries, men must recast their thinking about material need and question every single assumption of the artificial utilitarian production process whether it operates in a capitalist, communist or socialist society. Man must rediscover his true place in creation so that he ceases to exploit animal, vegetable and mineral nature beyond the limits of his conscientiously considered needs. Other measures must be found in the means of distribution and exchange so that justice and balance exist both between classes and between one part of the world and another. Opportunities for balanced and rounded human fulfilment must be extended so that they fully parallel and complement the bounty which modern knowledge can make available to all mankind. The vast stores of knowledge itself which systematic research and investigation yield, must be exposed increasingly to disciplined public view as well as being incorporated into public institutions in an orderly and critical way, so that the institutional line of our condition may keep abreast of the new knowledge which continues to outstrip by far our enjoyment and use of it and knowledge itself be kept within the bounds of the human capacity to understand and evaluate it.

But central to the question of progress and balance and sanity must lie adequate consideration of the nature of man, and of the ambiguity of the nature of man. He is the centre of production, of knowledge and innovation and of the institutionalisation of these. Yet he is more of an imponderable than all the rest. He is himself a limitation upon himself. And this ultimate resides in the ambiguity of his character. Thus he has to adjust himself, not only to the more easily understood limitations imposed by three-quarters of the field, but also to his own ambiguous nature which forms the last barrier.

I laugh when I hear the fish in the water is thirsty.
Perceivest thou not how the god is in thine own house,
That thou wanderest from forest to forest so listlessly?
In thy home is the Truth. Go where thou wilt, to Benares or to Manthura;
If thy soul is a stranger to thee, the whole world is unhomely.

(Kabir, from Robert Bridges' *Spirit of Man*)

Chapter 9

The Free Man and His Fulfilment

The claim of the individual to live out his life in freedom has been given many names: self-determination, self-realisation and self-development are amongst those most often used, but they have acquired many implications in addition to the precise ones with which they were originally endowed. Probably self-fulfilment, besides being less philosophically loaded, better expresses what the typical twentieth-century individual expects to achieve with his freedom, and is, therefore, the most suitable term to investigate in the search of the free man for conditions to give his life significance and value. As a slogan, however, it is relatively unimportant and it can be dispensed with later if it is shown to stand in the way of more crucial perceptions.

SELF-FULFILMENT

The word 'fulfilment' on its own has many meanings. Hyphenated to 'self', there are at least six which contribute towards some sort of creative picture of the free man and his needs. In a passive sense it can mean the fulfilment of the individual as a receptive agent; he allows himself to be filled, as a vessel, with the content to which he is sympathetic and which therefore replenishes him. He listens to music, he looks at paintings, he watches a play, he sits in a garden, he beholds a view, he attends a lecture, he chooses a house, furnishings, pictures and ornaments that give him certain valuable feelings; or he simply enjoys contemplation. In all these experiences, his 'strong identity', his 'very self' is intensified, however slightly, as a result of his internal responses to external works of value which he permits to influence him. He is a receiver, an interpreter, or a worshipper; he only takes into himself as much of the external reality as he values or as is true to himself. Second, in an active sense and obversely to the first, it can mean filling a vessel to the full. Thus the individual is responsible both for the content, the quality and the degree of fullness which he gives to his life.

In the third place, it can mean achieving a promise or a potential: the positive qualities and abilities of an individual, as well as the combination of all his qualities into a distinctive entity, constitute potentialities which give rise to definite expectations. Using himself in some sense creatively, the individual will not only go some way towards realising his own potentialities but will also put to their best use the materials he chooses to employ in conjunction with them. He will bring both to a higher intensity. Close to this there is a fourth meaning – bringing to consummation. He puts his qualities and person to a definite and complete purpose, not necessarily achieving an ideal best, but fulfilling a purpose for which he has settled and which goes well with him. Nevertheless, the particular purpose lies well outside himself, much more than mere aspiration does, so that he can truly say, in achieving it, that his life has been consummated in it.

Fifth, fulfilment may mean carrying out and completing in material form, ideas, images or projects first shaped in the mind. A finished house, it will be remembered Marx noted,[1] is the fulfilment of an architect's plan that existed first as a blueprint in his head; the climbing of a difficult mountain by a particular route involving the organisation of a base-camp, equipment, stores and porters, is the fulfilment of a project formulated previously in the minds of all involved in the expedition. The growth of the person in his lifetime is the combined effect of fulfilling many such blueprints. This fifth usage is the fertile general one and includes most of the other active uses. Writers such as Marx, Weil and Sartre claim that this ability to form images of intentions and projects prior to purposeful action is one of the most important of all human qualities, one which is the origin

1. Marx, *Capital*, Vol. 1, p. 159.

of initiative. When, therefore, an individual is denied the opportunity of giving his projects material forms, he is robbed of part of his characteristically human freedom.

Finally, fulfilment of self can mean the individual becoming a complete person, an integrated and harmonious personality. This sense of the term adds to the other five usages the suggestion that besides achieving standards and fulfilling projects or aspirations true to himself, he has, because he belongs to a world of personality, to become at one with the aspirations of other personalities.

There is an everyday usage of fulfilled, rather than fulfilment or self-fulfilment, the meaning of which is difficult to capture precisely but which nevertheless might be helpful. This occurs, for example, when we say 'in his work at the club he was fulfilled as he was not elsewhere', or 'only after he retired, when he was with his children and grandchildren, was he really fulfilled'. These sentences express something more than simply happiness. Some qualities of the particular person have been put to good purpose as well; there is more than a slight suggestion of being appreciated. The whole person seems to have been involved, although not necessarily to the extent of every talent, skill and quality. The emphasis seems to be placed on the event, the situation or the mode of employment and by the person being possessed by the enjoyment of the experience rather than on any special effort made by him.

IDENTITY

In all these usages there is the suggestion that each successive act of fulfilment is a contribution towards the shaping of the man, so that at the end of his life the question might be asked, 'was he fulfilled or not?' This question can have two different meanings giving rise to two very different conceptions of freedom. The first is, 'did his life achieve the form, fullness and purpose it promised or towards which it appeared to be directed?' The second is, 'did he end up as a full human being, having taken up and enjoyed at least one of the many alternative forms of fulfilment open to him?'

The first conception is Greek in origin. The Greeks taught that there is something different within each of us, a unique pre-ordained purpose implanted in our minds, which an individual moral life consists in drawing out. The vessel which we fill with content is given to us at birth; small at first, it grows as we grow, but its shape never alters; all the freedom we have is to fill it with more or less content, a content, moreover, for which it is already fitted. Also implanted in our minds are the influences to which we shall be ready to respond, or the abstractions which will delight us, striking notes which our constitutions will find harmonious or repulsive. Something akin to this view was very popular amongst a certain section of intellectuals who gave their support to liberalism in the latter part of the last century and whose thought has contributed much to that of many democracies in this. Their aim was to recast Hegelianism into an acceptable and quasi-religious English mould. Freedom, they said, was synonymous with self-realisation. The self is a combination of qualities with a preordained mission to fulfil. Providence, or destiny directed the individual into a situation where he could achieve this mission. His duty was, by the exertion of his good will, to perform the tasks appropriate to that situation or station and not to look beyond that station. The doctrine of 'my station and its duties' stimulated, therefore, a functional view of society.[2] One baby is born as an acorn destined to be an oak-tree, and another, as a seed that can only grow into a cabbage. The right seedbed, the right method of culture, the right method of transplanting it into its adult habitat and the appropriate care and attention will ensure it becomes the best of its kind – oak or cabbage; but its freedom is limited to its being good, bad or indifferent of its kind, and no exertion of will or ingenuity will enable it to be anything else. 'The rich man in his castle, the poor man at his gate', is an example of the worst Victorian application of this doctrine; a planned industrial society, with entrances to its many specialised fields of activity determined by paper qualifications obtained from an examination system which, it is supposed, can grade innate capacity, is perhaps the most obvious reflection of this doctrine at the present day.

In reaction to such doctrines we might well think that the mission, the ends and the details of an individual's life are not preordained. Nevertheless, we have to admit there are some very important aspects of it over which he can never claim control at all, and these aspects exert very strong, almost crucial in-

2. F. H. Bradley, *Ethical Studies* (Oxford, 1870).

fluences. He cannot choose where or when he is born, neither the society, nation, culture, class or epoch. 'He is inserted by birth into a tapestry of social relationships which determine for him' – certainly in the early part of his life, if not so strongly later – 'the overwhelmingly greater part of his thoughts, feelings, values and reactions'.[3] Thus, if he is to use his freedom, and his own distinctive qualities to create a unique personality, it is very considerably out of an unchosen and 'alien reality' that he has to do so.

What might be termed the seed-acorn view of human freedom was thought to have been refuted by a bishop long ago, who, when observing a criminal being carried to execution at Tyburn, observed : 'there, but for the grace of God, go I.' It has since been attacked by existentialists, who argue that a man's existence is prior to his essence, or to the essential personality he eventually becomes, and, on other grounds, by philosophers holding the opinion that the concept of essence is contrary to scientific method. Inquiry into what anything essentially is, they say, will be fruitless : whereas investigation into behaviour and function, aiming at explanation, will yield results which will illuminate new areas of knowledge.

None of this is conclusive. The answer, for example, might very well be that explanation is the best way of adding to our knowledge of every category of nature except that of human beings and their values. It might also be reasonable to say that, whereas in the pure sciences a name is no more than a definitive label or reference indicating succinctly what is known of the functions and qualities of an object; in the humanities, and in describing individuals, values and aspirations, a name implies something more. What does one really mean by the good, by justice, by truth, or by compassion, charity, or virtue, and in what ways do these ideas have existences independent of their functions as labels for particular acts or states? To seek clearer and richer meanings for them is a typically human thing to do. Similarly when we attach a label or description to a person, describing his occupation, date and place of birth, heredity and nationality, or calling him boring or witty or kindly or clever or dull, can any label really convey all we know about him and all

3. Ladislaus Boros, *In Time of Temptation* (London, 1968), quoted in Neville Ward, *Five for Sorrow, Ten for Joy*, (London, 1971).

the promise for good or bad that his nature contains? Indeed, can we ever really know all about him?

Is the *persona* a mask of hardened clay worn by the actor whilst he plays a role; or is it a mask of softer clay worn always by the individual, which, as the years pass, his character and experience transform so that it comes to represent him completely – not then a mask, but a mould?

The basic perplexity with regard to the problem of personal identity is this: we all recognise changes in our own and other people's characters, and some of these taken together may amount to an 'essential' change – such as for example, compelled the American, Chessman, to deny that the self that was about to be executed bore any resemblance to the man convicted eleven years previously for rape. But at the same time we also recognise a continuous identity that is aware of each successive intention that we form and is somehow involved in its being carried out. Moreover, this identity changes no more than a person's finger-prints do. It is the subject, I. If, then, this 'I' is constant, can it yield any more than one type of personality? Was the bishop really saying that he was an episcopal criminal, or a criminally inclined person lucky to be disguised in a dog-collar and gaiters?

There is a story told of Leonardo da Vinci which may be more illuminating.[4] Leonardo had finished the painting of his fresco, 'The Last Supper', except for the two central figures, Christ and Judas, which he could do no more than sketch on the plaster, because he had been unable to find models for them. Some years passed before he found a man whom he judged suitable in physique, character and personality to be an ideal model for Christ. But he had still to find a Judas. Ten years later he was accosted in the street by a vile looking beggar, despicable in every way, to whom he refused alms, but offered a fee if he would sit for him. 'Willingly', said the beggar, 'and I know your fee, because I sat for you ten years ago.' He who had been Leonardo's Christ was now consenting to be his Judas: two different personalities, but the same set of finger-prints.

4. This episode in Leonardo's life is not recounted by Vasari. The story may be legendary; but it was a common experience for a painter to sketch his principal characters into a painting and then to search for suitable models.

One decision or action alone could hardly have caused the change; but some incident, some periods of time must have been more crucial than others – a deal with the high priest, or a kiss of betrayal from which there could be no going back. Leonardo may himself have been responsible for the man's deterioration : until he contemplated the second portrait, the beggar may even have seen himself as Christ asking for alms. Then, like Dorian Grey in Oscar Wilde's allegory written four centuries later, he took into himself the indestructible reality of the change that the Judas painting had finally made objective. However, even then there remains a doubt : when he saw the effect of his evil living, did not the man say, 'this is not my true self. It is not the image of Christ that I have betrayed, but myself. I never, with my whole self, willed this change.' In this way he might have claimed that his story was at one with the essence of most of the tragic figures of great drama like Macbeth and Othello who are tragic not because of what is done to them but because of what in the end they are.

FULFILMENT AS FREEDOM

The story of the painting, by virtue of its being such an anni-hilating example of non-fulfilment, seems to point to all the ingredients needed for true fulfilment. There is the self and perhaps this reveals two 'I's : the active agent involved in living who paints the portrait; and he whom Sartre called the 'I beyond I', at once the observer and the continuing identity, the principle that organises the separate elements of the individual's make-up into a recognisable unity and at the end pleads for understanding. There are native qualities, propensities and latent skills of the individual. No less, there are characteristic vanities that may lead to the corruption of all that is positive or potentially good. There is the will too; but somehow in thinking of the man who had once played the role of Christ, that is forgotten. Instead, one is overwhelmed by his total loneliness, the absence of any love either toward him or by him. 'For love is more than a coin in a beggar's cap, It is the eye of fellowship too.'

Finally, although apparently lacking in the beggar, there are the individual's beliefs and more specifically his aspirations and projects, some of them formed so early in life and so passionately that they often seem to be ingrained into the texture of the original identity itself – the pale indelible guide-lines on the canvas of the person he would become. It might be claimed that this analysis illustrates only two possibilities : either one faithful to the original guidelines, or the depraved one. The only answer to this claim that experience and observation is able to give is 'No'. Every critical decision of life seems to be a free one. If I had decided, or happened, to do that instead of this on innumerable occasions, go there instead of here, worked with that person instead of this one, I would have been a very different person. The consequences of different disciplines and occupations upon personality also appear to be prodigious. Moreover, affections alter the painting as much as actions, and it would be sheer romanticism to suppose that at any one time there was only one possible choice or only one person to love, or even only one possible good choice. Not only do people make conflicting claims on the affections, but so also do different projects, purposes and social causes. There seems to be an enormous variety of different goods that confront the individual; his life is short and he can only devote himself to a few of them. If he is to grow as a person he must make decisions and commit himself. One is reminded of T. S. Eliot's lines :

> Footfalls echo in the memory
> Down the passage which we did not take
> Towards the door we never opened
> Into the rose garden; other echoes
> Inhabit the garden. Shall we follow?
> (T. S. Eliot, 'Burnt Norton')

A man's freedom, then, in some quite real yet limited sense, is the freedom to create himself or diminish himself. Every man is an innovator with the initiative to do this. The eventual portrait of his personality is the outcome, the objectivisation of what in life he has stood for. But the range of possible self-portraits is limited. The individual's original qualities, both biological and mental, are restricted; and so is his range of material opportunities and 'the tapestry of social relationships' which determine such a large part of his thoughts and feelings. It may be that such limitations present the opportunity for a choice between a number of 'bests'. This conclusion probably corresponds with the reflections and experiences of most people; but they are, of course, unable to explain how and why it was in the course of their lives that they followed down certain passages and not others. We cannot tell. What we do know is that we have many experiences of freedom and that it is in them that we give effect to the realities of conscience. We know, too, that our interest in politics, in liberty and in the possibilities of change in social and industrial structures is mainly due to the appalling lack of opportunities for so many people to use their qualities towards any 'best' – of achieving any kind of personal fulfilment at all.

But it is not success or even achievement that makes the man. This is not simply because fortitude, patience and the ability to bear disappointments are virtues, but rather because there are scarcely any worthwhile projects that can be carried out exactly as they were intended, and no set of values that can be fully embodied within a specific and limited historical epoch. Because too, few people achieve the goals they set themselves. Martyrs do not die in flames when causes are won; nor are the most fulfilled personalities those whose achievements are necessarily spectacular or noteworthy. At the last it is not what a person has achieved, but what, through the way he has lived, he has come to be, which counts. The peasant woman in a village struggling to bring up a family, or the man and wife doing their best to make a lively and in some sense creative home for their children and friends may be fuller persons, indeed, more fulfilled, than an ambitious prime minister, or victorious general. In short, newspaper headlines are not written by recording angels.

> It is not seemly to be famous :
> Celebrity does not exalt;
> There is no need to hoard your writings
> And to preserve them in a vault.
>
> To give your all – this is creation,
> And not – to deafen and eclipse,
> How shameful, when you have no meaning,
> To be on everybody's lips !

Try not to live as a pretender
But so to manage your affairs
That you are loved by wide expanses
And hear the call of future years.

Another, step by step, will follow
The living imprint of your feet;
But you yourself must not distinguish
Your victory from your defeat.[5]

SELF-FULFILMENT AND GOOD AS DIRECTION

There are two questions left to ask : 'how suitable a term is self-fulfilment for all that has been expressed above?', and 'in pursuance of the point raised at the end of Chapter 6, is it yet possible to indicate in any way at all the objective good to which it is directed?'

It is certainly a term less loaded with confusing historical connotations than either self-realisation or self-determination, but it is not without ambiguities of its own. There is little merit to be acquired by the individual going round, often, it would seem, unattractively, obsessively seeking the achievement of a particular promise that he believes latent in himself; or by determining for himself, almost from a copybook, the type of person he would like to become and thereafter closing his mind to other influences. This presents an even less admirable figure than the hero of nineteenth-century individualism who, with a well thumbed copy of Smiles' *Self-Help* in his pocket, rose from the obscurity of the back street to the ostentation of wealth.

Another objectionable usage of self-fulfilment is when it is claimed as of right, or to gain sympathy as part of a hard-done-by plea that someone's principal functions, responsibilities or duties have prevented his or her self-fulfilment, meaning physical enjoyment and the satisfaction of blossoming into a fullness that everyone else can admire. Employed in this way, it conveys more than a hint of self-indulgence. There is also a whole range of meanings indicating the possibility of finding self-fulfilment, or

5. Boris Pasternak, *Fifty Poems*, trans. Lydia Pasternak Slater (London, 1963), p. 70.

again self-indulgence, through morally ugly, depraved or socially unacceptable means – D. H. Lawrence's praise of and exultation in carnality as the supreme means of self-fulfilment, for example; or the worm of self-corruption which is the theme of Dostoievsky's *Gambler*.

We must be clear, therefore, about what qualities of fulfilment and of positive freedom we require and their relationships to the other aims of life that we cherish. We must be able to say to the two schools of justification that freedom as we seek it requires no justification; and to those who see liberty divided between back- and front-garden, or between negative and positive spheres, that there are not two spheres but one. It is the essential condition and the essential value of a full human life, a whole life. Man's claim to freedom is indivisible. It is contradictory for him to assert that he is free and at the same time for him either to lease away the eight most vigorous hours of his day to the control of technical forces and to their impersonal 'laws', or for him to indulge one part of himself, his appetites and sensations, whilst allowing his other parts to become frustrated and atrophied. We also wish to be able to say that life is valuable for the opportunities it gives to the individual to live out the purposes of his own choice. His good and his freedom lie in the direction he faces and neither can be imposed upon him by an entity extraneous to himself or by any other individual.

But it should not be implied that, because he cannot be allowed to turn and face his good and his freedom in a direction forcibly chosen for him by an alien social entity or by someone else, the purposes of his own free choice should not be good in a socially or publicly recognisable sense. In Western countries at least, the ambition of the individual for many centuries has been to add to the world some value typical of himself and thus to leave his mark on it. It has not mattered how trivial in the total scheme of things this contribution has been : the ideal has been that it should add to the reality of the human world in the way that the individual wished that it should. More than likely it was but a tiny item on a heap of similar contributions. That it should be on the right heap and as perfect as he could make it is what has mattered in the most creative and outward looking periods of Western civilisation.

According to these counter-assertions, the character of what is good may be seen in at least two but not contradictory formulations. One is as instrumentality: that which, enjoyable or not in itself, leads to something good in itself; inevitably this is activity which enhances, adds something new to the existing, and is therefore creative. The other, the good in itself, can be understood as the direction a person faces; the light on his face with which he wishes to fill his being. Within this direction there will be many possibilities depending upon the personality of him who chooses and of those with whom he chooses. But evil cannot be considered in these terms at all. It is not, according to Martin Büber, any of the directions a man can face.

> I am inclined to think that you cannot do evil with your whole soul, and you can do good only with your whole soul . . . Good and Evil are not different, as are right and left; each is a different quality. Good is direction and evil is a will. You can take a direction only with your whole being – you go in this direction, not the other one.[6]

Evil is not even total, unlimited destruction. It is simply corruption, the chaos of the once created, the once orderly. There are two states of mind which lead most immediately to it; one is the depraved and the other is that which is set upon diminishing or belittling the existing or the possible.

Finally, how realistic is it to speak or write of self-fulfilment as though it were an aim to be achieved in entire independence? Even the most solitary occupations are yet dependent upon a thousand and one cooperations. The composer not only needs score-sheets and pen; he also requires training and a tradition of music. He can only score for instruments that already exist, or, of course, for those he designs himself, as Wagner did, and for skills already practised. He can hardly compose without audiences as well as orchestras in mind. Self-expression can acquire merit through the understanding of those with a similar temper of mind.

These protestations and reflections suggest that the term 'self-fulfilment' is a far from satisfactory one. It is in response to all the other of his experiences – the 'non-self' of his experiences, to

6. Martin Büber, 'On good and evil', *The Listener*, 18 January 1962.

all life on earth and especially to other people, to their aims and needs – that the individual fulfils himself as a person. The isolated individual is an abstraction. The man in relation to other men and to all that is external to his own self-consciousness – the person – is the real and concrete. The terms 'human fulfilment' and 'personal fulfilment' better express this concrete fact. 'To give your all – this is creation.'

The more perfection anything has, the more active and less passive it is: and contrariwise, the more active it is, the more perfect it becomes.

(Spinoza, *Ethics*)

Chapter 10

The Free Man in Activity

VALUE AND ACTION

The conception of positive freedom as a creative principle of action in society is not something new, born in reaction to affluence and better mass education, or to an older generation's complacent veneration of negative and procedural liberties. Indeed it has roots in the Old Testament as well as the New: to see visions on mountain tops is not enough; beliefs and values must be practised in the towns and valleys through work, practical charity and preaching itself. Greek influence, too, was considerable in giving men precise intellectual values to realise in their lives.

By the time of the Renaissance, Christian civilisation had refined these principles to set before men the further ideal of embodying belief and value in material things of beauty as well as of practical usefulness, and in the visual arts as well as in working institutions. This was the mission of the public and private citizen; of man the believer, the fabricator and builder, of man the innovator, craftsman and artist. The perfect – whether as truth, beauty or goodness – could not remain an abstraction and hover around to inspire Platonic contemplation and conversation; it had also to be used in an attempt to inform, shape and inspire the everyday activities of men. This conviction has subsequently been the basis of conscience and revolution alike.

The Protestant ethic of northern Europe, it is said by Weber and Tawney[1] and others, has narrowed this ideal by relating it almost exclusively to the satisfaction of material needs and by raising to a special dignity those virtues such as endeavour, perseverance, thrift, honesty, self-reliance and resourcefulness, which became the strongest elements of the character of the independent businessman – and perhaps the strongest factors in their successes and fortunes. Thus, Protestantism, it is said, established a new priority of values, which later, when further narrowed and particularised, became the basis of individualism. From this, many features of the utilitarian outlook developed. On the other hand, it must be asserted that without the Protestant virtues and scale of values, there is little likelihood that there would have been an Industrial Revolution, a welfare state, or concern with problems of poverty on a world-wide scale, or, indeed, the physical machinery for dealing with them.

Even so important a philosopher of human fulfilment as Marx found himself trapped in a cleft between the larger ideal of fulfilment through activity as seen by the men of the Renaissance and the lesser concept of work as material productivity, the energy basis of artificial utilitarianism. His early alienation writings, his chapter on labour in *Capital*, his idealisation of craftsmen and artists, as well as his Shakespeare-inspired strictures on the love of money, belong to the one; his legacy of crude utilitarian intimations, seized upon so avidly by Lenin, to the other.

Work, for Marx, has a dual purpose: it is both the means of man eventually overcoming physical necessity and also a true and necessary function of distinctive, or exclusive, human nature. Marx thus stretches the word, enlarges its meaning to include any consciously directed effort, so that even to have true perceptions of the material world man must put in work to verify or to refute the first impression of his senses. If, for example, a traveller in the desert sees what he believes to be water, he has to verify his visual perception by going up to it and touching it. This, in Marx's sense, is work.[2] Work, for him above all, is the

---

1. R. H. Tawney, *Religion and the Rise of Capitalism* (Harmondsworth, 1972), and M. Weber, *The Protestant Ethic and the Spirit of Capitalism* (London, 1930).
2. H. B. Acton, *The Illusion of the Epoch* (London, 1955), p. 35.

means by which men extend their thought and imagination into the material world. He saw a man-made thing very much as Aristotle had done, as an extension of human personality; it was the distinctive product of the maker's thought and personality.

INDUSTRIAL WORK

'Work', Marx says, 'is a process in which both men and nature participate, and in which man of his own accord starts, regulates and controls the material reaction between himself and nature; and by thus acting on the external world and changing it he at the same time changes his own nature.' In spite of much mis-understanding by Marx's followers, he himself is clear that conceptualisation comes before making.

> What distinguishes the worst architect from the best of bees is that the architect raises his structure in imagination before he erects it in reality; and at the end we get a result that existed in the imagination of the labourer at the beginning. He not only effects a change of form in the materials on which he works, but he also realises a purpose of his own that gives the law to his *modus operandi*, and to which he must subordinate his will.[3]

Thus, even if tools determine superstructure, both tools and structures themselves exist first as blueprints in their inventors' minds.

It was the minute sub-division of labour resulting from machine production, 'detail work', and the tendency to regard labour itself as well as its products exclusively in terms of exchange or money values that led to the fragmentation of personality and, therefore, to the destruction of all that was 'truly human' in men. The very basis of human freedom, the capacity of men to change this world by thought and intention, was jeopardised by machine production. The transformation of industry from individually controlled workshops to machinery-dominated manufacture so de-humanised the worker as to make the limbs or muscles needed for factory work representative of the man himself. The alienated part stood for the whole; the worker – is it not a term of our daily speech? – becomes a hand.

3. Karl Marx, *Capital*, Vol. 1, p. 157.

F

While simple co-operation leaves the mode of working by the individual for the most part unchanged, manufacture thoroughly revolutionises, and seizes labour power by its very roots . . . not only is the detail work distributed to the different individuals, but the individual himself is made the automatic motor of rational operation, and the absurd fable of Menenius Agrippa, which makes man a mere fragment of his own body, becomes realised.[4]

Even more realistic, perhaps, is the myth of the centaurs, horses with human heads, shoulders and arms, the embodiment of the ruthless Assyrian horsemen who descended upon ancient civilisation : not so much human beings as warriors possessed, taken over, by all the instincts and skills of the wild horses they rode. Today almost exactly the same kind of possession occurs in the case of tractor drivers. As individuals in the home or the cafe on the ground or the street, they may be amongst the most gentle and most human of men; but once on the seat of the tractor they become possessed by its power and inhumanity. The functions and *modus operandi* of the machine takes over the man and he becomes a ruthless, inhuman, destroyer of all that lies in the way that his tractor has selected for him to follow.

What Marx meant by detail work and how the 'absurd fable of Menenius Agrippa' came to be realised in nineteenth-century factories is clear if we read a justification of the division of labour in manufacture written by any of the classical economists, say Alfred Marshall, one of the more enlightened and humane :

4. *ibid*, p. 354. Alienation as described by Marx is really a much more complicated phenomenon than described here. See *Soviet Survey* 32, April–June 1960, pp. 21–5. A type of alienation which it would not have been possible for Marx to describe is that of the specialised, skilled mass-production worker. This is admirably described in Ottiero Ottieri's *The Men At the Gate*, trans. I. M. Rawson (London, 1962), p. 21:

    One immediately recognises the protagonist of mass-production; the worker who is halfway between craftsmanship and automation: a manual worker, but a specialised one, doing repetitive but skilled work. He is interchangeable like the parts he produces, but he is possessed of the carefulness and responsibility of a technician.

    It is this contradiction that worries us industrial psychologists, although it fascinates us : for it tends to break up the human personality while at the same time it places great responsibility upon the worker.

... Anyone who has to perform exactly the same set of operations day after day on things of exactly the same shape, gradually learns to move his fingers exactly as they are wanted, by almost automatic action and with greater rapidity than would be possible if every movement had to wait for a deliberate instruction of the will. One familiar instance is seen in the tying of threads by children in a cotton mill. Again, in a clothing or boot factory, a person who sews, whether by hand or machinery, just the same seam on a piece of cloth or leather of just the same size, hour after hour, day after day, is able to do it with far less effort and far more quickly than a worker with much greater quickness of eye and hand, and of a much higher order of general skill, who was accustomed to make the whole of a coat or the whole of a boot.[5]

This horrible and inhuman sub-division of labour described by Marshall may significantly be compared with Plato's description of a natural and acceptable division of labour.

We are not all alike, there are diversities of natures among us which are adapted to different occupations . . . And if so, we must infer that all things are produced more plentifully and easily and of a better quality when one man does one thing which is natural to him and does it at the right time, and leaves other things . . . for the husbandman will not make his own plough or mattock . . . neither will the builder make his own tools; . . . and in like manner the weaver and shoemaker.[6]

Mass manufacture was, then, the quintessence of that process which made Marx plead for the 'reversal of the object-subject relationship', perhaps the most striking and best remembered of all Marx's slogans: the plea for men no longer to be modelled by the machines they were employed to handle, but to be given machinery and productive conditions which would enable them to choose and work towards their own ends. The tragedy, how-

5. Alfred Marshall, *The Economics of Industry* (London, 1901), p. 142–3.
6. Plato, *The Republic*, Book 2, Jowett's translation Vol. 3, pp. 50–1.

ever, was that, when Marx came later in his writings to advocate specific industrial reforms, he found himself committed to prescribing in the name of collectivism even more extensive forms of mass-production than those he had condemned in capitalism; perhaps also to giving his readers reason to believe that he thought tools and machinery were determined by the mystique of an economic-historic procedure.

His belief in the possibility of achieving what he regarded as true freedom through the overcoming of physical necessity and his devotion to his somewhat eccentric conception of 'essential human nature' – an essence and an identity that but for the contradiction embedded in capitalist production he believed to be precisely the same in all men[7] – must be held responsible for the most disappointing inconsistency in his thought: only mass-social-production, he seemed to conclude, could overcome physical necessity and release men's identical and essential human nature to blossom without constraint. In extenuation, it must be remembered that in Marx's time the largest commercial undertaking was probably a shipyard, or an engineering combine then employing no more than say 3,000 men, whilst the largest mass-production factory may not have employed as many as a thousand workers.

Marx's position in regard to freedom in activity, to organisation of work, to tools and machinery display other inconsistencies which set his followers almost impossible tasks of reconciliation. He saw mass-production machinery to be the source of detail work, of fragmentation of personality and alienation; yet his theory of the relation of human will and knowledge towards nature, as well as his conception of human freedom as total exemption from necessity, make him a disciple of the view that progress and revolution are aimed inevitably towards 'greater modernity' – hence the support given by communist orthodoxy

---

7. This vision would appear to be more religious than political in origin. See comments on 'essential human nature', Chapter 12 below.

   For an ingenious and well argued account of how Marx envisaged the organisation of a society of free associated cooperative producers true to the intrinsic values of artists and thinkers see Eugene Kamenka, *The Ethical Foundations of Marxism* (London, 1962). Such a society was, of course, to come about after the proletarian revolution and after the withering away of the State.

to mass production, automation and the processing of all inventions aimed at greater efficiency and productivity; hence also its support of vast collectivist 'planning'. His human paradise was the enjoyment of the Athenian free man's life by all; yet the immense amount of time he invested in understanding Ricardo's theory of labour-value and his dedication to the ambition of standing Hegel on his head, led him and even more his principal apostles, into the inevitability of an enormous system of state organisation and oppression in order to control the means of work out of which exploitation and surplus values arose – hence the modern socialist state simply has had to become the super-exploiter, the super-capitalist.

Marx's greatness as a social scientist is best summarised by Simone Weil. 'Marx's truly great idea' she said, is that 'in human society as well as in nature nothing takes place otherwise than through material transformation'.[8] She saw necessity as the mighty force blowing upon the human world from the outside which men transform into more and more subtle forms of physical and social power. It was this conviction which drove her to work for a time in one of the enormous Renault factories and from there to depict industrial society as a vast arena of human power. In this arena, by virtue of organisations becoming larger, she saw that those in authority were able day by day to increase the distance between themselves and those whose functions rendered them servile. Studies designed to make management and administration more efficient, she believed, did not serve to improve industry or industrial relationships, nor even to increase productivity, rather increase the power of the controllers over the controlled. As Trevor Smith has noted: 'Alienation is further reinforced by the consequences of managerialism with its unceasing and single-minded pursuit of efficiency to the exclusion of democratic considerations.'[9]

Weil was not able to accept Marx's conception of ideal liberty as the absence of all necessity; nor did she find attractive his dream of machinery doing for modern men all the tasks which slaves might have been compelled to undertake in Athens.

8. Simone Weil, *Liberty and Oppression* (London, 1958), p. 45.
9. Trevor Smith, *Anti-Politics, Consensus, Reform and Protest in Britain* (London, 1972), p. 20.

The total absence of necessity would for her empty the world of all concrete meaning. 'It would not then represent for us that which when we are deprived of it takes away the value of life.'[10] She concluded that 'living man is a thinking creature.' He can choose between submitting himself to the spur of the blind necessity of the forces external to himself, which include social and human oppression as well as the more primitive oppression imposed by nature itself, 'or else adapt himself to the inner representation of them that he forms in his own mind : and it is in this that the contrast between servitude and liberty lies.'[11] Thus for her, work would always and rightly be a part of man's condition on earth. Man's true liberty, his mission, was to be discovered in a creative use, a creative transformation, of necessity. 'True liberty,' she said in an important passage, 'is not to be defined by a relationship between desire and its satisfaction but by a relationship between thought and action. The absolutely free man would be he whose every action proceeded from a preliminary judgment concerning the end which he set himself and the sequence of means suitable for attaining this end.' 'Pain and failure', she concluded, 'can make a man unhappy, but cannot humiliate him as long as it is he himself who disposes of his own capacity for action.'[12]

For her, it was essential that knowledge, imagination, skill and judgment should be used together both in the formation and in the realisation of a project; if not in the same person, then in a group where thoughts and purpose could run from mind to mind. In order that workers in cooperation with each other should be able to achieve this sequence of free actions, she prescribed that the size of the working unit ideally 'should never be sufficiently vast to pass outside the range of the human mind.'[13]

10. Simone Weil, *Liberty and Oppression*, p. 85.
11. *ibid*., p. 86.
12. *ibid*., p. 85.
13. *ibid*., p. 99. The quotation appears at the end of the following passage, which is a superb statement of the solution to the problem of the free man at work:
     The technique would have to be such as to make continual use of methodical thought; the analogy between the techniques employed in the various tasks would have to be sufficiently close, and technical education sufficiently widespread, to enable each worker to form a clear idea of all the specialised procedures; coordination would have to be arranged in a sufficiently simple manner to enable each

Her criticism that the organisation of modern industry creates ever-widening distances between the worker and the manager, between each and what he makes, and between man and the knowledge needed for his work, was expressed with considerable sensitivity by a writer more than a hundred years earlier and quoted by Marx in a footnote :

> The man of knowledge and the productive labourer come to be widely divided from each other, and knowledge, instead of remaining the handmaid of labour . . . has almost everywhere arrayed itself against labour, systematically deluding and leading them (the labourers) astray in order to render their muscular powers entirely mechanical and obedient.[14]

WORK AS A MODEL OF CREATIVE ACTION

This incursion into the writings of Marx and Weil reveals something of the limitations as well as the fullness of the satisfactions to be obtained from carrying out and completing an activity with a purpose beyond itself, whether formally called work or not.

Every project is in some sense typical of its originator, who is himself unique and carries something novel and distinctive into the first conception, or blueprint, of his intention. But very soon he has to adjust himself and his project to what Jung called 'the claim of the material' – to the nature of the raw materials which he plans to use; to the characteristics of the tools or machinery available to him; to the intentions, skills, qualities and personalities of those sharing his enthusiasm and intending to cooperate with him; to the framework of organisation in which that cooperation will take place, and finally to the needs of those who will use his product, or whatever other service the complete project will provide.

---

to continually have a precise knowledge of it, as concerns both cooperation between workers and exchange of products; collectivities would never be sufficiently vast to pass outside the range of a human mind.

14. W. Thompson, *An Inquiry into the Principles of Distribution of Wealth* (London, 1824), p. 274; quoted by Marx, *Capital*, Vol 1, p. 355.

This give-and-take in his mind and imagination – this 'mental negotiation' – alters the shape of the blueprint, as originally conceived, very much as a sculptor's preliminary intentions are altered by the character of his tools, or of the stone or metal which he has chosen to sculpt : or, if it is a piece of work that needs casting, then by the skills and arguments of the foundry men also. It hardly matters whether the project is concerned with industry, a profession, an artistic career, writing or trying to make a room in one's own house more attractive; the ingredients are alike : at the end of the creative negotiation, there is an objective blueprint existing in its own right, and its originator, if he wishes to succeed, must subordinate himself to it. But this subordination need only be in the disciplined way that Weil has described; that is, by assenting voluntarily to it in his mind and imagination as part of the exchange, or conversation, between his own thoughts, and afterwards following methodically through the sequence of means which he has already foreseen are needed for its completion in material form.

The limitations imposed by the claims of the materials, the tools and indeed also by the claims of the organisations in which projects are carried out, need not be inflexible or permanent. Man finds novel ways of overcoming what stands in the way of fulfilling his projects; and what are absolute obstacles one day become challenges to him the next; and sometime later, little more than items of historical interest. He is, as Marx described him, among many other things, a toolmaker; and the fundamental purposes of tools are to achieve purposes and to overcome specific problems. They are instruments of man's adaptability. Moreover, since Marx's day there has occurred a second Scientific Revolution, one of the results of which is that machine and tool makers can devise, very much more quickly than in the nineteenth century, new tools and machinery and invent new techniques obedient to the wishes of those who will use them. Of all the aphorisms that have been taken out of context from the writings of Marx, none has had more paralysing effects or given rise to more absurd superstitions than the one about the hand mill and the steam mill. Even if the doctrine has to be swallowed whole and uncritically, that one did give rise to feudal and the other to capitalist society, modern society is in no way obliged to accept as inevitable the vast plants and machines which the giant firms of industry have erected in order to maintain the power of their directors and managers and to perpetuate the vast impersonal forms of organisation which they now control. The fact is that the steam mill and the typically cumbersome machine of the nineteenth century have long since founded the fortunes of old-established firms of scrap metal merchants. Industrialists know this, but many political commentators prefer not to do so. If society really wishes to scrap inhuman 'detail work' and all that bores and frustrates the worker, it could, granted time for experiment and preparation in developing the tools, develop machinery and methods to do so.

Weil was no optimist and she would most likely have been astonished if she had been told that, within forty years of writing, her superb definition of liberty as the relation of thought, action and sequence of means, would have been at least theoretically realisable in a wide sector of industry; or that her criteria for the right-sized working unit would have found so many supporters.

Since the time she wrote, there have been enormous advances in techniques, knowledge and education which now make it possible to separate those kinds of work and forms of organisation to which her definitions could be applied from those to which they cannot be. It is possible to invent expressions and say that work which has – or, differently organised could have – a 'high think content', a 'high skill content' or 'high participation content' should be reorganised into 'Weil-sized units'. There are, of course, other sectors of industry, especially those dominated by the large plant and machine in which automation is a possibility, where other methods of finding freedom for the worker must be made explicit.

More remarkable still is the fact that within less than forty years of her writing her *Notebooks*, a report commissioned by the Conseil National du Patronat Français on the problems of the assembly-line worker investigated the very undertaking where she had worked as a labourer in order to gain experience for her writings. It concluded by condemning the policy of supposing that every strike could be overcome solely by offering increased wages. The basic problem was to find the means of ending the boredom of routine work by changing the philosophy of the assembly line and then to develop a less fragmented mode of working.[15]

Quite clearly, if we really do wish to reform much of our industrial system in accordance with the principles of creativity and fulfilment, machines and tools can be devised to fit more nearly Weil's ideal of liberty and to give workers the all-round satisfactions which she claimed for them. Granted a social outlook and the political will to challenge all those who derive satisfactions of power from the present giant-sized impersonal complexes of modern industry, it is possible to reorganise its structures or at least a considerable proportion of them, so that workshops and offices using these tools and machines are 'never so vast as to pass outside the range of a human mind'. It is worth an enormous effort to attempt to achieve this.

It is also theoretically conceivable and entirely practical in a world of educated and knowledgeable workers that the division of labour can be restored to what Plato understood it naturally to mean. If this were done, it would be necessary that much of the repetitive and 'detail work' should be turned over to automation, thus releasing once alienated workers for full creative work either in 'Weil-sized organisations', or to carry out activities of a different kind altogether. Aims such as these have become for many workers much more important than shorter hours of work.

To all these hopes, there is, however, a rider. Much is written pejoratively of a consumers' society and of a producers' society. The terms hardly matter. What does matter is a recognition of the fact that the ideals of freedom and creative work can only 'find their limits in each other' and both be adequately expressed if producers adapt their plans and skills to what consumers want to buy and if consumers become aware and then share the values which the creative worker wishes to embody in his production. This meeting point can only be made in a significantly different position from the present one fixed by the market of the artificial utilitarian outlook if both producers and consumers share in a

15. The report was mentioned in *New Left Review* 73, in an article called 'The Prison Factory' by Michael Bosquet. The report itself was commissioned by the Conseil National du Patronat Français (CNPF) and is entitled *The Problem of the Assembly-Line Worker*. It was published in November 1971.

creative and radically different outlook. For workers to produce articles of intrinsic value and workmanship, consumers must be willing to buy them and appreciate them.

The ordinary man does not claim to have the genius of a Michelangelo or a Chippendale, or a social reformer such as Booth or Webb – or even the qualities of a competent factory manager or probation officer. But he is capable of appreciating purposive intrinsic values and of expressing them. Moreover, it is possible to ask that, if he wants it, there should be work for him to do in factory, office or society where he can display his initiative, follow his interests and in conjunction with others realise his projects and become a more fulfilled and involved person. He is, even in a minimal sense, an innovator with the power to transform some area of his environment. Thus, in however humble a way, his work should provide him with an objective good to which he can devote himself; some intrinsically worthwhile task that he can undertake and enjoy, for some better reason than solely his pay packet at the end of the week. In a society that has so much capital wealth, so much inventiveness, such a variety of ingenious machinery, it should be possible to meet such claims. It should, at the very least, be possible for round pegs to find congenial round holes and for irregularly shaped ones to be given ground in which to dig their own.

For many, the attraction of satisfying work is neither its skill nor thought-content, but the opportunity it gives of fellowship, or of doing something and occupying some niche which, on grounds of personality as much as of function, can be regarded as indispensable. Both of these forms of satisfaction point again to the importance of the right sized organisation. Work is regarded by many as 'the club'. Weil's criterion of ideal size ought, therefore, to have added to it, 'and a size never so vast that people working in it cannot know each other and share the senses of fellowship and purpose'. Until all boring and repetitive work can be abolished altogether, this additional criterion, and the possibility of achieving 'the club spirit', must be important.

All these demands may be put forward independently of any external justification. It is not asserted, for example, that if they were met, work would be necessarily any more efficient or men any more productive; nor that the world, in any material sense, would be any more wealthy. No doubt arguments could be made out for or against all three of these positions; but they would be irrelevant. However, it is claimed that the world would be richer in one very important sense. The changes wrought in it and the things added to it would be the reflection of personal values, personal qualities and of personal initiatives. The ultimate ambition would be for the entire world of fabricated things, institutions and activities to be at once the reflections of the personalities that had lived or were living in it and a statement of common human values : not the dominion of nature by man, but a real cooperation of the two in which man's contribution was his humanity and his creativity.

This is not a vision that excites the expectation that a life of ease and plenty is close at hand or ever to be achieved. On the contrary, it tells plainly that only in the union of thought, outstanding purpose, cooperation towards common ends and sustained effort, can men confidently hope to seek their fulfilment.

> And wisdom's final word is this –
> He only merits life and liberty
> Who day by day must make them his.
> Thus here by perils girt, shall child and man
> And ag'd ones too live out their fruitful span.
> Such teeming life I long to see :
> Stand on free ground with beings who are free.
> Then to the moment I could say
> Remain ! Remain ! Thou art so fair !
>
> (Goethe, 'Faust')

Fulfilment through work, however, cannot be regarded as the sole example of worthwhile human fulfilment. The tragedy of Faust himself typifies the strain of attempting to make it so. It is important not always to be busy and preoccupied with achieving a serious purpose. 'Extreme business,' wrote R. L. Stevenson in *Virginibus Puerisque*, 'is a sign of deficient vitality'. Sometimes it is good simply to be with other people and to do casual things with them : at others to enjoy life spontaneously in whatever way the occasion prompts.

The ideal of fulfilment through activity, beginning in contemplation or an imaginative blueprint and resulting in a tangible and completed product, is only part of a very much larger ideal,

THE FREE MAN IN ACTIVITY

in which those with no visible results to show – prophets, priests, saints, doctors, social workers, administrators and countless millions of others attempting to serve their communities or simply to love their families – have contributed. It is such forms of direct service as these with vocations to flesh and blood people and to living communities that are very often the models for those who demand meaningful opportunities of 'participation' in contemporary society. Modern bureaucracies, aided by the expertise of the so-called 'sciences', they plead, especially in the very efficiently conducted representative democracies of the West, have tended to form such an abstract, artificial conception of what society is, and then to divide that conception out into neat, easily administered but utterly impersonal bundles, that the ordinary citizen has been made to feel that he has naught to do but pay his taxes and vote at election times for one of the nominees of a distant party caucus. The criteria of those who make these criticisms and who value participation as an aim of social reform are very much like those of Weil in respect of artisan-work : actions first thought out, then talked out and finally carried out by the same body of people in organisations never too large for participants, in their minds, hearts and imaginations at least, to be involved in every item of policy from initiation to completion.

Finally, therefore one wishes to ask : has all activity, in order to have merit, to be directed consciously or intentionally towards a purpose? Was there not in Marx himself the residue of zealot, puritan or Jansenist thought – perhaps of anxiety too? The Greek concept of praxis, at any rate as interpreted by Aristotle and Plato, contains the idea of activities which are good in themselves that is absent from Marx's understanding of the concept of work and activity. These need not be earnest or lofty undertakings. Conversations, friendship, life in the community, even parties deserve to be considered in this light; simply being happy too, doing things with other people whose company one likes very much without a thought in one's head about what purpose the activities are intended to produce.

A fulfilled man, we may conclude, is more than just his restless striving for visible achievements : his salvation cannot be obtained merely by activity undertaken for the sake of the tangible evidence it gives of a life well lived, or the rewards that measure it. Nor ought he to regard the world and its resources as existing solely for purposes conceived by him. Its animals, birds and insects, minerals and vegetation, hills, rivers and valleys are not simply objects on which to impose his wishes, however altruistically or even aesthetically intended. They too have their independent claims in a larger and unified view of all existence. The idea of activity includes that of contemplation. The man most free is one who is free because he has contemplated this larger view of existence and sees all his activities as being one with it.

Nevertheless, this larger vision of the free man, with dignity and time of his own to use as he wishes, in contemplation, leisure or purposeful activity, must not be allowed to detract from the urgency of devising tools, techniques and forms of organisation to give reality to Weil's conception of true liberty. Skill-intensive tools and machines are needed to satisfy men's hunger to use their skills and qualities of person in purposeful pursuits, just as automation is required to do the chores and really boring work. There must, therefore, be a well defined line drawn between what automated machinery and the computer can well do and what is the realm of activity that may be claimed as 'truly human'.

With what simplicity I would have demonstrated that man is naturally good and that it is only through these institutions that he becomes wicked.

(J. J. Rousseau, letter, *Oeuvres Complètes*, Vol. 10, p. 301)

Desire of Ease and Sensual Delight disposeth man to obey a common power.

(Thomas Hobbes, *Leviathan*)

Chapter 11

The Field of Limitations II: Human Ambiguity

So far in the discussion of the needs of the free man and the constraints of the field of limitations, we have been concerned to describe men and women pursuing ideal goals evenly throughout their lives. Except for the briefest references, the limitation of human ambiguity has been ignored; and it is this limitation, the limitation of man upon himself, which is crucial, for it is this which, unless most carefully taken into account, frustrates all plans for a more just society and greater freedom.

Men and women do not consistently seek what they love most; nor do they devote themselves solely to activities good in themselves; nor even do they pursue consistently their own aims and ambitions and so try to make the best of their lives. Their drives to give significance to what they do are often narrowly and egotistically conceived, and their quests for fulfilment as often as not do not spring from magnanimity or even a more moderate betrayal of consideration for others. They each seek union with other human beings or with purposes outside themselves and in doing so experience an ecstasy that no other achievement offers them, yet, almost as soon as such a union becomes a part of the pattern of their lives, they become dissatisfied with it, criticise it and start to analyse and reject it.

Abilities are unequally divided, but the least able often make up for their lack of ability in envy and cunning and often get what they want more quickly than their talented rivals. The strong rule the weak, often simply because the weak love security and ease and like being indulged by more ambitious, stronger personalities; thus the greed of the weak and the love of power of the strong are often more decisive motives of social behaviour than the desire to use skill, knowledge and imagination for the realisation of projects. Moreover, as the typical organisations of modern society become larger, the more cynical motives prevail, so that organisations become less the vehicles for the ordinary person's fulfilment and more the creatures of artificial utilitarian policies through which ambitious men are able to satisfy their desires for power and aggrandisement.

Even were men and women to overcome these kinds of difficulties, they would be immediately confronted by another set, namely an uncertainty about the rightness of their vision and about the extent to which they should make concessions to aims opposed to their own. Whether they live in socialist, capitalist or communist societies, their views and interests clash as often as they coincide. Human beings are neighbourly, helpful, perseverant, truth-seeking and cooperative, and they are capable of heroism, compassion and high ideals; but they are also lazy, envious, malicious, self-indulgent, deceitful and quarrelsome. And it is the mixture of this sympathy and contrariness, this desire to learn and inability to know, indeed, this ambiguity about human nature, that makes the prospect of a perfect society and perfectly fulfilled individuals a necessary but ultimately unrealisable ideal.

THE ROLE OF AMBIGUITY IN A REALISTIC VIEW OF SOCIETY

The refusal to face the facts of human ambiguity, the fallibility of men's moral as well as their intellectual natures, may well lie at the root of modern utilitarianism's false optimism – its belief, for example, despite the ups and downs of everyday events, in an inevitable law of progress. Men unfortunately often gain as much satisfaction from the exercise of their faults as their virtues; at times relishing the pleasures of being combative, uncooperative and self-indulgent and even rejoicing in their ignorance. All attempts, therefore, to define good exclusively in terms of satisfaction or individual happiness, still more to base an optimistic law of progress on such a definition of good, must lead to contradiction and disappointment.

The most important effects of human ambiguity which need to be considered may be seen in terms of two familiar truisms. The first is that man thinks and behaves both as a social animal and an isolated individual. In order to exist at all he needs human society; even to have the fact of his own existence or the objectivity of any of his ideas confirmed, he needs other men's affirmation. He is utterly dependent upon social institutions for his means of living and growth, as well as for the protection of law and order that they give; yet he is also, and always 'on his own'. Indeed, were he never on his own as in some 'closed societies', he would have nothing 'of his own' either for his society to approve or for his own benefit. He is born in isolation, dies in isolation and works out his salvation in defensive isolation which excludes even those most concerned for him. Although dependent on others, he yet believes and so often behaves as though he himself were totally responsible for himself, so that he at times carries in himself the most appalling worries about himself and his lack of achievement.

Man's social and individual natures do not easily combine nor find a happy and stable state of reconciliation. He wants willing cooperation from others for his own projects, but does not so freely give his cooperation to theirs, nor modify his own to adjust to theirs. He hides from them the conceit of his own imagined superiority while scheming to take from them more than what even he himself views as the just measure of his own deserts. He can justify his most deceitful actions and hypocritically use the existence of other men's values to do so. In spite of his boasting, fear of more forceful personalities and greed-for-money incentives quickly reduce him to positions of subservience, so that he will forgo his own originality and much else for the sake of the plans of stronger and wealthier individuals. He has goodwill, often an immense fund of it, but he is also apt to dissipate it over a wide variety of objects, often remote and impersonal ones, whilst those close to him he often ignores. In these circumstances, love of neighbour all too frequently, especially in the twentieth century, means for him an attempt to give loyalty to large anonymous organisations, whilst ignoring the claims of those much nearer home. The miracles of modern communication have come upon him so suddenly that he finds himself trying to love the whole telephone directory, or to immerse himself imaginatively in the lives of everyone whose stories are presented in every single television current affairs programme. He sees himself and his opinions as unique, but in large groups he is easily swayed and quickly loses his independence and reasonableness. Thus he is apt to allow himself to become the tool of every large impersonal organisation, the cannon-fodder for every battle, and the chorus for tragedy and comedy alike.

The second truism about human nature to take into account is that man is both an intelligence capable of abstraction and also a very imperfect material being. As a species, he is set midway between the animal kingdom and a potentiality he cannot achieve – or, as some say, he has both animal and spiritual natures. He hovers between both and rarely settles for long to follow the pattern of either. He may be described in physical and psychological terms – in terms of his body, his brain and instincts, which can be measured and recorded in much the same way that the physical mechanism of a dog or rat can be. But no mere physical description can exhaust his nature or explain his accomplishments. The other side of his nature, although it produces striking effects in the world of physical events and can be established quite objectively in his politics, history, art, affections and in all his efforts to invest articles of use with a beauty beyond that of function, or to gain a truth irrespective of advantage or consequence, is so mysterious and unsure that he is reluctant to name with certainty any of its universal qualities. Even when he does so, in the use of words such as good, value, beautiful or freedom, he is unable to specify precisely what he means; yet even in his agnosticism he is unable to regard them as less than truths of some order to which he owes an obligation. But the other side of his nature tells him that, even if they be called truths, they can be evaded or countered by the all too clearly and readily accepted facts and explanations of his physical and psychological make-up. Especially in the mass, where all the inhibitions with which on his own he strives to control his moral and personal life are released, man's inhumanity to man is far greater than any other species' cruelty to its own kind. At times a seeker of perfect conduct and expression, at others he is a wolf, and worse than a wolf, investing himself with

the clothing and the bleat of the self-righteous sheep. This knowledge of his divided nature is too much for him to bear; in order
not to admit it to himself he hides it from others unless they
should see him as he is. 'He shudders at his own naturalness',[1]
and clothes his own nakedness so that he may neither be seen
for what he is nor have to deal with himself as he is.

THE NEED FOR INSTITUTIONS

Society meets the facts of human ambiguity through institutions
of many kinds – government, law courts, learning, industry and
so on. And it is in their different attitudes to institutions that
political philosophers reflect the divisions of human opinion
about human ambiguity itself : whether human waywardness is
an accident that better institutions could have avoided altogether,
or whether it is an indelible defect of human nature that has to
be met by the coercive powers of government; whether man
is at heart a perfectible, friendly and cooperative creature,
frustrated and perverted by wrong institutions, or whether he is
essentially self-seeking, faithless and combative.

For the first class of thinkers, organised society fundamentally
expresses the friendly dispositions of men. Man in his original
state was good and cooperated spontaneously : all that need be
done to restore him to that state is to abolish the institutions that
embody the extraneous defects and contradictions that have
crept in to the human condition since; then to imitate in a
sophisticated way his recollection of that original paradise in the
form of institutions that are appropriate to his contemporary
techniques. A ruthless sweeping away of all defects and the
promotion of the right type of institutions, by virtue of their
fidelity to justice and rationality, will save man from any future
corrupting influences and will enable him to realise his latent
good, or, as Marx expresses it, his 'essential human nature'.

For the other class of thinkers, society is an artificial con-
struction that has grown up out of the mutual need of men to
place a check upon their natural hostility to one another. It is
a compact of truce, built upon self-interest, whereby they are
saved from the malice and egoism of one another and enabled
by artificial means to cooperate in affairs where it can be demon-

1. C. F. von Weizacker, quoted in Victor Gollancz, *Year of Grace* (London,
    1950), p. 191.

strated by appeal to fact or expedience that their interests coincide. Since cooperation is not an intrinsic part of their nature, they have to put themselves under the dominion of men of superior ability – princes in politics and sophists in the social sciences – and invent institutions to express what agreement is possible and desirable between them. For this school of thought, love of neighbour has to be converted into an artificial norm and obedience to it secured by penal exactions or by inducements directed to men's appetites, sensations and desires for power, prestige and position, whereas for the first school it is a natural inclination for statesmen to posit in framing all their laws or designing institutions.

There is a third, more natural and realistic approach that takes both points of view into account whilst showing that neither is sufficient by itself. Human nature cannot be defined exclusively in terms of its capacity for good on the one hand, or of its physical qualities and appetite on the other. Human goodness, according to this view, is grounded in propensities that can never be fully realised, because the human race is never likely to devote itself consistently and totally to them; because, too, different people's objects of good differ, and men exist in a world of material imperfections and can never possess total truth. There have, therefore, to be institutions to encourage men to achieve their best and to control their worst; both types of institution are necessary – those that restrain man's egoism, combativeness and duplicity – institutions of negative liberty; and those that encourage him and give him the opportunity of expressing constructively his creative, positive and cooperative qualities – institutions of positive liberty.

Social arrangements must realistically reflect both the ambiguity and fallibility of man. It is in this connection that, for example, Popper insists upon the importance of building into science, philosophy and politics a recognition of human fallibility. Cooperation, indeed, must be what he calls friendly-hostile; hostile, because it involves criticism; friendly, because it is useful. Criticism has for a very long time been confused with censure and social disapproval. In order to overcome this attitude we might indeed devise institutions that assume and reflect the basic fallibility of our human nature, by, for example, instituting that any scientist who is subject to a serious public criticism by a Fellow of the Royal Society is thereby made a corresponding member of that Society, that a politician attacked by opponents be regularly invited to talk to the local branch of the opponent, and so on. Here is a great field open for further study and application.[2]

The need for both positive and negative institutions is made clearer if one recalls the maxim, 'Civilisation is law'. An institution, it has to be emphasised, is not only an organisation, it is also a public arrangement which has, or needs, the support of law or of equivalent social sanctions : thus the family is an institution, friendship is not; established social customs are institutions, but conventions, such as hand-shaking or using a knife and fork at the table, are not.

Any mode of cooperation to be stable has to be institutionalised. Thus private arrangements, and informal relationships become formalised and are given the sanction of law. In the same way, recognition of rights and wrongs and definition of what is criminal have to be institutionalised and so to give rise to courts of law, systems of punishment and the concept of damages for injuries suffered. The meaning of institutions should not of course be confused with the word 'bureaucracy'. Indeed, as has already been suggested, much can be achieved by reforms taking away functions from bureaucracies and giving them back to small purposive groups, communities, families and individuals themselves. In doing this, of course, new institutions will thereby be created, many of them to help the smaller groups to establish and maintain themselves.

MAKING THE FIELD OF LIMITATIONS MORE HUMAN

Proportion must be restored to the human environment and to human life itself. Already we are apprehensive of untellable disaster. 'There was a time when we were on the land' says Ma, the heroine of Steinbeck's *The Grapes of Wrath*; 'there was a boundary to us then', life had limits and they were securely known. Now we sense that some of these boundaries are breaking apart at the corners where hitherto they were securely tied,

2. I am indebted to Professor Joseph Agassi for the ideas expressed in this paragraph.

and others where before they formed a continuous line. We have become greedy for knowledge of one particular kind; the kind that will lead to the limitless satisfaction of desire, appetite and sensation. We have ceased to try to understand the experience of life as a unity or the wisdom underlying our attempts to find value in it. Our efforts in one part of the world to overcome scarcity and to treat luxury as an everyday necessity have been undertaken at the expense of the resources of the rest. We lack adequate institutions of distribution, and all the while our need for spontaneous cooperation with each other gets lost in larger and larger and more unfeeling, insensitive, unwieldy organisations. The freedom and opportunities for true human fellowship and conviviality has shrunk to a smaller measure than perhaps at any other time in man's long history.

The field of our contemporary existence is, therefore, to be imagined as ugly and distorted and there are three immediate steps to be taken whereby these defects may be righted. The first is to iron out the excesses; this involves recognising what the excesses are and having standards by which to judge them. The second is to redistribute within the framework of existing society the fruits of all its many achievements. What is produced must be distributed more justly and institutions must be adapted or devised to do this. No less important, the means of production must be distributed differently so that those with the ability and the zeal to do so may have the opportunity of enjoying fulfilment in their work. But most important of all it is necessary to ensure that all the knowledge that civilisation possesses is open and public and available to all. There must be no secret knowledge, no trade secrets, no laboratory secrets, no secret know-how, nor little private groups using a monopoly of some particular facet of human knowledge to exploit the rest of mankind.

The third step needed to be taken is to introduce new features into the human situation – features in particular that amend that end of the field which is based on the limitations of human ambiguity. Only a little imagination is needed to see that this line, the human boundary, is not only very much narrower than the other three; it is also very much further away from its ultimate standard than the rest.

The initiative is with men both individually and socially, therefore, to acquire a new outlook that recognises the reality of their values and of the creative potentialities of human nature. When they have found this and established it with the same certainty with which they acclaim physical knowledge, it will be possible to approach the problems of finding new institutions and new techniques to translate this outlook into material opportunity.

Next a word must be said about the means whereby a more human outlook may be formulated. Sometimes it is asserted, with wistful envy for past ages when there existed a unity of action and belief, that no such outlook can take hold until a comprehensive and systematic political philosophy exists that first propounds it. On this view political philosophers are both the fire engines to extinguish the first smouldering of social disquiet and the manure carts to fertilise afresh exhausted patches of ground. Political philosophers are neither – and, indeed, are rarely able to give system and coherence to thought until after its elements have been sprouted by a variety of other more creative but less consistent thinkers. It is for more ordinary people to state their values with the help of those who specialise in these fields and feel deeply about them, and then for philosophers to rationalise these new statements and convictions.

With even less justification, men also look to experts with established reputations in other activities of public life to give them the details of the social and moral outlook they need – the television panel, consisting, say, of a fluent journalist, perhaps the very able London correspondent of a distinguished foreign newspaper, an up-and-coming young don in a recondite scientific subject at a redbrick university, a member of parliament, and the inevitable eminent after-dinner humorist, is one of the favourite forums for this question : 'What does the panel think children should be taught in schools about the moral assumptions of their civilisation?' Just as a film-star who does little or no housework is in no position to recommend household washing powder, so these men renowned in other walks of life are no better fitted to answer such a question than thousands of the viewers watching them. Indeed, the question is one to be answered by ordinary people rather than by experts in other unrelated areas of specialisation; and if an extraneous expert is to participate in the assessment of human values and their relevance to social outlook, it should be as an ordinary person and not as a public figure with all the influence of his prestige gained from another field.

The masses of ordinary people are conscious of their own bewilderment, of the conflict between the practices of their society and the values which its political institutions embody and on which its humane attitudes are based. They are conscious too of the narrow utilitarian and positivistic norms of the experts who lecture them – and at times confound them – with their brilliant superficiality. They are anxious too for a society of wider proportions and deeper foundations in which they themselves can achieve in practice a fuller human life. Their confusion and despondency is not due to the supposed fact that basic human values have suffered an eclipse, for these basic values and aspirations have not ceased to matter to ordinary men and women in their private reckonings. The same themes and the same conflicts between higher perceptions and more immediate impulses run through their private lives as ever did. But they live in an artificial society that has been able to function – though for how long it will be able to continue to do so is another matter – with the most amazing efficiency without taking these deeper insights into account at all. Hence ordinary people are subdued, incoherent and reluctant to speak. In such a mood and without speech they are in sullen rebellion, no longer identifying themselves with the progress of their civilisation. They are indifferent spectators of its mechanical development.

For we, which now behold these present days,
Have eyes to wonder, but lack tongues to praise.
(Shakespeare, Sonnet 106)

Chapter 12

A More Human Outlook

ESSENTIAL HUMAN NATURE

If human nature cannot be defined exclusively as good or bad, how are we to amend passages of thought and writing where such expressions occur as 'essential human nature', or 'fully human', 'truly human' or 'really human' and are intended to have favourable meanings? If 'essential human nature' is *not* a bundle of moral qualities that are consistent with each other and under favourable conditions cooperate with one another in the production of good conduct; if, on the other hand, it is a bundle of inconsistent qualities which, without constraint and regulation, set men at war with each other, would not less committed and less ambiguous expressions declare more precisely what this term is intended to convey? Would not words such as 'typical' or 'best human qualities' and, in other circumstances, 'human dignity', 'undivided personality', or the more dated expression 'the whole man', have more reliable meanings? We must know the answers to these questions, because in these Marxian expressions, now used as extensively by Christians and liberals, and even benevolent social democrats calling themselves liberal, as by Marxists themselves, we had hoped to find the link between the individual's search for freedom and his own significance on the one hand, and liberty as a policy of collective humanity on the other. Moreover, without answers we cannot have any clear idea of what a more human outlook would be.

In Chapter 9, we have referred to the central place which the idea of essential human nature plays in one of Marx's key doctrines. According to him, contradictory economic forces, embodied in the institution of private property, alone prevent the identical display of essential human nature in everyone. Men do, of course, have different secondary qualities such as character, skill, ability, intelligence, personality; but inside each person, locked up and unreleased because of the repressions of private property, is this essential human nature, this essence, this potentiality for freedom and identical good – almost absolute good in itself. 'Communism,' he wrote, 'is the abolition of private property, of human alienation, and thus the real appropriation of human nature (or the human essence), through and for man. It is therefore the return of man himself as a social, that is, a really human being; a complete and conscious return which assimilates all the wealth of previous development.'[1]

This vision of a universal human nature awaiting certain specific conditions to be released in the lives of all men would appear to be more religious than political in origin. In assuming the possibility of a final and apocalyptic negation of all negations, Marx was inviting belief in the possibility of establishing heaven on earth.

Perhaps in this case one should trace the origin of his idea to St Paul rather than to Hegel or Aristotle. In communist society men would be members in each other, limbs of the same body, living the life of the same essence : 'For by one spirit are we all baptised into one body. . . . But now there are many members yet but one body. And the eye cannot say unto the hand, I have no need of thee, nor again to the feet, I have no need of you. Nay, much more those members of the body, which seem to be more feeble, are necessary.'[2]

But short of the nature of the spiritual body of the Christian Church or a universal communist party with all its members living unambiguous lives, what are we to mean by a 'really human being'? It is clear that we do use this and similar expressions in different ways to mean at least three different things. The

1. Karl Marx, *Economic and Philosophical Manuscripts of 1844*, in *Karl Marx: Early Writings*, trans. and ed. T. B. Bottomore (London, 1963), p. 155.
2. 1 Cor. xii: 21 and 22.

first is as St Paul and Marx do to mean the essence of human nature that can only be fully expressed, fully lived, in an ideal society, a society yet to come, free of contradiction and ambiguity. We can also think of this as absolute integrity, the whole and undivided personality existing with none of the ambiguity of human nature. It is best to reserve the expression, 'essential human nature' or 'the essentially human' for this range of meanings.

Secondly, we use it and similar expressions when wanting to make lists of those qualities or mixtures of qualities which we regard as distinctively human or characteristically human; when, for example, Hobbes says that whenever man conceives of anything, he is apt to inquire into the consequences of it and what he can do with them,[3] or when Marx claims that man is essentially a toolmaker, and in contrast to animals 'makes his life-activities themselves an object of his willing and of his consciousness, so that he alone has conscious life-activities', or that 'man alone is a producer of his concepts, ideas' and so on,[4] these statements tend to be anthropocentric and there are no certain means of knowing them to be true. It is wiser, therefore, to keep the list of 'distinctively human qualities' to a minimum and to regard every item on it as contingent. Even before these qualities claimed by Hobbes and Marx, awareness of justice and of truth as categories would be on everyone's list; also love in a specifically human sense; probably also the capacity to recognise differences as such, otherwise how would justice and truth as principles operate and be seen to be distinctively human? The awareness of differences as such, of course, enables man to be aware of the ambiguities of his nature and conduct. Rooted in both are two of the most characteristic of all human qualities, so often startlingly present in the same person. One is pride and the other is humility.

Pride may be seen as the habit of over-valuing oneself, over-emphasising the importance of one's own individuality and place and honour, or as *The Concise Oxford Dictionary* defines it, 'an overweening opinion of our own excellence'. Humility is too

3. Thomas Hobbes, *Leviathan* (Oxford, 1960), p. 27.
4. Bottomore, *Karl Marx: Early Writings*, pp. 127–8. Animals produce only under compulsion of physical need, whilst man is 'free in face of his product' and constructs also 'in accordance with the laws of beauty'.

difficult to define precisely, yet everyone knows individuals in whom it exists supremely.

There are, of course, a number of other seemingly distinctive human qualities. To be endowed with reason in a wider sense than Hobbes' definition comes first to mind. Almost on a par with it is the capacity for passion and concern. Men have passion and concern not simply for the generalities they form which seem to them to be most consistently reasonable and needed; but also for those convictions, causes and aims which they value most and for the people who share them, as well as for those they love or about whose plight they are anxious. This fellowship of shared concern arouses compassion as well as passion and leads on to one of the most striking and (for empirical and sceptical thinkers especially) difficult of all distinctive human characteristics: the obsession to identify with generalities and with fellow beings of the same conviction to the extent of being willing to die for them. In the distinctively human man are the bowels of compassion and he not only ought to be, but nearly always is, willing 'to lay down his life for his brethren'. Unhappily, human ambivalence so often intervenes that this same man is hardly less willing to kill the brethren of others. But in the end the truly human man must clearly be seen to stand for something. He must be able to recognise goodness and truthfulness so as, despite his ambiguity, to try to attain them within himself and he must be able to give his ultimate loyalty and support to those who stand for, or strive after, the same things.

So far as the theme of this book is concerned, there are five other distinctively human qualities especially to emphasise. First is the power of conversation and exchange of ideas. Second is the capacity for creativity: not simply making things, but also introducing through the medium of ideas the new into the human situation. Human beings have the power to make plans and to project them into the future, so that constantly they can change their situations and reach the goals that they have set themselves. Often to do this they may have to revise many times their original plans and choice of means. Third, therefore, is the capacity to adapt, repair, improvise and to deal quickly with emergencies by *ad hoc* measures. Probably no man could repeat the geometrical perfection of a spider's web, yet spiders cannot repair the damage done to even one tiny section of it. Fourth, is an apparent inability to accept for long what is claimed to be, or even recognised to be, a state of perfection. Almost as soon as any art form or even political form is perfected, men seem to want to abandon it and to search for another with which to supersede it. 'Here there is no abiding city.' There is no final solution. Men seem to have a well-founded instinct that a perfectly organised society would soon become a fossilised one : one perfect custom or habit would corrupt :

> The old order changeth, yielding place to new,
> And God fulfils himself in many ways,
> Lest one good custom should corrupt the world.[5]

The fifth of these distinctively human qualities is that man is an all-rounder and with a little training is able to do a great many things reasonably well. This capacity is, of course, irritating to utilitarian perfectionists who are anxious for specialists to work out men's solutions for them and to leave them with few causes of spontaneous and responsible action outside their special- ism. Nevertheless, it is by making good their mistakes, turning their hands to many things, following their own aspirations and balancing out the needs of their natures in many ways in the company of those most congenial to them, that men can overcome the worst consequences of their own ambiguity. In this way they can enter imaginatively into the difficulties other people have with theirs. Here is an important field for educational as well as social reformers.

THE FULLY HUMAN

Most of the qualities that normally and unthinkingly we call 'really human' go on the third list to which the description 'fully human' applies. These are typically human qualities without which we should regard no man as 'fully human'; but many of which, such as bravery or perseverance, or the ability to bear pain well, we know animals to share. We are able of course to dress up many of them and include terms such as 'honesty with oneself' or 'true to oneself' and so make them appear to be dis-

5. Tennyson, 'Idylls of the King', l. 407.

tinctively human; although in fact animal species would appear to be instinctively true to the nature of their species, whereas most humans often find it hard to be true even to what they consider their own particular nature to be, let alone to that of the human species. What really entitles one to call another person 'fully human' is the mixture of many qualities in him; some of which may be considered exclusive to human nature, but others not. The 'fully human' man must have, it would seem, courage, fairmindedness, generosity, loyalty, intelligence, resourcefulness and other positive qualities, but also a fairly wide range of defects. The capacity for anger must be part of him. He is one who has certainly not overcome the ambiguity of human nature. Brutus, according to Mark Anthony, was such a man. His virtues and vices were those compounded from the sanguine, the choleric, the melancholic and the phlegmatic.

> His life was gentle, and the elements
> So mix'd in him that Nature might stand up
> And say to all the world, 'This was a man'.[6]

To be immediately recognisable the fully human man must be genuine in himself and sincere – without wax to conceal the bruises and scars of his defects. He must be one who is unable to 'offer incense to the unworthy': but on the other hand, be generous, even to a fault. He must be magnanimous – perhaps Churchill's most attractive quality. Although with clear moral judgments and decided opinions of his own, he is always, on first being approached, open and fair minded; accessible to and with an equal regard for all men; and a warm humility in his manner counts far more than any special ability or distinction. Being moved matters very much, whether it is by someone else or by an aesthetic experience.

Some human qualities of the fully human seem more fundamental than others and it is this combination of generosity, humility and awareness which makes them so: to be aware that one is living in an order of people and things and in a universe infinitely larger than oneself; to have that generosity of response

6. Shakespeare, *Julius Caesar*, Act V Scene iii, l. 71.

which is more than is strictly called for by the situation, circumstances or predicament, from these more fundamental attitudes it
would seem that a certain kind of sensuousness is desirable –
sensuousness which is a generalisable attitude to the whole
material order as well as a particular response to the touch,
texture, colour and shape of a particular item in it. Anyone
concerned with the preservation of the human environment, or
with fitting the right kind of buildings and cities into it, must
be sensuous in this way. He must have feeling and a sense of the
appropriate. Before all else he must be capable of standing
still and being filled with awe and wonder – the *thumos* of
Plato.

A quality – more social than individual – which deserves to
be high among 'fully human' characteristics is, as we have seen
in considering the distinctively human, the capacity for fellowship – participating in relationships of feeling with other human
beings. This is not the same as friendship, which is a form of
exclusive love between two or at least a very limited number of
people, and probably belongs to the distinctively human; but it
has many of friendship's characteristics. It is feeling of identity
and of separateness too. It is something humans share in some
respects with animal species, but it is capable of being much more
highly developed in humans, because of their apparent greater
self-consciousness, because of their powers to exchange ideas, to
recognise their interests, their values, their priorities and to do
things intentionally with and for others : because, too, of their
apparently greater capacity to display their emotions and consciously to seek enjoyment with each other. The idea contains
large elements of self-conscious fun, enjoyment of something for
its own sake, spontaneity and caring. An area of sympathy lies
on one side of it and conviviality on the other. Fellowship,
conviviality and feelings of sympathy are possible with strangers
of the same disposition; it is even possible to tell quickly on
encountering a group whether it has people in it with whom
one will be able to experience a happy state of fellowship. Because
doing things together, furthering common purposes, putting
cherished values above self-centred aims and living with one's
fellow beings in a spirit of open good will are very much activities at the centre of the idea of fellowship, it is all the more
surprising that, in spite of attempts by the French revolutionaries,

it has never become an important concept of political thought and activity.[7]

There are two concepts which, in conjunction with each other and each in a particular sense, constitute the specific condition of living the fully human life : fully rather than distinctively, because, although they are not shared by animal life, they are manifestly not characteristic of all human life and relationships. Indeed their realisation, or attempted realisation, as a unified working principle in any society at any single period of time has been exceedingly rare. One is freedom and the other is equality : freedom in the fullest moral sense – the freedom to choose responsibly and effectively, as well as to put a ranging order of value on all the possible objects of choice and on alternative courses of action, belief and conduct; equality as the equality which, in spite of all the manifest differences of each individual life, gives each man the dignity and the regard of other men, also the means of being fully human – the equality which makes the very fact of each man and woman, being a different personality with different characteristics, the basis of the equal regard and treatment which it postulates.

'God alone knows the truth. To man he has given freedom' : this ancient insight combines the essential fallibility of man with the practice of the full range of values and virtues which he acknowledges. But it is only man himself who can give equality to his fellow men. It is the most free of all things any man can do; because only in the deepest sense of a kinship in a common humanity are all men equal. As such it is the basis of all 'face-to-face relationships', of one man holding the attention of another in his eyes. It is also, however, the basis of all radical demands for changes in society – changes that go against the empirically verifiable facts of inequality. Thus, freedom and equality, welded into a single precept and weapon of principle and policy,

7. Marx also wished to develop the idea of fellowship :
     The fellowship from which a worker is isolated is a fellowship of a scope and order of reality quite different from that of the political fellowship. The fellowship from which his own labour separates the worker is life itself, physical and intellectual life, morality and customs, human activity, human satisfaction, being human. Being human is the true fellowship of men. (Marx/Engels, *Correspondence*, Section 1, 3, 21–3).

constitute a mystery at the core of man's social, political life which is a truth between men and the criterion of all fully human revolutionary change. It points to the meeting place of religion and politics. But equality postulated by itself, without being joined to freedom or bedded in the fully human, is a dangerous tool which, in fact, whenever it has been so employed, has frustrated or destroyed every potential revolution of liberty to which it has been applied – the French Revolution is an example.

Finally, it is necessary to return to the theme of ambiguity as the quality of human character that inevitably sets the limits of any new outlook that would seek to be practical and to change society from being primarily utilitarian and materialistic to one that is creative and compassionate. This theme belongs more to the distinctively or truly human, than to the fully human, because it views man as he is different from other species, ambivalent towards them and to the whole of nature. Seen from one aspect man is part of the world and totally dependent upon it for his material existence, maintenance and preservation. He is limited by the scarcity of its resources, just as every other living animal is. Seen from another he is separate from it and from the rest of the universe. He 'stands over against' both. It is this consciousness that gives him his desire for knowledge, so as to know the truth of that which is strange to him. It is this too which makes him, at any rate in his more natural condition, a worshipper. It gives him his awareness of beauty and arouses in him awe and response. It gives him also his idea of order which is contrasted so starkly with the disorder produced by his unwillingness to cooperate fully with other men. And then also there is his awareness of his own imperfections, his own lack of completeness. Thus again we reach the four limitations of the human condition : scarcity, ignorance, lack of cooperation and human ambiguity. The severity of their effects can be reduced; but their existence is as lasting as man's life on earth itself.

A MORE HUMAN OUTLOOK

For the purposes of a more natural human outlook we need the idea of the distinctively human because of the many threats to characteristic human qualities implicit in the petty perfectionist tendencies of artificial utilitarian processes and of the bureaucratic procedures of utilitarian society. All the more we need

G

it because without the concepts of justice, mercy, charity, truth and reason, men would cease to be human. The idea of the 'fully human' we need because of its warmth, its full-bodiedness and its positive qualities which we shall find are stimulating in provoking practical thoughts about the kind of future society and the kind of communities we want. We need also the concept of the 'essentially human' – the human essence or spirit – of Marx and St Paul. The ideal of the whole man or undivided personality is an indispensable criterion for the formation of an adequate critique of artificial utilitarianism and the bringing to birth of a more natural and creative outlook with which to replace it.

But how is man to grapple with the problem of his wholeness, his integrity, not so much with a view to attaining his elusive moral perfection but so as, at the least, to give to the life he leads in society, the work he does, his politics and all his other social activities, the mark of being distinctively and more fully human? How can he gather the practical as well as the moral equipment to oppose the prevailing artificial utilitarian outlook with one that is natural and balanced? These questions are of prime importance, and we need to agree with Kant that 'first politics must do homage to morals',[8] or, as Popper has restated the proposition, 'we must moralise our politics rather than politicise our morality.'[9]

At root, the problem of human ambiguity, the problem of the whole man, of holiness, is the problem of all religions. This fact in itself, at a time when religion is singled out for special attack and when, as a result, people lack confidence in religious beliefs, makes it difficult, but none the less all the more desirable, to state what is required to make more whole – or holy – creatures. God is a concept people are reluctant or embarrassed to use in public discussion. None the less, even if only as the personalisation of intrinsic value or of man's highest standards – for

---

8. Kant, *Perpetual Peace*: see also Kant's third formulation of the moral principle 'the conception of the will of every rational being as a universally legislative will'. As Ross notes, this formulation contains the ambiguity of the idea of a self-imposed law, and suggests that 'the dignity of human nature is more effectively asserted if it is described as the maker of its own laws'. *Kant's Ethical Theory*, p. 95.
9. Popper, *The Open Society and Its Enemies*, Vol. 1, p. 173.

example, of goodness, truth, justice, freedom and beauty and
love of his fellow men, also those of self-sacrifice and honesty with
oneself – it is the clearest concept that can be used economically
to show what is required for men to live more whole lives. To
understand the concept of God, used in this human and minimal
way, is not a difficult intellectual or emotional undertaking.
Beethoven is said to have had framed on his desk an inscription
copied from an Indian temple :

I am that which is. I am all what is, what was, what will be; no
mortal man has lifted my veil.[10]

'To know God', said Socrates, 'men have first to live God' : to
live a life of practical virtue and to seek beauty within the
natural order.[11] The Hebrew prophet Jeremiah was more down to
earth. 'He judged the cause of the poor and needy, then it
was well with him : was not this to know me ? saith the Lord.'[12]
Both Jewish and Christian teaching at the present time would
agree that a man who does well the work he undertakes, whatever it is, whether he is paid for it or not, and does it so that
others may enjoy its consequences, has no need to think that he
knows God less or praises him less than the most famous theo-
logians or devout priests.

Men's social systems should be so designed that they themselves
can play direct parts in remedying injustices and misfortunes
which are within their reach to remedy : in helping personally
and directly the handicapped and in bringing the warmth of
affection and practical aid to children without parents, to the old
and the deprived; in using their own hands, if that can be organised, to help repair houses for the homeless, or wherever else
they can be compassionately employed. Even these words are
wrong and patronising, yet in a utilitarian society it is impossible
to use others without losing the identities of those classes needed
to be included within the community. In a truly human community, these classes would hardly exist as separate categories.

10. George Marek, *Beethoven* (London, 1970), p. 413.
11. *Republic* 519; see also *Meno* 99 and 100, *Symposium* 24.
12. Jeremiah xxii: 16.

It would simply be recognised that all need fellowship and that this takes many forms.

The utilitarian system, with its faith in legislation and impersonal departmentalised arrangements, has taken away from the world of spontaneous personal concern all these natural, instinctive, neighbourly forms of caring for others. Public institutions are needed, but to complement community and personal effort, not to supersede them, nor to put books of rules where the heart should be. It was in demanding the right for direct personal action in ways such as these that the movements of protest, revolt and direct personal action in the 60s and 70s have given concrete evidence of people's desires for more constructive, sympathetic, face-to-face social outlook as the basis for radical change.

Such prescriptions are vital parts of the Western tradition and easy to understand. Men should discover their obligations, their talents, their skills and interests and their all-roundedness too; then find activity to carry out – not necessarily work in a formal sense – so as to practise these qualities as much for the well-being of other people or for the activities' own sake, or for the greater glory of the world itself. They can then forget the quest for fulfilment. It simply happens. The good has many forms of expressions and there are a great many routes to it.

But in the end it is who the person is that matters most to creation – the entire being he is; not what he may, or may not, have done. Moreover, no man can be considered as fully human or entire whose life has not been affected by an aim outside itself, beyond the finite and material. Thus, for example, Bertrand Russell claimed (*Principles of Social Reconstruction*, London, 1916, p. 245): 'Life devoted only to life is animal, without any real human value, incapable of preserving men permanently from weariness and the feeling that all is vanity. If life is to be fully human it must serve some end which seems, in some sense, outside human life, some end which is impersonal and above mankind, such as God or truth or beauty. Those who best promote life do not have life for their purpose. They aim rather at what seems like a gradual incarnation, a bringing into our human existence of something eternal, something that appears to imagination to live in a heaven remote from strife and failure and the devouring jaws of Time.'

A beautiful object, whether it be a living organism or any whole composed of parts, must not only have an orderly arrangement of parts, but must also be of a certain magnitude; for beauty depends on magnitude and order.

(Aristotle, *Poetics*, vii, 4)

Chapter 13

The Free Man in Society

All human beings, it appears, have a need to identify with an organised group or community. The question may be asked: 'What, for different purposes, are the right human-sized organisations?' and, arising from this, the further question, 'what is the right human-sized community?' The answers will in the first place be biased towards the medium and small and towards the principle of decentralisation. But in showing that there are different activities and purposes, it will become apparent that many basically small- or medium-sized independent groups work best and give their members the liveliest sense of freedom when they are joined together, however loosely, into larger wholes representative of their purposes but not able to dictate what these purposes should be or how they should be achieved.

REASONS FOR PREFERRING THE MEDIUM OR SMALL TO THE LARGE

There are three well-established and fairly obvious criteria by which any organisation may be considered to have become either too large or over-centralised. The first is when the individuals making it up cease to count or to matter to it and to each other. In organisations of such size, rules and bureaucratic procedures take the place of human relationships. The second is when initiatives, decision-making and control activity generally are taken away from individuals or small natural associations or purposive groups and given to a central command organisation, as a rule functioning in the same way as the hierarchy of command of an army is imagined to operate in war time. The third is when size is primarily a function of power. Some commercial amalgamations and mergers may make sound economic sense but the majority, on closer examination, will be found to have been undertaken for a reason connected with the pursuit of power. The chairman or managing director wants more power for himself, or the board of directors as a whole for themselves; if they did not swallow up smaller companies, they believe that they themselves would be swallowed by a larger one. Then again, as Weil observed, size enables top management to create greater distances between themselves and their work forces, and the greater this distance the greater is the reality as well as the appearance of power. The third criterion for an organisation of any kind being too large is also connected with power : that degree of monopoly or concentration which gives its possessors the prospect of a totally objectionable centralisation of power over the rest of the community. This monopoly or concentration may be economic or political. When it is both – concentrated politico-economic power – a stage of tyranny or potential tyranny will have been reached which would be almost impossible to overthrow without extreme violence. It is against this danger that all objections to undue size, undue centralisation, too many mergers, are ultimately directed.

Some degree and some forms of power are inevitable in all social, economic and political relationships. So far as the world outside a given, or a number of given, organisations is concerned, power in the objectionable sense (for different senses of power, see Chapter 16) can only be effectively controlled when there are a great many centres of initiative and decision making and a large number of different kinds of organisation and counter-vailing power existing under the supremacy of a totally independent law. But so far as the inside world of any organisation is concerned, there are other more easily approached remedies. The best and most immediate of all is familiarity. When the chairman and his directors are all known personally by the workers, undue ostentation and display of power can be seen to be absurd and be ridiculed very quickly. When managers and specialists work with groups of relatively small numbers and the groups themselves have intelligible purposes to fulfil skilfully, power is usually closely related to purpose and confined by the relationships within the group.

Other reasons for the desirable size of the purposive workgroups being small and the firm being small to medium sized, have been given in Chapter 10. There is, therefore, no need here to consider again the advantage of the small- and medium-sized unit of work. Weil's criteria of size may, however, with suitable adaptations, be used for assessing the optimum sizes of other organisations. They should never be so vast that anyone belonging to them or living in them is not able to comprehend in his mind and imagination what is done of common interest within them and what his own relationship is both to what is being done and to the other members belonging.

The other reasons for preferring small- and medium-sized units are mainly personal and moral. But the general point has first to be made that the words 'small', 'medium-sized', 'large', or even 'mammoth' have different meanings according to the entity being considered. A very large orchestra is the size of a small village; a mammoth firm, hardly that of a small city and so on. In general it may be found that 'doing-groups' tend to be called large very much sooner than either living units or composite bodies made up of a number of independent or quasi-independent or subsidiary units.

The personal reasons for preferring, subject to the above qualifications about the relative usages of the words, small- and medium-sized groups to larger ones are many. In the small- and medium-sized group the individual can be effective in the realisation of his own projects and of those he shares with others. If the group is a creative one, it is of course almost certain that the project as first conceived will be improved upon; all belonging to the group will contribute to the understanding and discussion of it as well as to its carrying out. In this way the original concept will be changed for the good. Nor is it easy for any single person's point of view to be shouted down or ignored; as in Aristotle's *polis*, men can know each other's characters, anticipate one another's actions and all be familiar with the thinking of each other so that there is much less need for formal rules and rigid procedures. There is an easy understanding and a ready give and take. Small groups exist for specific purposes, the attaining of ends agreed upon by their members and to which they are devoted. The group therefore need not make demands on them beyond these limits. Loyalties thrive between the members as fellows of each other and not of an anonymous collective with its propaganda and moral hypocrisy. Thus the structure of the small group exists for the purposes of the men in it, rather than the men in it being subservient to its needs for continuity, expansion and survival.

The typical large impersonal organisation, on the other hand, asserts through its hierarchy of command its own purposes, demands its own survival and is ambitious of expanding its territory at the expense of other groups. In the end it is the same as with armies; only survival of the organisation matters; its original aims and purposes are forgotten and left behind. Those working in large organisations are obliged to serve ends they have not chosen and do not understand as well as to accept commands solely for the sake of their attainment. They quickly lose their status as persons and assume the role of tools; they revert to the subject-object relationship and have little zest for the work they are given to do. The best that they could have contributed as whole men, intelligently absorbed in spontaneous activities and in occupations fitted to their skills and temperaments, is lost to society. Instead society has to accept the lesser – the reluctant and often disgruntled fragmentary contributions exacted from them by the impersonal disciplines exerted by remote controllers. How much violence in politics, how many sudden strikes, how much less productivity and how much shoddy workmanship in the big firms is due to large impersonal units of organisation and to individual workers in them unable to realise their own aspirations or to identify with the massive organisations by which they are employed?

The moral reasons are similar.[1] In small groups, where equality

1. Compare Jung:
    A large company that is made up of entirely admirable people resembles, in respect to its morality and intelligence, an unwieldy, stupid and violent animal. Hence the larger the organisation, the more is its immorality and blind stupidity inevitable. (*Senatus bestia, senatores boni viri.*) By automatically stressing the collective qualities in its individual representatives, society will necessarily set a premium on everything that is average and that tends to vegetate in an easy, irresponsible way.
    Two Essays on Analytical Psychology, trans. H. G. and C. F. Baynes (London and New York, 1928), p. 148.

exists between the members, the decisions made are all personal ones, and their being carried out depends upon the sense of responsibility of each member to all the others. They are discussed or debated at a personal level, and each member subscribing to them does so with a full awareness of the commitment he has made. In large groups, even in conditions of formal equality, or in democracies, the decisions carried out are collective ones : the majority governs but this does not necessarily mean that the minority accepts either their ends or their means of attaining them. Moreover, groups beyond a certain size are affected by irrational psychological phenomena associated with collectives, such as mass suggestion, adulation of leadership personalities, mass hysteria and the imperatives to expand and survive. By way of examples, one can think of the differences in function and climate between, say, a branch meeting of a trade union and a national congress of the same union, and of the differences between the meeting of a local religious group, church or chapel and the national assembly of the same body: resolutions are passed, but there remains the difficulty of getting in the one instance the rank-and-file membership and in the other the men and women in the pews to accept them as personal decisions. The very distance between the local and national body dulls the urgency and vividness of the local point of view and condemns it to insignificance even before it is ventilated. Thus the once generous member loses heart and abandons his sense of personal responsibility. If he continues to belong to the body, it is an unthinking commitment; he becomes a passenger who pays his fare willy-nilly without caring greatly whether he goes by one route or by another.

Springing from these reasons, and also because of the liberty in the Weilian sense which they give, small and medium sized groups are the sources of originality, invention and new values in society. In them, too, cultures are preserved and developed in a lively way; dialects and traditions kept fresh. A large number of small groups and small communities existing side by side, with their complexes of face-to-face and kinship relationships and continuity of living styles, provide a country or a region with enviable variety. But not everything is on the credit side of the account. The very word 'parochial' describes most of the items on the other side; inward-looking, censorious and interfering, apt to be untouched by important issues of the time – sometimes complacent and more than a little narrow-minded.

Some groups can be too small. Often they are far less democratically organised or sensitive to minority opinions than larger ones. Not only villages, but also sects, associations and small organisations of many different kinds can be parochial and given over to vices such as gossiping, henpecking and pharisaism. Very small departments of provincial universities can be the most crippling, claustrophobic, vicious communities; so too the small intellectual society, the long established voluntary body surviving under the tyrannical control of a self-perpetuating committee. What is wrong with bodies such as these, however, is not so much the fact of their size, as that their structures and their relationships to larger, more central organisations and communities are wrongly conceived. The essence of the value of the small group or community is its potentiality for fellowship. A small group, voluntary society or university department, in order to gain the most value from its size, has to be animated by a sense of purpose more important than its own survival and organisational preoccupations. It is this sense of purpose and awareness of issues larger than those with which it can deal on its own that relates it to other groups both small and large; it gives it a sense of belonging to an identity of wider horizons than the mere parochial. In the utilitarian and fragmented society in which we live it has to be admitted that these conditions do not often obtain. Moreover, the more intellectual and sometimes the more exalted the *raison d'être* of the group or association, the more isolated it tends to become from the rest of society.

The emphasis upon the small cannot therefore be made to the exclusion of the claims of the complementary larger entity or those of society as a whole. Often the small is the writing room or rehearsal platform for that which is eventually intended to be played before and to influence the large – the political movement begun in the front parlour of a small-town villa; the research experiments and innovations pioneered in the back room and often perfected in a complex organisation of factories and offices, or the new thought first discussed in the seminar. Ultimately the contributions of the small are intended to come into the large; the brooks join the rivers and the rivers reach the sea.

The large creative entity is often better viewed as made up

of smaller independent parts and these then integrated into a lively unity. It would be mistaken, for example, to assume that all activities carried out in large towns and capital cities were large-scale ones. On the contrary, the very fact of their being large provides opportunities for all kinds of small enterprises not possible in lesser centres of population. It is indeed their size which makes possible the button shops, the antique dealers specialising in their chosen periods, the many art galleries each concentrating on a separate school of artists, the cafés with their different cuisines, one, perhaps, setting out to attract intellec-tuals, another, beat groups, while yet another, more solid citizenry.

THE LARGE: THE CENTRAL AND THE CULT OF GIGANTISM

Contemporary discussion about size and the economies of scale is often confused by the uncritical assumption that the large and the central organisation are interchangeable terms, and also by the supposition that all large organisations are necessarily made up of a single unit under the command of a single hierarchy of control. Some central bodies whose purpose is to coordinate and consider critically the work of a great number of small and medium sized decentralised organisations, such, for example, as the pre-1948 Electricity Commission, may be very much smaller than some of the bodies whose activities it coordinates. The Electricity Commission, for example, employed a staff of about fifty, the Central Electricity Board, under it, some 1,500, and the industry as a whole more than ten times that number. Then again, many large organisations are made up of a greater number of quasi-independent smaller units. A university with perhaps 25,000 staff and students and comprising many colleges and faculties may have few of the disadvantages of size that would cripple a command commercial organisation of half that size. To give another example, many imaginative and vast engineering projects are often carried out by seventy or eighty sub-contractors working in harmony under the leadership of a main coordinating contractor.

The capital city, provided it is not too large and it is possible to forget for a moment its traffic noises and other disturbing features, is an excellent example of the functions of the large and central in reinforcing the initiatives and intimacies of the small. It enables roles to be performed for which the demand is not great enough in the smaller community. It has room for specialists – legal or medical – whom people from smaller towns come to consult. It offers facilities that can only be offered economically in a large centre of population. The larger the city the more market places for different commodities it has, the more shops catering for the greater variety of wants, the more theatres, sports grounds, concert halls, restaurants, museums, art galleries and public meeting places. Then in capital cities there are also the centres of government and the headquarters of the nation's or province's administrative departments. Each one of these places has a function to play in relation to the activities of the smaller groups scattered all over the country. The capital city, too, is the headquarters of national movements, of political parties and of trade unions. Although these have already been criticised for doing too much and for deciding questions which are better decided locally, there are none the less many services that they should rightly provide. They are there to coordinate and give coherence to local decisions and to offer leadership on larger ones.

There are some people who thrive in cities – provided the cities are not too large and have the facilities they want – just as there are others who feel most at ease in small places. There are many races, Anglo-Saxons especially, who have never learnt to enjoy city life in the way that the Mediterranean races with their city cultures have; for example, the nightly parading in the square and main streets of an Italian city that allows each con- sciously well-dressed citizen to see and be seen, thus asserting and reinforcing his individuality. The street, the bar and the café are public places where discussions and friendships are end- lessly possible. But in all races there are perhaps typical metro- politan personalities and typical small-town personalities. Some- times the latter has a feeling of greater self-importance – liking to be, as it is said, a big fish in a small pool – than the former, who may well be attracted by the feeling of the anonymity that the city sometimes gives to its inhabitants. The small-town man, especially the petty official and sometimes the mayor or chairman of the council himself, is often intolerant of other people's opinions and likes everything to be clearcut and in his favour.

The metropolitan man, in contrast, is usually someone who finds particularly stimulating the variety of the large city with its different 'quarters', different classes and groups, and perhaps even different nationalities. He likes the tolerance of city life. Most people however are probably neither typically large- nor small-town personalities; in their youth they find the city congenial or challenging and later take with them their experiences and enjoyment of it to the smaller community where they spend the rest of their lives.

These reflections apply sometimes just as well to small and large countries. Contrary to expectation, some small countries although efficient democracies, are often more intolerant of minority beliefs and attitudes than large undemocratic countries, especially the centres of large cosmopolitan empires; for example, Austria before 1914.

The small and the large complement each other, but are subject to two riders. The first is that by the large is not meant the too large – the mammoth and the megapolitan, if this new word may be used to express the new large centres of population counted in millions rather than thousands: what the megaton bomb is to the older TNT bomb, so the megapolis is to the older capital city. The second is that all units large and small alike, come under the rules of justice. There must be an independent law and corresponding courts to whom the aggrieved person suffering from the vendetta or pettiness of the small-town mayor or council can appeal; to whom equally the individual in the large city can go if his 'papers are lost' and he is suffering injustice or anxiety as a result. The local council, the commune and the *sindaco* must be answerable to some body above them no less than the large commercial organisation or regional body – minimally to a court of law that is free and able with the minimum delay to interpret all fact and actions as well as to apply the articles of a constitutional code.

GIGANTISM AND THE LOST SPIRIT OF COMMUNITY

This attempt to assign suitable roles to the large and small and to the central and decentral, using the advantages and disadvantages of large and small towns as models for other problems of scale, cannot be interpreted as justification for three pernicious dehumanising tendencies of modern utilitarian society. The

first two are the cults of gigantism and centralism which combine to produce the problem *par excellence* of artificial utilitarian
life – the vast, overcrowded sprawling shapeless megapolis – five,
ten, or twenty times larger than the largest ideally sized city. The
third is the tendency of people to segregate themselves into separate groups, quasi-independent collectives and communities
without any regard or affection at all for the community or
society in which they are placed.

The evils and problems of the megapolis – Greater London,
Tokyo, New York, Calcutta – are too well known to require
repetition. For the individual, loneliness is the most conspicuous.
This is the basis of the neuroses, petty crime, drug addiction and
violence of the vast centre of population. The lonely bedsitters,
the tower blocks, the ghettos, the contrasting overcrowded forest
of office blocks and the total absence of the spontaneity of natural
life are perhaps the most common physical features of all such
places. It is here that many of the most typical spiritual and
psychological diseases of civilisation begin.

Only a little less frightening is the tendency accompanying
the cult of gigantism and centralism for the creation in every
industrialised country of a very few headquarter towns and the
demotion of a great many once prosperous and happy, full,
occupied and integrated towns and cities to the status of 'branch'
and 'factory' towns. This tendency is the counterpart of big
business, mergers and amalgamation and of the drive for personal power by some of the most able industrial leaders. The
disagreeable and often dehumanising conditions of life in the
'headquarter cities' are well known and the subject of a large
literature. What is not often thought about is the plight of the
branch and factory towns. Most of the people who used to take
leading roles in their social and political activities have been
drained away to the headquarter towns, or live a disturbed life
being unrooted and moved from one branch town to another. The
more fitted they are to play a part in local culture, the more
likely it is that they will be made to play what can best be described as industrial musical chairs. The pay of the managers and
executives who fill these roles is modest rather than good, so that
they have little extra to spend in the local shops which gradually
become more and more like each other until they are 'taken
over' and, too, become branches of remote parent companies.

Combined with the alienation of the detail workers employed by the factories, the effect on the morale, politics and culture of local life is most depressing. Perhaps nowhere is the dehumanising influence of the artificial outlook more immediately apparent.

The third pernicious tendency is one which does not concern towns and cities alone. It is for each small community or each small group of shared purposes and inward-looking collective to hive itself off emotionally from the rest of the community and to ignore the existence of any common interests or bonds. At the best in the modern alienated utilitarian world, each group or unit, whether large or small, accepts, but is not interested in, or stimulated by, the aims of others. Most treat the government of their own society as no more than a roof-covering to protect them, and, except in times of national crisis, one which needs very little attention from them at all. It is impossible, therefore, to achieve a really creative understanding of all the many problems of size unless account is also taken of the community of which small and large alike are part. When everyone is gripped by a positive social outlook that acknowledges the due importance and complementary role of the other, the waters from each tiny centre of purpose flow into a common stream which in turn feeds tributaries that flow into one wider river. But when there is no such outlook, no common recognition of the interests nor indeed of the existence of each other, nor of any value other than those of the production-process and of private preoccupation, then there is also no awareness of any entity, concrete or abstract, more important than the mythical unity of 'the firm' or the over-serious collective, the inward-looking committee, the parish or the two or three streets that make up the estate. Then the waters from each little organisation, each little centre of self-conceit, do not flow towards any mainstream at all; instead each one is drained away into one small reservoir for the use of its members only.

The entirety of no man living can rightly be confined to city walls, factory gates, or indeed frontier lines. The sickness which affects all industrial societies and the actual physical poverty of the remainder of the world must be faced and their causes recognised. Each individual has within him a life of his own to live, talents to develop and give. But there must be common values and outlook, common policies and goodwill. Only when such have been found can the impersonal and faceless giants of artificial utilitarianism be vanquished, and the small, and the medium-sized and large be made complementary to each other in a wider pattern of lively human purpose. The present tendencies of artificial utilitarian society are the reverse of all these aims. It will serve its establishments well, therefore, to remember that there is an optimum size, although not easy to detect, of all human groups and organisations. When that size is exceeded they either generate an insupportable degree of violence and destroy themselves, or, as more often happens, they slowly become extinct like the colossal and over specialised mammals of prehistory.

DECENTRALISATION ON A WORLD SCALE

One very difficult contemporary problem of size, excessive specialisation and over-centralisation will serve to illustrate the above conclusions and to raise some of the complex issues that challenge the contemporary world. This is the problem of population congestion caused in non-Asiatic countries by industrial concentration in places of traditional expertise and skills.

The population of Greater London is very little smaller than that of a vast country such as Kenya or the whole continent of Australia; that of south-east England than that of Canada, which, next to the USSR, is the largest country in the world. The area of New Zealand is greater than that of the British Isles; its population, less than a quarter that of Greater London. The USA is about a quarter the size of the whole of Africa and its population is approximately the same size; within its borders, the majority live around such areas of industrial production and commerce as New York, Chicago, Detroit and Los Angeles. More than two-thirds of the world's land surface is not cultivated adequately at all and much of the remainder is under-cultivated; yet the fertility of other parts is so intensively exploited that in all probability many areas are close to exhaustion, so that, for example, deserts may be formed in parts of India, in the midwest of the United States, or even perhaps in the mid-eastern counties of England, as in Roman times they were in North Africa (many North African deserts were, of course, formerly the corn fields of the Roman Empire).

The need of medium-term policy, not the distant ideal, is for men's centres of living, villages, towns, cities, provinces to be suitable environments of fully human living and to be knit together in economically and ecologically sound patterns. If the world community is to make a balanced use of its resources, and if its towns and cities, with the factories and farms surrounding them, are to be of the sizes and balanced constituency to correspond with men's values, natural interests and needs of each other then very drastic changes must be entertained. On other grounds also, especially on those of the alleged probability of a population explosion early in the next millennium, it is urgent for these problems to be faced. However, it is no more practical to ask countries of excessive productive concentration drastically to restrict their human breeding arrangements so that they have a net reproduction rate of substantially less than their mortality rate, than it is to ask the underdeveloped countries to increase theirs by all the means in their power and to acquire no less quickly the basic skills so that they can build advanced industrial cities in the shortest possible time. It would be more sensible to plan orderly population movements from areas of industrial concentration to thinly-populated areas; to build new centres of population and to develop thriving agriculture around them. But such proposals would be met by the forbidding prejudices and intolerances of national and ethnic groups and of conflicting cultures and religions.

No move to solve any of these most urgent of all problems can be made until men and women of all races and of all ideologies have shown that they are able to understand the true principle of toleration,[2] which is that, however important their differences

---

2. For Acton's references to toleration see HF, pp. 84, 157, 182; HE, pp. 63 and 121; and LMH, pp. 10–11, 136, and 200–1:
   The true apostles of toleration are not those who sought protection for their own beliefs, or who had none to protect, but men to whom, irrespective of their cause, it was a political, a moral and a theological dogma, a question of conscience involving both religion and policy. (LMH, p. 10)
He considered Penn's contribution to the development of the principle far superior to Locke's (Fasnacht, and Add. Mss. 4955). Acton described Penn as 'the greatest historical figure of the age' (LMH, p. 223). His (Acton's) strictures on Calvin for intolerance and his account of the first Protestant pamphlet in favour of toleration – *De haereticis an sint persequende*, 1554 – are fascinating (HF, pp. 181–7). See also his entire essay on nationality (HF, pp. 270–300); but especially pp. 291–2,

of identity, belief or opinion, they must never reject each other as fellow human beings; on the contrary, they should be interested in examining and discussing the differences that exist between them. Beliefs are supremely important, but in the interests of greater and more generalisable truth, differences of belief should be discussed between people who share conviction in the values of the essentially, distinctively and truly human. Such must be one of the cornerstones of any new outlook capable of giving men and women the moral material needed to resolve many of the basic problems facing the world as it crosses from the one millennium to the next. These conditions sound idealistic, and to suppose that they can be met indescribably optimistic. Yet, except to watch large numbers of the human race perishing from hunger and from violence induced by over-crowding and other unbearable circumstances — as indeed in areas of great intolerance is likely — what alternatives are there? The suggestion to decentralise the industrial belt and to create a large number of city-size communities with balanced agricultures surrounding them, may be taken several steps forward and argued on pragmatic grounds. On a twenty-five or thirty-year view there are two batches of problems concerned with food that will become crucial to the survival of the masses of mankind. The first show up the need for centralised planning on a world scale if the earth's surface is to be fertile enough to support its population: reafforestation of desert areas in order to increase rainfall and to bring about conditions for soil formation and the sowing of crops; irrigation, drainage and reclamation of wet and marshy areas, and the refurbishing of land at present cultivated but where soil erosion and excessive planting will in a few years create wastelands and deserts. Only central planning and the investment of vast sums

---

'Christianity rejoices at the mixture of races', p. 293 'There is a moral and political country . . . distinct from the geographical', and p. 297 'the greatest adversary of the rights of nationality is the modern theory of nationality' (we would say nationalism). Those interested in the study of toleration, however, will find his notice on von Hefele's *Life of Cardinal Ximenes* very suggestive. Here the excessive intolerance of the Spanish Visigoths under Lewigild and Recared, leading to the first Inquisition in Spanish history inaugurated at the Council of Toledo in 633, is compared with the excessive toleration of Theoderic (Recared's cousin) which eventually lost him the Lombard throne. *Essays on Church and State* (London, 1952) pp. 381–94.

of money as acts of international policy can achieve these three objectives. Within a quarter of a century since the end of the Second World War, in spite of vast sums of money being spent, the land lost through soil erosion and structural collapse has far exceeded that reclaimed from desert and marshland. If these problems are to be tackled, therefore, on anything approaching the scale needed, mankind will have to give up for the time being expensive space flights, sophisticated instruments of warfare and a great many items of ordinary luxury. Money intended to be spent in instruments for man's destruction will literally have to be converted into plough shares and the chemicals of war into fertilisers.

The second batch of problems concern what can only be done locally. Here there are four main problems : fertilisers; skilled and knowledgeable manpower; the right kind of tools adapted to local traditions and cultures; and machinery and transport. Not enough artificial fertilisers can be converted from other forms of energy such as coal to provide anything approaching the quantities required. Phosphates must come from the recycling of sewage and the waste products of industry from local centres of population, and nitrogen from the intelligent ploughing back of suitable plants, such as many kinds of beans, possibly after they have been cropped. All this requires a very intelligently managed agriculture, provided with labour, intensive machinery designed for local needs and supported by industries and professions as intelligently conducted. It requires, too, nearby towns and cities with sufficient attractions and facilities for university trained personnel; also electricity generation and supply and many other local services. Finally there is the problem of transport. Not only do its direct costs – the vehicles, their fuel and their drivers' and co-drivers' wages and salaries – increase all the time; so also do the indirect costs – roadmaking, congestion on roads and the damage to the physical and human environment from fumes. Populations in future will have to live very much closer to their food supplies. They will certainly find life more enjoyable.

All this argues incontrovertibly for small- to medium-sized decentralised units of population balanced between agriculture, industry and service occupations. The case becomes even stronger as soon as the tensions and neuroses of megapolitan life are introduced into it. It may not be possible to say that, unless all these problems are solved, mankind will destroy itself; but it seems almost beyond doubt, that, unless they are, there will be disasters of unprecedented magnitude because of the very size of populations in many parts of the world. The solution will inevitably entail the reduction of the material exploitation set by the artificial modern outlook of Western industrial countries. But there will be immediate compensations in the form of more fulfilled, more free and happier human beings living in closer relationships to each other. This is not simply the vision of a believer in a decentralised society; it is no less a vision dictated by the necessity of physical nature and the needs of human nature.

In connection with the points raised in this last section and the plea made earlier for communities of lively purpose with which individuals can identify, the importance of nationality, a common heritage of language, traditions and moral attitudes, as well as of written and oral literature, has to be understood. Granted the existence of larger coordinating international political units and the condemnation of nationalism interpreted as exclusiveness, fanaticism or chauvinism, then the ideal, the aim, would be many more, rather than less, adequately recognised and separately organised political units and sub-units. Different cultures, or different groups aspiring to a separate culture and living style, would be given a compatible form of political independence within a larger nation state and that nation itself would belong to a still larger grouping of nations sharing traditions and values as well as being united by common economic and political interests.

Assuming that this aim were to be accepted, the difficulties of new nations and new groupings would have to be treated sympathetically. It has not been easy, for example, for new African nations to grow out of the colonies formed by the accidents of British, French, Portuguese, Belgian and German trading policies. Almost certainly the boundaries are wrongly drawn and the models for the idea of nationality which the politicians of the new state follow, are wrong. But, in any event, the difficulties of creating new group-identities must not be dismissed. It is no more easy to give a common life to people living in a new political territory without their first sharing a common heritage, than it is for a new town corporation to give a sense of shared citizenship to the people migrating to it from other parts of the same country.

To all these hesitations and questions there is an optimistic rejoinder to make. The developing countries at the present time in many ways throw up in an easily recognisable and uncomplicated form what will very soon be acknowledged as the basic problems of all mankind. All the countries of the world, affluent and poor alike, will soon be faced, if they are not already, with the need to create new balanced centres of population and to foster in them – mainly by moral means – spirits of genuine community and fellowship. They will be faced too with the cry of those whom automation and the conveyor belt have dispossessed of their right to use their minds and hands in purposive actions of coordinated creativity. A new knowledge of man and of his needs, of physical knowledge and its ability to satisfy those needs moderately and well, will of necessity have to develop throughout the nation; and on this there will grow up a relevant 'intermediate technology' capable of devising techniques suited to the new outlook's assessment of man and his genuine need. This ferment will be world wide and may well in the first place grow out of the actual physical and economic necessities of the poorer countries of Africa and Asia.

There is then a possibility, as yet no more than a possibility, of a world-wide new politics – the politics of concern.

PART IV

LIBERTY AS REVOLUTION

Liberty is the revolutionary principle supplemented by the constitutional.

(Fasnacht, Acton's Political Philosophy)

The government may be called free and its institutions firm and secure; when, having good laws for its basis and good regulations for carrying them into effect, it needs not, like others, the virtue of one man for its maintenance.

(Machiavelli, History of Florence)

I know many have been taught to think that moderation in a case
like this, is a sort of treason.

(Burke, *Letter to the Sheriffs of Bristol*)

Chapter 14

The Human Jury

THE TENSIONS

If we trace the argument back through Part III to the original
sorting out at the end of Part II of the concept of positive liberty
into two quests contained within the same model of thought –
one, the search of individuals in all walks of life for freedom and
personal significance; and the other, the public policy of liberty,
envisaged as the reshaping of the field of human existence where
the present limitations of physical and human nature most restrict it, and the excesses of materialism and the artificial outlook
most distort it – if we do this, then we discover tensions at the
centre of the type of dynamic liberal thought which we have
been describing. It is these tensions which have to be experienced
imaginatively as well as intellectually and one by one resolved as
decisive steps in the forming of a policy for the new outlook that
can be put forward with conviction. A critique of existing society
and a convincing vision of a more human and creative society,
although separate, have to proceed together. Both then have to
be reinforced by expertise to render their arguments practical
and sharp-pointed.

At the beginning, both critique and vision have to be founded
on a shared set of moral assumptions and values. More than this,
these assumptions and values have to arise out of the same image
of human purpose, significance and stature *vis-à-vis* nature and
vis-à-vis the artificiality which man has shown himself to be
capable of creating, but not of controlling, out of scientific
knowledge. Starting from this commitment to belief, we can
follow through a succession of these tensions and a number of

apparent contradictions until we reach the final ambiguity of
revolutionary liberal thought – its ultimate equal attachment to
the principles of freedom and authority.

How can the beliefs and values intended to flourish in a
changed society, we may begin by asking, be practised until the
new society exists? Men and women in utilitarian society have
suffered so long from living the life of the lie; from the neuroses
associated with professing a set of values yet hardly being able
to carry out a fraction of them, that it would appear that, apart
from divine salvation, man's only way to his redemption as a
species is, as Marx might have described it, by practising his way
out of the society he condemns – that is, by playing an appropriate part in the transformation of existing society into something
more worthy of God and man. Yet the tension still remains. How,
and even where, except in private and familiar relationships,
or perhaps in little groups of ever-self-conscious people
into which his particular abilities may not necessarily fit, can
anyone except the pioneers themselves play any part?
And whilst artificial utilitarian structures remain and
constrict all his activities, can anyone fill any part fully and
effectively?

The goal of a transformed society is the cause of another
tension. It is a collective goal and the organisation of the means
of reaching it must be the work at first of a mass political movement growing all the time; then later, of the impersonal central
organs of society, applying the principles of the new outlook to
activity. Once again, it would appear, another set of alien,
depersonalising and vast structures must be created to stand
over against the individual. How is he ever to escape the huge
shadows of alienating structures?

The very mention of alienating structures presents another set
of tensions. Large plants and undertakings are one of the factors
in the successes of modern technology in releasing men for more
creative work. Nobody would suggest returning to a world entirely
made up of small workshops and businesses; or indeed of creating
a society composed exclusively of 'Weil-sized' units. Even Marx's
dream of a society of associated producers, although very attractive, no longer seems practical. Again we have to ask, 'can the
individual possibly hope to discover his significance, positively
practise his freedom, or put his own special skills and qualities

to any satisfying purpose at all, in such an environment?'

We can counter all this simply by asking for a solution that will make the best of both worlds. Automation must be used to take over the really large plants made necessary wherever there is a proven need of technology on the grand scale;[1] then small- and medium-sized firms, in which the individual can participate according to inclination and capacity, for the rest.

But there is another doubt. It arises from the tension between two sets of policies; one, the Weilian solution, here outlined, to the deeper problems posed by alienation based on disenchantment at work; the other, those that apparently must be devised to meet that other set of challenges that have stirred the popular imagination – pollution and conservation. If one of the ways of individuals' recovering their significance and true freedom is to be found in small 'Weil-sized' purposive groups and in rethinking many types of work so that each stage of production will have the maximum 'thought-content' or 'skill-content', the question has to be asked, 'will not a great number of very enthusiastic worker-owned firms, that is, firms owned by everyone working responsibly and permanently in them, increase rather than decrease the very evils most condemned in the utilitarian system of production?' The worker-owned firm, in the moral and material conditions of contemporary society, might very easily be at least as greedy and self-seeking as is the subsidiary of the conglomerate or the giant of industry itself, and might well be the cause of an even greater waste of resources.

How can governments and departments of state established to encourage decentralisation possibly be expected to control all this? Then another doubt emerges, fundamental to the idea of excess itself; has not man always exploited nature; done violence to it in order to obtain the materials for his creativity – marble and stone from the hills and wood from the forest? The more the desirability of creativity is stressed, the more the doubt grows.

There is yet another aspect of these tensions which is crucial to the carrying out of all the measures needed to rediscover human significance and to recreate an environment on a human scale. This concerns authority. It would seem that the difference

1. See Appendix I for detailed description of the economies and dis-economies of scale.

in policies between the measures required on the one hand to expand the area of human values, initiatives and actions and those, on the other, to control the very essence of utilitarian industrialism, constitute a dividing line which runs through the very centre of the area of the authority required by the state to assure its continuing existence and to guarantee the order and justice on which civilisation, let alone liberal revolution itself, depends. One set of measures undermines the central authority of the state, and the other requires it.

How is this deadlock to be broken? It is not possible to say, as the discussion so far might suggest, that whereas the changes needed in society are political, the activities in which men wish to recover their sense of significance are economic; therefore, let each have its independent realm and the authority of the state be used to support each. On the contrary, the changes needed in society are at least as much economic as political, and the activities which the ordinary man claims for his personal involvement and participation in small-scale units are just as much political as economic. Nor are these the only categories involved. A large measure of the crisis of society is concerned with moral arguments. The ordinary man has suddenly found the words to ask that the knowledge-seekers with all their formidable qualifications and manifest distinctions of intellect and social standing should not be left free to evaluate their own discoveries, not to adduce practical applications from them, without first having them discussed quite humbly in a great number of human seminars and finally assessed, although it is not yet clear as to how precisely this would be constituted, by some kind of human jury. This is the kind of democracy and the kind of vigilant watchfulness over scientific application to everyday life that ordinary people begin to expect.

A great many campaigns of direct action,[2] but in different contexts, are taken up daily against establishments of all kinds; against governments, local authorities, large corporations, against the military. Protesters stop airports from being built; houses from being pulled down to make way for motorways; trees from being felled to clear space for new factories. Some forms of direct

2. Robert Benewick and Trevor Smith (eds.), *Direct Action and Democratic Politics* (London, 1973).

action are too hastily embarked upon and others foolhardily executed; but that many of the people who lead them and form the resolute core of them are possessed by an urgent sense of concern cannot be doubted. No less can it be doubted that they are all too often supported by many followers who do them discredit and an even greater number of hangers-on with no really decided opinions of any kind about anything.

All this presents a challenge to authority in every form; to political, moral, economic, academic and intellectual authority. Nobody who did not recognise this could understand the present age. But how are the fundamental and radical, often indeed revolutionary changes which are essential if society is to throw off its artificiality and regain human proportions, to be carried out without the support of the most precise authority in all these spheres? The question is a simple one.

The answer seems simple too. Contemporary authority simply has to shake off its old fashioned and artificial utilitarian mantle, to do away with its faceless mask and so reduce the distance between itself and those whom it governs. Authority has to catch up with the spirit of the age and to be on the side of those whose rebellion is just and directed sincerely towards a more free and sane future.

But this solution by no means ends the doubts and causes of tension. Indeed, it revives the most disturbing of all. When authority lends itself to supporting campaigns of the street and gutter, does it not threaten every genuine freedom which the forces of liberty have fought so hard to establish over so many generations? Does not the idea of authority catching up with the spirit of the age convey a picture of governments conniving at political hostages being held for bargaining purposes, hijacking airliners, and of free institutions, because of their bourgeois associations, being extinguished? And does it not suggest, too, authority supporting fanaticism of another kind – the kind prevalent in many parts of the USA – finding so much in modern society to condemn that all the most vital industrial and scientific institutions of civilisation will soon come under the threat of being dismantled? In short, is not the undermining of authority by what Acton called 'the minorities of liberty' destroying the very means, in the end the only means, by which many of these wrongs can be righted? Moreover, all these challenges come from a new concept of democracy, one relying far more on 'participation' than representation :

> The liberal language and representative institutions no longer enjoy the near monopoly of legitimacy they were once accorded. A new mood is emerging, to be seen in various manifestations of political protest, which feels that representative democracy stands not so much in need of reform as of being replaced, if not entirely then at least in large measure by forms of direct action or participation.[3]

If there is contradiction between the minorities of liberty and the authority needed to carry out the policies of liberty, this is it and it must be resolved.

These fears can also be shown to be groundless. We can refer again to the crime of excess, also to the virtues of proportion and to the need of strong institutions of government, all of which the principles of the field of limitations are designed to illustrate. Besides authority catching up with the spirit of the age, that spirit itself has to become responsible, consistent and morally based. The popular outlook has to become alert, knowledgeable and just, and even at its most rebellious, to be disciplined by the goal of the free finding its limits in the just, so that excess of any kind will always be loathed. We have to remember all that was said in Chapter 8 about the ultimate principle of the sanctity of human life imposing a limit upon all rebellion, and of what was quoted from Camus' *Rebel* that freedom has to have a limit in the just and in the human. 'Freedom has its limits wherever a human being is to be found – that limit being precisely that human being's power to rebel.'[4]

We can summon Simone de Beauvoir to our aid as well. 'One cannot lightheartedly accept resorting to force; it is the mark of failure for which nothing can make amends.'[5] And again : 'freedom that is exercised to deny freedom is itself so scandalous that the scandal of the violence then used to combat it is almost annulled.'[6]

3. Trevor Smith, *Anti-Politics, Consensus* . . ., p. 166.
4. Camus, *The Rebel*, p. 248.
5. Simone de Beauvoir, *Pyrrhus et Cinéas*, pp. 140–5.
6. Simone de Beauvoir, *Pour une morale de l'ambiguité*, pp. 362–3.

Liberal revolution can deny neither justice nor freedom. It is evils, not persons, at which it strikes. Challenges to old forms of authority before the new have been created are inevitable. But when the new is coming into existence those who were previously in limited rebellion have to be on its side – the side of authority of liberty. There can be no possibility of liberty being accepted as 'a continuing state of revolution' unless this is agreed.

THE TRULY HUMAN SOCIETY

But in spite of all that has been said, there is still an impression of an inherent incompatibility between the philosophies of centralism and of decentralism; also between the claims of the small and of the large to the same territory. The fear is that these incompatibilities are basic. The focus and the attitudes of the typical small group which, it is assumed, is creative and yet also self-determined and ruthless, is feared to be at total variance with the focus and the attitude of the larger society which, it is assumed, is uncreative and hostile to all aspiration. Society, because it is composed of a very great number of people, has somehow come to be regarded as just another large-scale organisation with all that body's typical defects.

How can these two views be reconciled? This is not a practical or legal, or constitutional question; the next chapter but one will answer that. It is a question rather of communication, and one of whether the two sets of aims can really assimilate each other and be integrated into a consistent political outlook.

The first point to make clear is how, from the point of view of the outlook we are putting forward, society itself should be described. The ideal is to think of it as a human brotherhood, a humanity in common, corresponding to the vision of the essentially human of Marx and St Paul. At the very least it must be described as a kingdom in which justice, order and community, freedom, knowledge and compassion meet and are recognised. If fellowship is the fitting term for the sharing of purpose and conviviality[7] within the small, and community for

7. It has been brought to my attention too late for me to include in this book any consideration of the writings of Ivan Illich on this subject. He has published *Deschooling Society* and *Celebration of Awareness* – a collection of essays. They are all relevant and readers may note a similarity of concepts used. See Appendix 2.

the larger living unity within which true communication is possible; then society is the word which expresses the joining together[8] of the purposes of the groups, communities and individuals that share basic convictions of value under the aegis and rule of a commonly acknowledged authority. If sharing the cup is the most appropriate image for fellowship, then the seamless robe is the one most appropriate for society. Although the robe be conceived as being made up of the brilliant and colourful differences of human personality and of the groupings to which individuals belong, it is yet seamless. This seamlessness represents the distinctively human qualities of men's characters and those common aspirations directed towards the 'essentially human' which bind them and make all their searchings ultimately one.

A society conceived in this way cannot, at this time, simply be called 'the human community'. This is for at least three sets of reasons. One is that it has to be a political unity, even if only an all-embracing one, with common institutions different from those of other political unities. The second is that it has to have a shared, or at the very least, a merging history and shared or merging traditions, and also a culture with a literature or number of literatures read throughout its territory: a single nation, or just as easily a coming together, or commonwealth, of several nations. The third is that it has to cover a territory, a concrete or abstract territory, of shared moral language and attitudes, even if these are in the course of being critically changed; the assumption is that the changes will be supported by the shared experience of the same reforming enthusiasm. Then, too, those living in this territory, because of this common moral currency, have to be capable of recognising each other when key issues are raised. They have, for example, to expect freedom and justice to be applied in the same style and to react decisively when they are not.

Because this society is thus restricted and exclusive, it has a strong identity and it confers this identity on those belonging to it. It is this which binds the diversity of smaller entities and interests into the shape of a robe capable of enfolding all its members. The robe might in this way enfold a number of nations

8. The word 'society' is derived from the Latin verb *sociare* meaning to join together, to unite, to associate.

and distinctive political units sharing the same values and wishing to understand each other's traditions and histories.

The greatest contrast to such a society is the fragmented one; a society such as artificial utilitarian industrial society, broken up into interest-groups, each having very little in common with, and communicating very little with, each other, or with society as a whole. The fragmentation of society is an even worse evil than the fragmentation of individual personality. It is worse, because if society is healthily whole, a sick personality has something with which eventually to identify itself and in its own time may become whole again; but if human society is fragmented, then everyone in it and every group and collective within it, becomes affected by its divisions.

In such a society men and women owe their primary allegiances to their interest-groups and only when their society, the society made up of all these fragments, is dramatically threatened, do they heed it. If the tenets of the artificial utilitarianism are accepted, this is the right view of society to hold; an artefact put together solely for the material advantage of its members. This explains why utilitarian socialism is as alienating as utilitarian capitalism. Each model classifies individuals primarily according to the occupations and the organisations to which they belong, so that ideally, as at most utilitarian conferences, the information should be worn uniformly and all the time on the individual's chest. Then it could at once be seen with which fragment of utilitarian society he should be identified and of which he spoke the language.

THE CREATIVE CHAIN

In what terms, remembering our initial problem of showing how the aims of small groups may be rendered compatible with those of society at large, and how the ethos of the small pioneering group can be transferred to the whole of the society of which it is part, should the actual relationships of the small creative group to society be described? It is said – although it is almost certainly not true – that in the formative stages of a society, the creative elite, the ruling elite, passes its messages, including its values, downwards, so that there is no difficulty of either communication or obedience. How, in the type of advanced society in which we

H

live, where there are problems both of communication and obedience, is the passage of value and originality from the founders of a new outlook to the rest of society to be described? There are four separate problems implied by this question :

1. *Spread of outlook*. How can an outlook – a set of values, a unique point of view of man and his relationship to society and the natural order – be transmitted from those who first adopt and define it to society at large?

2. *Community of interests*. How can solutions pioneered in small groups, or small-scale experiments if successful – the ideas and projects of creative minorities – be impressed upon society at large?

3. *The Human Jury*. How can new knowledge and novelty generally be judged according to the tenets of this outlook? How can the moral assessments implied in it so affect the projects of small-interest groups and society at large that the imagery of a seamless robe made of many patterns and colours be retained?

4. *Authority*. How in each of these three different chains of communication is authority itself affected? How may it be absorbed fully into both creative and moral roles?

Because the spread of outlook and the community of interest problems have much in common, they can be discussed together. Both start from the basis of the new outlook, from its assessment of the human role in the world and its critique of the old decadent society. The content of their messages – in the one case, its values, priorities and general policies, and, in the other, the projects, ideas and models of practice – spread horizontally across society from one centre of interest to another, then only after they have made an impact on society as a whole do they travel upwards to its authority. When this has happened, their problems of growth at least are over. For every separate interest, for every project separately pioneered, for the different policies as well as the value content of the outlook itself, there will be different strands of communication. But these will all travel in the same direction, horizontally from group to group until the attention of society at large is captured and its authority is altered. So intertwined will these strands be that they can be regarded as links in a creative chain of purpose.

The simplest analogy to adopt is to that of a large stone dropped in the centre of the lake causing ever-widening circles that
keep touching rocks jutting up out of the water. If each rock
can be supposed to represent another centre of actual or potential
interest, then it has to be capable of causing at least as much
energy or force as the original stone. It must be able to give new
impetus to the ripples when they touch it, so that when they
ultimately wash the shores of society as a whole they do so with
even more force than that imparted by the shock of the stone
when first dropped in the lake. When this happens the interests
of the originating pioneer groups become the interests of society
as a whole.

The spread of a new religion is the best example of such
forceful spread of message from one point of impact to another.
The transmission of the religion is nearly always from one group
to another, probably all within the urban lower middle classes.
However, after a sufficient impact on society at large has been
made, the messages of the new religion begin to travel upwards to
higher intellectual and social classes. Then inter-actions and
reactions take place and the religion becomes intellectualised.
The small cells under these influences, then increase in number,
reproducing themselves into larger cells until later they are joined
together in major centres of combined interests, values and purposes, which transmit outwards messages of greater and greater
complexity to all levels of society.

It is interesting at this point to draw attention to an unexpected
quality of nearly all those powerful ideas that have really transformed society. This is that the more powerful and influential
they are, the less they are loaded with specific or detailed content.
They are supremely adaptable. What content they have is rather
by way of precept than prescription. They gain definition from
the actual membership of the cells to which they are transmitted
or the situations to which they are applied. But, it has to be
observed too, that those who are truly possessed by a great idea
never regard themselves as tied by circumstances. They mix their
labours with it, so that the idea itself is capable of an upsurge
of renewal or a fundamental reorientation as a response to
changed circumstances. It is the power and veracity of the idea
that matters, not one or two local applications or prescriptions of
the moment. This observation draws attention to the contrary :

those detailed ideas and prescriptions, usually rather shallow ones, that are wrapped or cocooned in the typical illusions of an epoch. It is easy temporally to persuade majorities of their rightness and in this way they catch on and steam-roll alternative views. But at the end of their course it is usually found that they have left hardly any permanent mark at all upon society. Men become ashamed of them and recoil from their influences.

Another question, arising from these observations, which it is important to ask, is in what circumstances do the small groups with originating purposes – cells – stay as isolated centres of particular interests, and in what circumstances do they become major centres of combined interests and eventually parts of chains of creative social communication? The answer would seem to lie in the timeliness of the ideas they embody and their relevance to social needs. Sometimes, it would appear that they are destined to exist for a considerable period in isolation without very much social or political relevance; then suddenly to become immensely relevant and within a few years, the basis of radical social changes. For example, first the Desert Fathers, then the early monasteries created cells of this kind in north Africa and southern Europe which survived the collapse of the Roman Empire and, when threatened from time to time, moved into northern Europe and Ireland. But they did not have any considerable impact on society at large until shortly before the millennium, when political and other factors gave them timely messages of a social as well as religious nature to transmit and they became parts of one of the two chains of communication upon which the structures and institutions of the Middle Ages were built. (On this view, chains of communication are at least as significant forces as techniques in shaping superstructures.) Similarly, the knightly cells created by Charles Martell at the time of the battle of Poitiers (AD 720) – the giving by him of small estates to certain knights so as to enable them to pay for their armour, horses and armed retinue[9] – did not, except for a brief period during the life of his grandson Charlemagne, form an effective chain of communication until just after the millennium. Yet by the time of the first crusade, 1095, these two chains of

9. Hugh Trevor-Roper, *The Rise of Christian Europe* (London, 1965), pp. 195ff.

communication had already created the basis of the familiar system of feudalism.

A slightly different example occurred in the history of the United States. From the earliest days of British colonisation local committees existed to express the common interests of their members; sectarian committees, committees of lawyers, traders and business men, and committees to express agricultural, literary interests and the like. When later colonies' boundaries were made definite and given to governors and each colony had its own laws making it difficult and dangerous for individuals to cross boundaries, each local committee of interest corresponded with its opposite numbers both within its own state and in other states. It was not, however, until the decade before the War of Independence that a common feature of the letters passing came to be the expression of grievances against the British – the London government, the soldiery, the governor and so on. The number of these 'Committees of Correspondence',[10] as they came to be called, increased and finally stretched from Boston to Williamsburg. But this chain of communication did not become creative, or effective in a military and revolutionary sense, until the harbour of Boston was occupied by a permanent garrison of four

---

10. See *The Listener*, 7 December 1972, for Alistair Cooke's *Making A Revolution*. There is a voluminous literature on the growth of the Committees of Correspondence, and of their formalisation into a revolutionary chain of communication. Most accessible is probably R. B. Nye and J. E. Morpurgo, *The Birth of the USA* (Harmondsworth, 1955); p. 177 contains a description of the coming together of various interest group committees into what was to be the Central Co-ordinating Committee of Correspondence at Boston on 28 October 1772. This would be the equivalent of a 'centre of combined interests' in terms of my analysis. Starting from an unquoted source, the authors say:

It was moved by Mr Samuel Adams that a Committee of Correspondence be appointed, to consist of twenty-one persons, to state the Rights of the Colonists and of this Province in particular, as men, as Christians, and as subjects; to communicate the same to the several towns in this province, and to the World, as the sense of this Town, with the infringements and violations thereof that have been, or from time to time may be made – also requesting of each Town a free communication of their sentiments on this subject.

The request was met; in each town, in each colony, similar Committees were set up with the means of communication between them. Before long intra- and inter-colonial conventions of committees were organised; the machinery for revolution was keeping pace with the urge to make revolution.

British regiments. It then became the decisive factor in the organisation of the War of Independence.

In both the above sets of examples, a final series of almost accidental happenings, as well as a more rationally understandable growth of moral and political climate, created the conditions for the small, independent, quasi-private cells to replicate themselves on a wide public scale, then for some of them to coalesce into larger, more central nodal organisations and societies which were the basis of very radical changes indeed. Moreover, these changes reflected the structures of the original pioneering cells. They became the most typical and characteristic facts of the new society.

The lesson would seem to be that small creative groups, reinforced by appropriate techniques devised to answer the urgencies of contemporary needs, form chains of purposive communication when times are ready, conditions relevant and there are messages to convey with a strong moral basis already discussed and shared by the most active people in that society. More important than the hand mill in originating the structures of feudal society and the steam mill in originating those of early independent American capitalism, were the stirrup, the sword and the spur. The hurrying herald – the messenger – is the real originator of social change. *Quadripedante putrem sonitu quatit ungula campum*[11] (free translation: The hooves with four-footed sound pounded in pieces the trembling ground).

THE HUMAN JURY

Perhaps everyone is capable of seeing that the new outlook which we now seek must begin by a people, especially its own elite, being seized by an attitude of awe and value for the whole living order of creation. In addition, the need for policies and for a political movement as well as the role of its pioneers will be accepted. Nor is it difficult to think of types of the radical people fitted to fill these roles: partisans of liberty whom Acton in his time admired so greatly and once in an excess of candour described as sometimes needing to be superficially dishonest: 'Every doctrine to become popular must be made superficial,

11. Virgil, *Aeneid* VIII, l. 596.

exaggerated, untrue.'[12] What are not so easy to identify are those with this outlook, yet without the assumed superficiality and who have the gifts of judgment and moral persuasion to make public opinion effective and capable of fulfilling the formidable functions which liberty considered as revolution casts upon it – those whom we have tentatively called 'the human jury', men of sound moral judgment.

Pericles pointed to the ideal that the whole electorate should form such a jury: 'We consider a man who takes no interest in the state not as harmless but as useless; and although only a few may originate a policy we are all able to judge it.'[13] But the electorate of Athens was an elite of 30,000 free men in a population of over 500,000. Clearly everyone whose views are sought in a television current affairs programme is not suited to qualify. For one thing television condescends and for another, there is no genuine communication; simply a one way transmission of viewpoint from the box to those sitting in the room. The quickest flesh and blood way of indicating the kind of people who might in the present days be members of the human jury is to refer, by way of example, to those who up to 1914 made up what was called 'the nonconformist conscience', a term that at one time included a high church prime minister and his radically minded Whig Roman Catholic confidant protesting at the pronouncements of the first Vatican Council, as well as all who preached political sermons on Sundays and were stirred by moral issues – people who acknowledge the supremacy of the same ends and are fired by the same urgencies.

The membership of this jury is certainly made up of experienced and therefore probably older men. But, no less certainly, young people have important roles to perform, sometimes in bringing issues to the attention of the older men, and at other times, in acting passionately to see that justice is done to a particular point of view. Not all members are, in the formal use of the word, educated. The image of the pub as well as the club has to be brought in. The observer or philosopher at the street corner – the flower seller and newspaper vendor – and those who gather

12. Fasnacht, *Acton's Political Philosophy*, p. 236, analysis of Acton Add. Mss. 4955.
13. Quoted in Popper, *The Open Society and Its Enemies*, Vol 1, p. 163. This is Popper's translation.

round him, have also to be included. So also the carpenter and cab-driver, the editor and man respected in his community. If such as these be the members, formal meetings in any one place at any certain time cannot be arranged; yet issues arise all the time for the human jury to discuss and to decide. Here again, the roles of the herald and of the messenger hurrying from group to group, of the towncrier and the summonser to the assize, are relevant. It is the judge as well as Lars Porsena of Clusium who

> Bids his messenger ride forth
> East and west, south and north
> To summon his array.
>
> (Macaulay, 'Lays of Ancient Rome')

The issues which first concern the human jury are those which press most acutely upon human freedom, belittle human significance, or affect human values and aspirations. Then there are all those items which lie in those fields where knowledge itself has yet to be perfected, let alone any practical application of it developed – test-tube babies and the many other questions stemming from the study of biochemistry : should parents be able to determine the sex of their children; should hereditary defects be eliminated in the foetus, thus preparing the way for a human super-race? Besides these questions, there are those concerned with the application of science to new techniques that, when developed, pundits claim to be the basis of the inevitable – a communication system, for example, that would allow the gas-man to read everyone's meter from his office, and 'Big Brother' to be watching us and listening to all that goes on in our homes by 1984.[14] Other sciences yield other questions – space flights, bugging devices or chemical farming. The human jury should almost certainly have its attention directed towards such presently topical problems as pollution, conservation, population control and the use of public funds for scientific research into inhuman methods of warfare.

14. The coaxial cable has been developed to perfect a technique of distributing wide-band information. It has been tested in a number of small towns in England and Northern Ireland. The wide-band coaxial cable would not only provide piped radio, television and telephone to the householder, but also with the addition of a viewphone terminal would make possible all the invasions of privacy foreseen in George Orwell's *Nineteen Eighty-Four*.

From all these questions, the really important issue arises of how much knowledge can mankind properly and adequately digest in any single generation. Knowledge to be adequately digested and to nourish human life has to be evaluated and its implications for the entire human condition imaginatively, sensitively understood. Too much knowledge hastily acquired is like too much food too quickly eaten.

It might be asked why parliament itself is unable to undertake many of these functions. But this question presupposes that Members have both the time and the facilities for face-to-face discussions with their constituents, especially those of their constituents with moral concerns, and that constituencies are small enough for this to be possible. It presupposes, too, that on important moral issues Members are willing, as they were in the eighteenth and nineteenth centuries, to break away from conventional party alignments and to form fresh alliances which may bring down one government and create another. The House of Commons is now not constituted in this way. Ought it to be reformed to correspond more closely to its original functions, or is there a need for other types of political structures, besides parliament, to make moral judgments to be the decisive factor in decision-making of many kinds? It may be that this is the role that a reformed second chamber should undertake.

What is important is that the criterion 'truly human' should be established and that every issue with all moral implications should be discussed and judged to it. Even when the new policies of liberty have been formulated and there has been a new constitution of liberty, the human jury and the human seminars must remain independent and critical. Otherwise the policy of liberty as one of continuing revolution would come to an end.

EFFECTIVE PUBLIC OPINION
The eventual goal is to influence the vital elements in public opinion itself. Those anxious to change the style of a society are always apt to underestimate the force of lively public opinion. Government and informed public opinion acting together can often be very effective. Numerous examples come quickly to mind. How soon after London became a 'smokeless zone' did London's fog, infamous for more than two

centuries, disappear? How soon after local authorities, public opinion and private industry acted together to reduce pollution in the river Thames, did it take for bird and fish life to return to the river? Sometimes, too, informed public opinion can force governments to act or desist from acting: town-planning and conservation examples come quickly to mind.

Scientific expertise, public opinion and authority acting together can be very effective in being able to cope with the many issues and emergencies these pages have raised. If enlightened and morally stimulated public opinion is jury and scientific opinion expert witness, then authority is the judge. And the judge must sit at the bench above both the jury benches and the witness box. But it has always to be remembered that this authority is founded in and sanctioned by popular consent. For public opinion to be informed and zealous, alert and resolute is immensely important; there can be no revolutions of liberty without public opinion being won over to its side.

The changes required by a new outlook, if on anything approaching the scale discussed in the last few chapters, are enormous. They simply could not be carried out without the enthusiasm of intelligent public support sustained over a very long period – over a great many years, not simply from one July to the next or from one October to another. So extensive are they that they cannot be described in detail, nor be put down in any one or any number of blueprints. The need for a multitude of them cannot yet be foreseen in any detail at all.

In this connection, it is necessary to be clear about the distinction between a social and a political outlook. A social outlook is the spirit of the age, the epoch; a spirit to which in a lively society sharing a sense of community and purpose, both governing and opposition parties are obedient over a very long period. A political outlook has a shorter, more precise and practical vision. Its first objective is to make possible the wider aims of the social and to clear out of the way all the monolithic structures that would otherwise impede the realisation of its intentions. The political outlook has to create the conditions to free men and women for the new spirit to work in them and through them in society at large. There has to be, therefore, a pioneering movement, a radical and revolutionary one at that, and a pioneering political party to take up and gain the objectives that have been specified for it. 'They that have turned the world upside down have come hither also.'

There has to be a critical time when a series of emphatic and fundamental changes take place, when all can see that the wheel has revolved; when all can acknowledge that a new style of society has been brought about that will affect the style and manners of everything else for the entire duration of the new era. This critical time has to be of such a character that man afterwards can look back on it and say that it was for the better, that it was the means of releasing human activity and of making creativity possible again. The political movement has to be such that men can see that it has driven oppression out of privileged enclaves and opened up enormous vistas of freedom. When the sun has set on such a time of intense creative political activity – that day, or week, or year – people can wake up on the morrow and not only know that the wheel cannot be turned back, but be glad that it cannot be: not simply those who are politically active, but all be glad, acknowledging the anxieties that have been quietened and looking forward with a new vigour to the possibilities it has released.

All excesses must be eliminated: those of all contemporary political systems, of all forms of oppression and exploitation, of fanaticism as well as of materialism; above all those of artificial utilitarianism. It is only such a revolution that, when the ground for it has been adequately prepared, will command the universal and enthusiastic support of public opinion. In the world as it is, this is the only true form of revolution, because it is the only one which aspires to bringing about a genuine change of style and of fundamental attitudes which men and women will not later want to reverse. It is the only form of revolution that of its nature cannot provoke counter-revolution: it is a revolution which genuinely has liberty as its objective.

The word revolution applies only to revolutions which have liberty
for their object.

(Condorcet, *Sur le sens du mot Revolutionnaire*)

Chapter 15

Liberty as Revolution

IDEOLOGICAL REVOLUTIONS AND REVOLUTIONS OF LIBERTY

Political outlooks, both critical of the values of the society in
which they are formulated and determined to alter some of its
more typical and basic features, may be said to be revolutionary.
This is so, not because of a programme of violence that they
may or may not entail, but because of the irrevocable change
of attitude, of outlook and of regime perhaps – change of the
social or political life style – which they are set upon bringing
about. A revolution in this sense is ideally the cycle of a wheel
that has been turned but cannot be moved back. But there are,
of course, counter-revolutions which do in fact turn back the
wheel at least some of the way that it has come. Also there are
violent episodes to which most people give the title 'revolution'
that in fact turn back the wheel of what Acton repeatedly called
'the continuing revolution of liberty'. It is indeed doubtful
whether any revolution of this century has not had this
effect; although possibly there are some aspects of Nasser's
revolution and Mao's which do not deserve to be dismissed so
peremptorily.

The word 'revolution' has in recent years been used to cover
a wider range of action and not all political so-called revolutions
aspire to changing the style of a society in any significant way.
Many, such as in Latin America and sometimes in Africa, can
simply be recognised by an abrupt change of ruling regime. These
may be considered as palace or military revolutions. Then there
are those which aim to change both style and regime, but not in

accordance with any previously well-worked out and consistent outlook. The Colonels' revolution in Greece falls into this class: the Egyptian revolution began in this way but, during the time of Nasser's leadership, gained both in outlook and consistency. Finally there are revolutions which are rooted in well-prepared and consistent strategies, or founded in a political theory such as Leninism or social democracy, and are pioneered by an active minority determined to change both style and regime as well as to alter basic institutions. These revolutions may be classified from a theoretical point of view as either ideological revolutions or revolutions of liberty – episodes of liberal revolution.[1]

Ideological revolutions are based upon the logical development of a single idea or thesis. It is this idea which, interpreted by those convinced of its rightness, is the starting point of their critique of existing society, and, when developed, names the defective institutions to be replaced, becomes the basis of a particular revolution's blueprints for the new structures which it intends, decides its strategies and settles, in theory at any rate, its entire course. Revolutions of liberty, on the other hand, are based on belief in the power of a whole and growing group of ideas, of the unity of general ideas, ideas strongly rooted in and clarified by common reason, and the power of values in general; not a single idea nor a single value, nor necessarily a logically developed set of ideas and values. The unity of general ideas, once clear, Acton posits in the theory of liberal revolution which can be constructed from his writings, is the currency of revolutionary change, the coinage of which is valid world-wide. Hence liberty in this sense is, amongst much else, the state or

---

1. The word liberal was first used in about 1807 and found in Spain in 1811. 'The rise of Liberalism in Europe followed the suppression of the Spanish Constitution in 1823. So an international system was formed which was not Whig. Its basis was as to the ideals of 1789 controlled by ten years – equal to centuries of experience – together with the example – idealised – of England – and the practical example of America' (Acton, Add. Mss. 4955; Fasnacht, *Acton's Political Philosophy*, p. 238).

The term 'liberal revolution' is therefore, in as much as it can be applied to revolutions before 1823, used here anachronistically. As a developed concept it owes much to English Common Law tradition and to the political revolution in Britain embodied in the Reform Act of 1832. Acton uses the terms 'revolution' to express the suddenness and irrevocability of change brought about by 'the reign of general ideas'.

condition for the competition of ideas with each other; it is also the state or condition for the realisation of those which, clearly expressed and rigorously tested, have the humanity and the appropriateness to social and other circumstances to survive.

Out of the tensions caused by these many ideas and out of the matching tendencies provoked by their reaching towards new unities of thought and practice, revolutions of liberty and their policies are born and new orders are shaped. These revolutions are the products no less of physical and intellectual discovery than of people's reaction to it in terms of aspirations, or of new forms of 'ideal right' which they can achieve with it. Thus, it is legitimate to speak in the same breath of the revolution of the age of discovery associated with such names as Columbus, and Vasco da Gama, of the Copernican revolution, of the scientific and industrial revolutions and political revolutions such as the English, American and French. All are revolutions caused by ideas, however generated and all together help to constitute what Acton calls the revolution. It is indeed the advent of 'the reign of general ideas' which marks the beginning of the modern era and its continuous, although uneven, association with the advancement of liberty, at any rate up to the year 1895 when Acton delivered his Inaugural Lecture. In its opening epoch,

Columbus subverted the notions of the world and reversed the conditions of production, wealth and power; in those days Machiavelli released governments from the restraints of law, Erasmus diverted the current of learning from profane into Christian channels; Luther broke the chain of authority and tradition at its strongest link; and Copernicus erected an invincible power that set for ever the mark of progress upon the time that was to come. . . . the unity of the new [age] is manifest in the universal spirit of investigation and discovery . . . the advent of the reign of general ideas which we call the Revolution at length prevailed . . . ideas that give life and motion, thus take wings and traverse the seas.[2]

The creative minority of men and women dedicated to free-dom, those whom contemporary Latin writers might call partisans

2. Inaugural Lecture to Cambridge University, June 1895, LMH, p. 314.

of liberty and whom Acton called 'sincere friends of freedom', become revolutionaries very easily. Conscience is their compelling motive; 'doctrine laden with storm and havoc, which is . . . the indestructible soul of revolution.'[3] An apt example of this readiness for revolution on a relatively slight pretext was provided by the tiny minority who led the resort to arms against British rule in North America. 'In them is a principle of revolution, if not aggression. Any attempt to upset any government [they] do not deem legitimate must attract [them].'[4] Acton saw, therefore, as did Condorcet, an inevitable and reciprocal relationship between liberty and revolution and 'the development of ideas'.[5] If revolution were the texture of the outside of the shell and liberty were its substance and inner skin, then general ideas were its kernel.

The analogy of revolution appropriate to liberal revolution is not that of the wheel revolving in empty air; but that of the revolving of the wheel on a road going in a well-decided direction. The point is often made that the road indicated by Acton and his like simply leads to 'progress' – to what Kumar would call 'greater modernity'.[6] But Acton did not see the end of the road either as greater modernity or as material development simply for the sake of the satisfactions that it gave. But he did see the revolution of the wheel on the road optimistically; because for him the wheel revolved under a carriage that took society towards increased freedom. That for him was the best of all possible worlds, the state of optimism itself, and as far distant from the utilitarian utopia of a materialist panacea as it was possible to be.

Increase of freedom in the state may sometimes promote mediocrity and give vitality to prejudice; it may even retard useful legislation, diminish the capacity for war and restrict the boundaries of Empire . . . A generous spirit prefers that his country should be poor and weak, and of no account, but

3. LMH, p. 10–11.
4. Fasnacht, *Acton's Political Philosophy*, p. 240.
5. Compare 'Ancient Europe opened its mind to two new ideas – that Revolution with very little provocation may be just; and that democracy in very large dimensions may be safe', HF, p. 85.
6. Krishan Kumar, *Revolution: The Theory and Practice of a European Idea* (London, 1971).

free, rather than powerful, prosperous and enslaved.[7]

As we shall see, the principle of legitimacy was crucial to Acton's concept of liberty; but in judging whether a government was good or bad, legitimate or not, Acton advised the partisans of freedom on exactly what their standards of judgment should be :

> The great question is to discover, not what governments prescribe, but what they ought to prescribe; for no prescription is valid against the conscience of mankind.[8]

> To resist oppression is to make league with heaven and all things are oppressive that resist the natural order of freedom.[9]

These were moral and creative, not material standards. Yet material things were needed for people to attain the moral and creative ends they choose for themselves; be they things or be they only the tools and pieces of material with which they could contribute the best of their personal skills to the natural order of freedom. Personal property in some sense was an indispensable part of the mechanism of personal choice and freedom. It was Harrington who discovered 'the law by which power follows property,'[10] which Acton regarded as 'the most important discovery since the invention of printing.'[11] Accordingly its possession in the hands of a few had to be attacked as aggressively as the concentration of political power. 'The assault on the restricted distribution of power involved an assault on the concentration of wealth. The connection of the two ideas is the secret motive of the revolution.' But property has another function. Its possession is 'the first element of freedom'.[12] Accordingly, his remedy was not its abolition, but its enforced redistribution.

7. HF, p. 23.
8. HF, p. 24. It was the Stoics who bridged the chasm that separated the ancient from the Christian world and 'led the way to freedom'.
9. FR, p. 13.
10. Harrington, *Oceana*, 1656.
11. FR, pp. 53–4.
12. HF, p. 297.

FROM REVOLUTION TO CONSTITUTION

When Acton developed the theme of liberal revolution in his Inaugural Lecture, he was startled by the logic of his own rhetoric.

> If the supreme conquests of society are won more often by violence than lenient acts . . . if the world owes religious liberty to the Dutch Revolution, constitutional government to the English, federal republicanism to America, political equality to the French and its successors, what is to become of us . . . students of the past? The triumph of the Revolutionist annuls the historian.[13]

He did not answer this question directly in the Inaugural Lecture. But he did elsewhere. He had three 'doctrines' to expound, whereby revolutions could become part of a more orderly and less violent process; commonwealth, constitution and the principle of continuity.[14] First, commonwealth:

> The Commonwealth is the second stage on the road of revolution . . . and is the centre of the history of the modern world . . . And its ideas became efficacious and masterful by denying their origin. For at first they were religious, not political theories. When they renounced their theological parentage, and were translated into the scientific terms of politics, they conquered and spread over the nations, as general truths, not as British exports.

> Our topic is, how absolute monarchy, which just then succeeded so brilliantly over the Channel, when attempted in England, under conditions of no apparent danger, failed and failed at a great cost. And how, in the course of the struggle, ideas were developed which proved ultimately strong enough, as well as sufficiently lasting, to carry out an entirely new structure of constitutional government.[15]

This last sentence represents Acton's strongest conviction of the

13. LMH, pp. 13–14.
14. HF, p. 361. *De lex continui* was discovered by Leibnitz and was his anticipation both of Darwin and of Hegel.
15. LMH, p. 205.

development of liberal ideas : constitutions must be strong enough to contain and express revolutionary ideas – 'The true course of liberty is from revolution to constitution.' Constitution was his second answer to violence : 'Nothing but a constitution can avert arbitrary power.'[16] The expression of this second piece of wisdom is Fénelon's, the saintly seventeenth-century statesman and ecclesiastic, but few words could convey more tellingly Acton's own devotion to the principle of constitution; or of his attitude to power, which has been so widely misunderstood because of his observation that all power tends to corrupt and absolute power tends to corrupt absolutely.[17] In this way the principle of constitution, mediated by that of commonwealth, became for Acton more comprehensive and less formal and inflexible than it has been for Montesquieu. It was not simply a framework of legality, counter-balancing powers and order – but a definite rule for the limiting of the governing power. It was also all that is given permanence within such a framework, the power of political society adapting itself to the changing moral climate of the times. An orderly constitution stitches with two threads in its hand, the one cut from the past and the other drawn from revolutionary ideas. Whatever is creative and strongly believed in the old society must be carried into the new and form part of its foundations. A society must stand for something. In the process of transforming its style and institutions it will discover what this is and its members will identify with it.

The metaphor of a constitution 'cutting and sewing' was the means of Acton introducing another of his favourite expressions, 'the principle of continuity' – his third answer to violence and arbitrariness. He praised Burke as greatly for his devotion to it as he condemned him for his deplorable praise of expediency, and as much as he condemned members of Gladstone's entourage such as Morley for their deplorable devotion to compromise as a principle. A society must stand for something, it must have an

16. FR, p. 4.
17. This aphorism has to be placed in the context in which it was written – a private letter to Crichton disputing the view that rulers and members of governments should not be subject to the same moral standards as the rest of mankind. 'Torture and murder, in whatever capacity they are done or commanded, are vile acts and their perpetrators abominable.'

irreducible moral content. In the process of transforming its style and institutions, especially in times of revolutionary change, it discovers what this is and its members are able to identify themselves with the experience of giving it more concrete and relevant expression.

THE RELATIONSHIP OF REVOLUTIONS TO THE REVOLUTION

These passages from Acton's writings, together with the descriptions of revolution, reign of ideas and liberty as concepts that are fixed in complementary relationships to each other, pose a number of questions. What is the nature of these relationships? What is the relationship of the revolution to specific revolutions and to episodes of revolutions? What is the relationship of ideas to each other? How, if at all, do the aggregate ideas of any given historical period differ from 'the reign of general ideas' and what is the connection of each bunch of ideas to 'the doctrine of clear ideas'?

What is the revolution? When did it begin; has it ended or merely been interrupted by the reaction and sterile utilitarianism of this century? It would seem to have stemmed from the sack of Constantinople in 1453 from which an immense flow of ideas flooded over mankind and gradually became condensed into one 'clear idea' after another. What Acton meant by the doctrine of clear ideas was the very optimistic moral theory of Leibniz – the doctrine of general and clear ideas that are part of the moral order's inbuilt capacity, when invoked by men, to help them towards 'the best possible of all possible worlds'. In becoming more clear, ideas become more general, become more simple and hence also more apt and decisive as instruments of the good and the free. This process of clarification and sharpening might be viewed as the contrary to what happens to ideas at present conveyed through the mass media, where those which are capable of being clarified are instead prematurely generalised in order to reach a mass public immediately. As a result they lose their sharp edges as well as their potential clarity. At best they become slogans and images of well-intentioned fantasy stimulating a low level of action and discussion; at worst, the prematurely born infants of enthusiasm that are incapable of surviving the discontents of a single winter.

The flood of ideas released from Constantinople in 1453 seems to have become codified into a new outlook by about 1492, and this outlook can be associated with characters of such diverse ideas as Columbus, Savonarola, Cosimo de Medici or Galileo. It is remarkable that the gap 1453–92 is the forty years of which Keynes writes in *The General Theory*[18] the time taken for the 'distillations' of the philosophers and madman of one epoch to become the general outlook of the next. The revolution of liberty so begun by about 1492 lasted almost exactly to the end of Acton's own life in 1902, certainly not later than 1910. The question of whether it can be revived is one for us in this generation, with our own free wills and inherent sense of the ideal, as well as the opportunities offered us by scientific discovery to answer. It is not science itself, but what we ask of it and how we wish to use it that are the crucial issues.

Next, what is the relationship of the general idea of the revolution as a transforming current either made up of, or carrying, the different but unified ideas of liberty through the societies of Europe and North America from the fifteenth century to the opening five or ten years of the twentieth century, after which the tide has apparently turned and regressed?

It is fairly easy to see in terms already discussed in Chapter 7, under the heading of 'liberty as public policy', that the consequences of the Scientific and Industrial Revolutions were liberalising simply because the leadership of society at those times in Great Britain, where both revolutions were pioneered, was in the hands of men of liberty who saw to it that material benefits were used for moral and optimistic ends. Liberty was regarded by these men as a policy aimed at lessening the servitude of all men and women to the limitations imposed by the human condition. But what of the political? Here we must distinguish those revolutions which Kumar sees as interrupting the revolution from those that clarify and accelerate the current that carries it. The first set, illustrated by the Russian Revolution, he would tend to see in some contradictory Hegelian way, both as bringing to an artificial peak, or possibly to a false or unnatural crisis, the development of the revolution at that time and, therefore, as

---

18. J. M. Keynes, *The General Theory of Employment, Interest and Money* (London, 1938).

negating its entire course. So, on this view, some revolutions, possibly those which are intended or contrived to act as catalysts on history by reducing its development to the logic of one single idea, may be regarded as a species of Antichrist, as belonging to the mode of counter revolution.

Again, we are left with those revolutions that belong to the class of liberal revolution. Why should each one appear to be so very different from each of the others and yet to be capable of being shown as related to the uniforming and transforming current of general ideas which Acton and other writers of his genre call 'the revolution'. In a very undisciplined and unargued way one might relate each such revolution to a particular notion which its course helped to clarify and to introduce into the human moral and political vocabulary :

c. 1650	Dutch – the idea of religious liberty
1649	English – the idea of commonwealth
1689	English – the idea of toleration, political and religious, and of constitution
1789	French – the ideas of liberty, political equality and fraternity
1849	French – the idea of socialism and of the widespread distribution of property as the best means of attaining it

If these correlations exist then each revolutionary period releases at least one general idea from the kingdom of ideas, what Popper calls the 'third world of knowing'. In the course of the revolution itself this idea becomes clarified and generalised – operationalised might not be too practical a term – so as to be added to the kingdom of ideas on earth which the reign of general ideas and the reign of liberty are both intended to illustrate. This new general idea, as it descends on the earth, in practical form gives to that period of history a 'change of style' – a distinctive appearance to the years that follow it – and is responsible for structural changes as well as fundamental alterations in assumptions of thought and behaviour. All these many changes together and reacting upon each other, constitute a revolution of the wheel of society which cannot be reversed. Kant with his concept of a metaphysical kingdom of morals approached through the individual's practical duty to generalise the judgments of his own conscience before acting, rather than Hegel or Rousseau, may have been Acton's model here.

At this point it will be helpful to return to Acton's expression, 'the principle of continuity' – psychology may be a more useful word than principle – and also to recall the discussion in the last chapter about chains of purposive communication being formed by joining together separate cells of creative interest. Both help to explain the trigger mechanism of revolution, especially the class of liberal revolution.

The principal ideas and images on which political revolutions are founded usually have settled many years previously in the cells stretching across society formed in all probability for other purposes. Nevertheless the values which underlay these purposes were part of the fund of value in the society in which they existed. It was because of this that they attracted the new, more important, socially transforming ideas.

The interval of time between the cells being possessed by these creative ideas and the happening of a revolution in conformity with it, can also be explained in already familiar terms. The original ideas of those with the new political message have first to raise images and projects in the minds of their followers and these have then to be negotiated in the realm of the practical, before realistic policies can emerge. In the second place, times and circumstances have to be propitious. In the third place, the ideas and images of policy have to filter through from the followers to the masses.

It is easy to see the role of a psychology of continuity in conjunction with the occurrence of events that favour the revolutionary party, therefore, being the trigger mechanism of revolution. 'My conscience is aroused in this period, now, at this point of time,' a leader of radical liberal change might say. 'The law is being applied in such an irrelevant and ineffectual way by those in government and by others who act in their names, that it has been made absurd. There is a series of injustices against which I am reacting now and there is something definite and concrete which I must do about them. But the values, prejudgments and images of the right and fitting were formed in me long ago and I have been adapting them ever since I made my first commitment to the political cause which I now lead. These values had their roots in the culture and the political tradition to which I belong. They have implanted in my mind a logic which hurries me forward and impels me to ridicule the inappropriateness of the laws that are being applied.'

'Also,' he might continue, 'my wish is just, I recognise, not simply because of my own sympathies; but also because of the expectations that the people have been given by the entire political, social and cultural process and I share the premises by which they judge the wrong. Their very education and up-bringing – all the rhetoric and poetry that have ever affected them – have led them to suppose a future of a certain shape and content. These images are being denied to them at the very time when the state of knowledge and the possibilities of the epoch, when technical and other developments, make it seem that they should begin to come to be.'

This imaginary analysis of his own motives by a political leader on the eve of a revolution serves many purposes; but none so immediately apparent as to show that Acton's many reflections and generalisations about liberty as a revolutionary principle, beginning in conscience and ending in constitution, are only really convincingly coherent pieces of the same pattern, when put into the context of the traditions of the Netherlands and Great Britain. Nowhere else do his principles, doctrines, aphorisms and metaphors merge into a consistent and possible interpretation of the past leading up to a recognisable complex of events, policies and developments, in which the good and optimistic predominate over that other set of influences – the reactionary and counter-revolutionary. The Age of Discovery, the doctrine of clear ideas, the reign of general ideas, the principle of continuity, the metaphor of stitching and sewing, commonwealth – the second stage of revolution, legitimacy and so on; even in these two countries these principles must be seen as idealisations of motive that drove forward the creative minority of freedom seekers, rather than as components of a concise explanatory theory of history that fits every episode and sequence of events. These countries too had their reactionaries and periods of re-action. It was really a theory of political thought rather than one of history. Nevertheless, only in them and those societies overseas adopting their constitutional, legal and political systems, is it possible to think of such principles inspiring policies and achieving revolutions of liberty – the revolution – with violence.

The fact, at first sight, is all the more remarkable when it is seen how immensely powerful has been the part played by ideas, values and beliefs in the political traditions of the two countries, whereas their philosophical traditions have been notoriously empirical and pragmatic. The explanation may well lie in their adoption at different times, but each at a crucial period of its history (in Britain when 'parliament gave the crown on conditions'[19] to their Dutch King William and his Stuart wife Mary) of a very particular doctrine of toleration. This doctrine may be expressed as follows : allowing the expression in both words and practice of very great differences of belief, opinion and conviction; but however opposed or hostile to each other those beliefs, opinions and convictions may be, never allowing the holders of them to reject one another as persons born in the image of God. It is this doctrine from which are derived all the political values associated with personality, believed in until the beginning of this century so strenuously by the Dutch and British societies, although unfortunately never applied by them to the industrial sphere. The truth of the image of man is greater than the truth of anything else about him.

LIBERAL AND IDEOLOGICAL REVOLUTIONS COMPARED

Unlike ideological revolutions, liberal revolution is not committed to any one panacea, or towards bringing about changes solely in political and economic structures, changes that can be undone or even reversed. Yet the liberal revolutionary wants political and economic change; but also much more. He wants change of outlook : change of ideas that matter to society, change of the average individual's estimation of his own potential and of his relationship to other individuals, to the community as a whole and to the worlds of nature and things. Then, flowing from this change of outlook, he demands the changes in economic and social and political structures that are implied by it as well as the tools, machinery and other means to make them effective. No less is he conscious of the need for laws to ensure that the in-

19. LMH, p. 231.

dividual's liberty to do as he pleases with his own is not abused.

No one-party state, no dictatorship, nor any system of government not steeped in an outlook which is shared with people and which in a sense the people themselves have done much to make, can possibly promise or even reasonably expect to achieve any of this. Dictatorships and parties of violence can achieve power; that is undeniable. Possibly they may also be able to implement some of the first batch of their promises; but after that they cannot. Their ability to execute a consistent purpose peters out : they cannot, after the initial acts of revolution, if they are honest, genuinely offer any prospects at all. They become more and more the victims of their own arbitrary nature, of their leaders' own fears and their party's imperatives to survive. In reality, as history shows, a strong centralist dictatorship, whether of a single party or of one man, if rationally judged, is the very last system of government, especially when supported by violence, to be able to carry through the content of a popular outlook or to fulfil its pledges and programmes. It is as certain as anything in history can be that it will provoke, either within its own hierarchy or from outside, a counter-revolution.

Liberal revolution neither triggers off counter-revolutions nor allows them to happen. Nor does it create conditions of decentralised anarchy. Its philosophy is that there should be a permanent state of tension between decentralised organisations and initiatives on the one side and centralised institutions and the centralised administration of strong laws on the other, so that the constitution which it achieves is one that embodies in a certain sense a division in the sovereign power of society – a division between the sovereignty of the state and the rights of other bodies composing it. Indeed it is doubtful if in the tradition of English liberty, sovereignty, in the strict sense employed by continental thinkers, such as Bodin,[20] has any place at all. 'Prerogative I know is part of the law', said Lord Justice Coke, 'but sovereignty is no parliamentary word.'

All these comparisons show that the one-party autocratic state, as a progressive idea of libertarians or any other genuine idealists, except possibly in countries such as those in Africa attempting to

---

20. Bodin, *Six livres de la republique*, 1756. See also Preston King's forthcoming book *Ideology and Order*, to be published by Allen and Unwin for the Acton Society.

catch up on the basic economic installations of modern civilisation, is dead. Stalin proved an old lesson of history that autocratic states become dictatorships become merciless tyrannies. The rule of Pompey, Caesar and Crassus ended in the dictatorship of Caesar, from whom some seventeen or more Caesars, mostly exceedingly drab and incompetent (there were notably liberal and great exceptions) descended : the rule of Lenin, Trotsky and Stalin was succeeded by the bloody dictatorship of Stalin. No revolutionary or radical party in Europe, probably in any part of the world that has achieved an advanced degree of civilisation and self-government, is likely to forget that lesson quickly. The revolution needed in the modern world is a continuing revolution, a continuing policy based on freedom and justice always poised to make fresh and greater demands in every change of circumstances and every advance of knowledge.

No revolution occurring in the complicated and diverse conditions of the modern world and having regard to the dynamic condition of its frontiers of knowledge and moral responsibility, can expect to achieve any of its aims if it allows itself to be crystallised or petrified by one party seizing power and imposing its will on time, as though men by calling themselves revolutionaries could make history stand still whilst they become bold. Liberty must have its constitution and this constitution must embody in it the dynamic principles to which all in society must be obedient and the principles from which the identity of that society itself is derived.

The Liberal view of revolution is an organic view. It revivifies societies' broken roots and plants seeds in the ground waiting for the spring to bring the thaw and make even the surface broken by winter.

> April is the cruellest month, breeding
> Lilacs out of the dead land, mixing
> Memory and desire, stirring
> Dull roots with spring rain.
>
> (T. S. Eliot, 'The Waste Land')

THE STRUCTURES TO OVERTHROW

Since the First World War, there has occurred in nearly every industrially advanced country what has been termed 'the corporate revolution'. More accurately, since it has reversed many of the revolutionary tendencies of the nineteenth century away from corporate privilege, it should be called 'the corporate counter-revolution'. In capitalist countries, the typical mammoth-sized modern industrial corporation has come to exist as a body which, in practice although not in legal theory, is owned by no-one, is responsible to no-one and has not even one consistent long-term specialism or objective purpose. Its first concern is no longer economic efficiency, optimum production or profit maxi-misation, but power, achieved through successful aggression and expansion and through the delicate handling of the conflicting interests which form its foundations. In economic jargon, it seeks oligopolistic stability. In conception more like a medieval domain with princes, emperors, and usurpers succeeding each other than a textbook economic entity, its forms of organisation and strategies often seem to be copies from manuals of modern politico-military techniques with their theories of command hierarchies and the importance they attach to size and bargaining strength. The corporation understood in this wider sense is an infinitely more direct source of personal power than landed property, stocks and shares, or the wider range of property relationships that Marx called bourgeois property.

The corporate revolution, or counter-revolution, has followed the same course in most of the socialist and communist countries of the West as it has under capitalism. Nowhere has 'the new socialism' developed in the direction of distributing wealth. On the contrary, wealth and the power of social control are far more concentrated, in countries under socialist rule, except pos-sibly Yugoslavia, than ever they were before. With its centralised bureaucracies and giant-sized command organisations, socialism has adapted itself to the values and dictates of the utilitarian industrial process, sometimes paying but scant regard to the principles of its origins; its organisations are not a whit less ruthless than those of the monopolies and conglomerates of capitalism. The structures of communism in the USSR and of those countries imitating it are even more monolithic and highly centralised; and its commercial and political values as pragmatic and utilitarian as those of American capitalism. Indeed this monolithic quality of the soviet model has been recognised by such revolutionaries as Mao, Che and Tito.

Of all the ideas associated with liberty, property is the most easily abused and the most easy to confuse with policies that end up with the great masses of people having less freedom than before they were exercised. A revolution, therefore, which transfers the function of controlling key organisations, or 'the ownership of the means of production', from one political group or class to another, will not increase the worker's rights or opportunities, fulfilment or freedom one iota; will not cause any fundamental alteration in the nature of relationships of work, on which Marx and Engels relied so greatly for the realisation of their vision. Nor will it produce any fundamental change in the style of society. Such a revolution taking place in the condition of contemporary societies is best described as a non-revolution.

It is a fallacy to suppose that, if property is socialised, the power implicit in its ownership can be enjoyed by everyone. In such circumstances the only people to enjoy its power are the mandarins created by the state to control its use. Harrington's discovery at least puts us on our guard against that solution. There is no liberty to be found in, nor any true socialism to be created by, it. The outcome is for the state itself to become capitalist – a super capitalist with monopoly powers which no-one can, nor even dare, deny.

Acton had a much more realistic and severe vision. He welcomed 'the new socialists' because he believed they would distribute property rights and thus ensure that the poor and relatively deprived would have the physical means of using their freedom in the manner of their own choice.

As surely as the long reign of the rich has been employed in promoting the accumulation of wealth, the advent of the poor to power will be followed by schemes for diffusing it . . . Liberty, for the mass, is not happiness; and institutions are are not an end but a means. The thing they seek is a force sufficient to sweep away scruples . . . The principle of equality, besides being as easily applied to property as to power, opposes the existence of persons exempt from the common law, and independent of the common will.[21]

21. HF, p. 94.

The only form of revolution which can ensure permanent change consistent with its own promises is one which qualifies, limits and guarantees fairness in the distribution of all rights – those derived from property, those derived from government and those derived from the functions of controlling any key organisation. Every right and every person in society, ruler and ruled, must be subject to a common law. Power is inevitable; power, indeed, is necessary to achieve any human purpose. But it must be limited by strong laws, limited both in quality and degree to that which is appropriate to its purpose, and the structures of society must be built on these laws – decentralised structures in which individuals and groups can develop interests and initiatives of their own.

Besides the growth of the power of centralised organisations, another conspicuous feature of contemporary society is a limited form of rebellion; rebellion in the name of certain positive values, rather than in the name of any particular solution or new kind of economic or political structure. In almost every industrially advanced country, there is, regardless of formal political alignments, the same conflict between the utilitarian, economic values of its Establishments and the awakening human values of the most sensitive members of its population; the same contrast between the sophisticated power-structure desired by the one and the simple conception of a free life in daily activity sought by the other. In every such country, too, there is an intelligent minority, however small and for the most part as yet unorganised, who see that modern knowledge, together with a selective use of the applied techniques derived from it, can and indeed must be used to achieve this more simple conception. It ought to be possible for men not only to associate freely in order to form and realise common, socially relevant projects; but also for them in their private lives to have increasingly the means of achieving their chosen ends; of their acting together and doing things with and for each other in a quite different spirit of community from that which utilitarianism, with its private and public or back- and front-garden interpretation of liberty, has encouraged. But men ought not to be concerned exclusively with their own and each other's aspirations. The world, both natural and man-made, surrounding them claims their consideration and care; and the world of moral and aesthetic values makes wide claims on them.

Irrespective of regime, this sensitive minority is anxious to break away from the centralised monolithic structures of artificial utilitarian industrial society and to find the decentralised purposive units of industry and government responsive to basic human interests, aspirations and values; responsive alike to the needs of the community and the individual. In addition, it is beginning to be aware of the possibility, created by automation and the labour-saving devices of invention, of revolt against the minute divisions of labour forced upon workers by the artificial utilitarian productive process. Not as Luddites in heroic despair, but as realistic appraisers of innovation and invention, it can foresee the end of the servitude imposed by 'detail work', which Marx so bitterly condemned but could find no means of replacing; the end of the servitude, also, to the smug standards imposed by utilitarian manufacturers and advertising agencies.

The power of this minority is all the greater because of the immense improvements in the educational structure that have taken place since 1945. Unlike the children of the working masses in the nineteenth century and the early part of this, people of talent now go through the educational system. They are not only seized by a much wider vision of the possibility of the human future than their parents and grandparents were; but also they are intellectually equipped, or could be so equipped, to play specific roles in helping to approach it. Yet at the present time when they leave school, technical college or university, they are faced by high walls of frustration wherever they turn. This factor alone makes it almost certain that the strength of this minority will grow and will make its aims more precise, positive and determined.

It is the activities which this minority claims as its own which may be seen as examples of the kind of functions which, in a revolutionary liberal society, must be decentralised and which, when decentralised, sustain that tension between central and decentral that is at the very heart of liberty conceived as continuing revolution.

There is nothing better for a man than that he should eat and drink and that he should make his soul enjoy good in his labour.

(Ecclesiastes ii. 24)

Chapter 16

A Sketch of the Free Industrial Society

TWO SENSES OF POWER

How is a revolution in economic and social structure to be brought about, so that beyond all doubt it does achieve the changes it has set out to achieve, and does not simply begin another series of violent events followed by even greater repression than before? The views put forward so far may be summarised and it will be seen that taken together they give rise to a problem which, when solved, creates the conditions and provides the framework for the outlook which these pages have attempted to describe.

After it has achieved power, the first act of what for want of a better shorthand term we have called liberal revolution, is a constitution, or, in a country such as Britain, a series of legislative acts at the beginning of a new regime, securing its power and putting into effect its intentions. This initial legislation must be concerned to do four separate things. First, the revolution must ensure that its own power-base is secure and at the same time guarantee the conditions for free institutions generally and for the free competition of ideas. It must not only give the state power to enforce the priorities of the new outlook, but also be sure that the power-base and characteristic institutions of the old society have been destroyed.

Second, property rights have to be redistributed and shorn of their powers of exploitation. All members of society must be given the right to receive their appropriate share of the new values of wealth which their work brings about. Then everyone will have the means to use their freedom effectively. In this way, too, the objectionable features of the old decadent society will be broken down and stronger social foundations will be created to bear the weight of the new. This second requirement raises, of course, questions about the exploitation implicit in the means of production and other forms of property.

Third, a framework of institutions, spreading out from the central apparatus of the state, strengthened but radically slimmed, must be created to enable individuals affected by the spirit of the new outlook to sort out its application to their own particular and specialised fields. Within the pyramidical framework, at the apex of which is the law, all the subsequent legislative and administrative acts of the new regime will be conducted. It is especially in reference to these institutional reforms that Popper's warning of the fallacies and dangers of utopian engineering is most relevant. There must be a phase when individual aspirations and material tendencies are reconciled to each other in painstaking piecemeal measures. The unforeseen consequences and unintended effects of even the best blueprints become cumulative; so that too rigid adherence to any long-term plan which does not allow for profiting from the experience of mistakes will very soon destroy the basis of every noble aspiration of an utopian regime.

Fourth, the constitution of the state, the law itself, must ensure balance between all the many classes in interest, right and aspiration in the community. It must also ensure that these, whether belonging to persons, groups, classes or corporate entities, large and small, are conducted within the perimeter of its own declared moral and aesthetic assumptions.

If the above four groups of legislative and state action are looked at again, it will be seen that each group, and then the four taken as a whole, is the basis of a practical conflict between the principles of centralisation and decentralisation, between public rights and private rights, and public and private control exercised over the same items; between a centralised and revolutionary legal system and a decentralised economic political system.

This is the conflict which has already been discussed as a question of principle and theory in Chapter 14. When it is resolved in practical, legal terms as well as in those of communication and community of interest, it gives liberal revolution its distinctive method of approaching the crucial problems of public and private rights. When not resolved, or wrongly resolved, it drives the enlightened progress of contemporary socialism into a cul-de-sac. The issue of centralism versus decentralism, of public authority and private purpose, plays on two ways in which we normally use the word 'power': one, approvingly, meaning motive-power, the ability of any agent to move anything, to do or to act, to effect any purpose at all; the other, pejoratively, or at least with apprehension, when we speak of someone's power to compel or influence or harm another – his power over another. In the first usage, people need power to pursue any aspiration, or to seek any good of their own choice; it is intimately associated with liberty itself, and some thinkers invariably treat liberty and power as synonymous subjects. In the second, the personnel of the state need the coercive powers which it confers on them to enforce political objectives; for example, to maintain its cohesion and inviolability, or to put into effect the legislation settled upon. The conflict is thus reduced to the difference between 'the power to' and 'the power over': between the power associated with liberty and power associated with authority.[1]

Liberal thought is divided about its attitude to power in this second usage. What we might call the school of liberal revolution accepts that it is as inevitable as Necessity itself; but is anxious that those on whom it is conferred should not be privileged, either politically or socially, to use it for their own ends or so as to place themselves in their personal capacities at the advantage of the rest of the community. Because the temptation of office holders and of the wealthy to use political and social powers for their private advantage is very great indeed, this school of thought seeks first to limit their rights to that which is strictly necessary for the efficient performance of their offices, and, second, by means which will be discussed below, to divide the rights and duties both of office holders and owners of other rights, so that the powers attached to these rights and duties will balance each other. The classic example is, of course, the division of powers between the executive, the judiciary and the administrative

1. Preston King, *Fear of Power* (London, 1968).

I

organs of the state. It is this principle which needs extending to other areas besides that of government.

The other section of liberal thought regards power in the first usage – that is, the ability and the means to achieve the determination of the will – as desirable without limit, but in the second sense – that is, as coercion or command – as almost totally objectionable. Thus liberty means for this school autonomy, and it only needs authority tempered by justice as an auxiliary principle, in very small quantities, to protect and guarantee the individual's right to the use of this autonomy. Different members of this school of thought see autonomy as implying different forms of government ranging from federalism through individualism to anarchy, so that for each there is one ideal constitution of liberty. Dr Preston King, in his book *Fear of Power*, describes the thoughts of de Tocqueville, Sorel and Proudhon, in order to analyse the intellectual and practical impasses into which different members of this school are driven :

> For, if liberty (in one sense) means justice conceived as 'rights' protection, or constitutional guarantees, then clearly it must frequently demand, rather than preclude the resort to authority, to force the imposition (and the acceptance) of restraints; while this conception of authority is not compatible with liberty conceived as autonomy. Because liberty can change its meaning, the change permits it to be balanced, to be 'limited' (but ultimately 'realised') by or through authority. Given this notion of balance and given that liberty *qua* autonomy remains a prior ideal, then the balance must be informed by the principle that there must be as much liberty as possible, and the corollary that authority is a necessary evil.[2]

The same indictment could be laid at the door of many writers, for example Hayek in this century, who extol freedom as individualism or pursuit of self-interest.

The policy of liberty as revolution is saved from such a dilemma because it sees the principles of justice and freedom as lying side by side in the human conscience, always ready to provoke fresh acts of the continuing revolution of liberty, as

2. *ibid.*, p. 132.

historical conditions, new knowledge and new forms of expertise make them possible. In order to achieve the positive purposes of each new revolution, as well as to maintain the formal freedoms of negative liberty, power must be conferred on office holders and of course upon the judiciary and those who enforce its judgment.

Possibly the source of the most important differences between liberal and Marxian revolution is the acceptance by the former of the inevitability of power in both usages of the word, therefore recognising the need to come to qualify and control its rightful exercise; and the belief by Marx that under true communism, necessity could be overcome, thereby freeing true liberty for ever from its entanglement with power, but leaving a little of the scaffolding of what used to be the coercive state to help in 'the administration of things'. In short, the liberal revolutionary does not believe that the state can, or ought to, wither away, or that human order can be sustained without justice, both as fairness between one person and another, and as law. There is no utopia, no heaven on earth – and no possibility of either until the end of time. The next best state of affairs is one created by liberty under truly just laws; and these laws have to have adequate sanctions and the authority to make that liberty possible and lasting. There can be no liberty without law; and no secure society of associated producers without justice and an enforceable framework of cooperation.

ECONOMIC POWER

Power is, of course, exercised in many ways and the means of doing so are derived from many sources, legal, political, military, religious, psychological and economic. It is the last source which has especially worried people actively concerned with politics in this century and this has concentrated attention on the actual economic systems in competing for public esteem. From the point of view of liberal revolution, both capitalist and socialist models suffer from glaring defects; and it is these which, whatever the system, the above analysis would aim either to remove entirely, or to reduce to such manageable proportions as to bring true liberty in the economic realm within the means of every man.

The socialist system, so it would appear, implies the central ownership of the means of production. In the USSR and other advanced socialist economies this has led in practice, as would be expected, to an economic dictatorship, to the central bureaucracy having power over the life and limb of the worker and to no worker being able to follow within the economic sphere independent aspirations of his own choice. It has also led to oppression outside the realm of work and economics; to the repression, for example, of literature and the persecution of writers and artists. On the other hand, the capitalist system, as Marx prophesied it would, is passing through a stage of mergers and amalgamations so that soon, it would seem, all 'big business' in the Western world will be in the control of a very few companies – a state of affairs only marginally better than state socialism : marginally better, because the exercise of political and economic power would not be united in one legal entity. Even at its most enlightened, the capitalist system only attempts to correct at the level of central government in an impersonal, random and general way, the exploitation and personal injustices which occur at factory and office level : taxation and welfare policies cannot really remedy personal injustices any more than state ownership can.

We have next to inquire, therefore, how it is possible to use the analysis of the two senses of power made out above, so as to embody in one set of proposals the truths that both systems aim at expressing, however much they may be responsible for different kinds of disadvantages on other grounds. Is it possible to avoid exploitation and to achieve social justice on the one hand, whilst on the other giving purposive groups the means and independence to work at their own projects in ways typical of their members' skills and qualities? The introduction of automation in many basic industries, and the fact that in both socialist and capitalist countries most important branches of industry are already, or are rapidly becoming, integrated, and therefore more easy to reorganise, may well be two positive factors in helping to give encouraging answers to this question. If this be so, then the time to realise the ideals of the free man in activity may be much closer than the present utilitarian organisations and methods of work in both capitalist and socialist countries would lead one to suppose.

If we return to the distinction raised earlier between the two usages of the word 'power' – the power to move something, to act or achieve a purpose, and the power of command, or the power over, someone else – we can think of a situation when a person acquiring the means to use power in the first sense eventually employs it as power in the second. In fact, whenever power in the first sense needs physical means to implement it, it is possible for this situation to arise : for all physical means of doing things – tools, materials, money (capital, in short) – are always and everywhere scarce. And in these conditions of scarcity, what one person has, another wants and will often be willing to render himself servile to obtain. The problem arises, therefore, of how the much-needed power to achieve an end or a good of the individual's own choice can be conferred on the great mass of people without at the same time conferring on them power in the sense of exploitation, that is, of the possessor bending the unpossessed to his will. It is this problem to which the distinctive formula of liberal revolution has specific relevance.

The need for formal institutions, for a strong constitution and for a system of both vigilant and constructive laws, implies a centralised society and a state with strong coercive powers. Belief in the most widespread enjoyment of their liberties by the masses of the people, in the validity of individual aspirations, in the value of small purposive groups and the conviction that powers and privileges are most oppressive when concentrated : all this implies a decentralised society and people being given the means, institutional and material, to carry out their realistic projects and aspirations. How are the two sets of need to be met ? The answer to this question is very simply to divide into separate parts, into clear legal entities, those rights which other systems of thought regard as indivisible; to qualify by legal definition each right so divided, and, thereafter, to confer one set upon decentralised bodies, or groups, or individuals, and the other upon the central apparatus of the state, divided out into separate organs and departments for them to administer, to control or to interpret. All rights, all liberties are individual or corporate until, in the exercising of them, the point is reached when either they conflict with each other or threaten a larger good, or are needed to be subordinated to a wider purpose. At these points, the legislatures, the courts, the policeman's or the central government's functions begin. And all these functions both belong to the central apparatus of the state and cover the entire society with absolute objectivity and fairness. Thus, under the strongest possible umbrella of public qualification, interpretation and protection, private rights can grow; personal liberties flourish and people enjoy initiatives which were not open to them before. In these ways, too, those who man institutions can be given originating as well as negative and restraining functions in order to promote the widespread and positive enjoyment of personal initiatives and liberties.

A useful example of this method is provided by a description of some of the actual laws and conditions that affect the owner-ship of land. There is, first, a considerable body of statutes and common law determining the rights and relationships of the owners and tenants of landed interests towards each other as well as to the public. Second, there are more specific laws such as Town Planning Acts, which precisely prescribe the uses to which particular areas of the land and the buildings on them may be put; some even state that buildings of great historic or artistic interest must be preserved and maintained by their owners whether they want to do so or not. All these laws limit or qualify powers of individual ownership and create two sets of rights, public and private, in the same physical entity. Another impor-tant fact is that owners themselves can impose restrictions on their own and their neighbour's land by agreeing to common restrictive covenants for their mutual benefit. Moreover, a great variety of different rights can be created within the same piece of privately owned land : building leases, unfurnished and fur-nished tenancies, shooting, fishing, mineral rights and so on; each form of right having its particular legal definition, protection and enforcement. In a similar way it is possible to think of a large mansion converted into separate flats or maisonettes or even houses held on very long leases. The owner of each lease has cross covenants with the other owners and also, perhaps, with a company retaining the freehold and managing the common services on behalf of all.

These same principles could, granted the necessary legislation, be applied to all the many reforms which former chapters have shown to be necessary. Rights of ownership of industrial property, for example, can be divided in the same way as rights in landed property with different parts corresponding to the different functions exercised by different agents, and these rights can be duly qualified exactly as landed rights are : limited and qualified rights for organisers, managers, workers, technicians and inventors, each enforceable against each other. Each separated part or share of ownership will have its own rights and privileges, functions and duties, so that each factor will have a legal claim to the proportionate increase in wealth brought about by its contribution to the total, and will also have corresponding rights to make decisions or to participate in the organisation of the whole.

Large firms can be broken up into small and medium 'Weil-sized' firms in the same way that mansions are sometimes divided into flats and separate houses; or large landed estates are compounded of many separate legal entities. The independent units will simply pay rents, calculated either as fixed or variable interest payments, to their former parent companies in respect of the assets taken over by them, and of any services which the company continues to render as a coordinating or services unit.

THE ECONOMIES OF SCALE

The argument for these and many other desirable changes in favour of smaller units are challenged by technical arguments concerning the 'economies of scale', the alleged advantage of large-scale production, brought to public attention by financial journalists and other pundits of the mass media attempting to prove the inevitability of giant organisations. There are a great many economies of scale, and, what is no less important, many very influential diseconomies – the economic disadvantages of large-scale operation. Each group of economies, considered in relation to the diseconomies does, in fact, indicate a different sized optimum unit, some corresponding perhaps to the size of even a continent; some to that of a nation and so on down to very small areas indeed.[3] This point is pursued in greater detail in Appendix I. Here only one piece of economic analysis need be introduced, and this is one that matches the analysis already made of the method of liberal revolution. Just as it is possible to separate those aspects of rights and liberties which are best attributed to central administrative or judicial bodies, so also it is possible to divide the economies of a business or any other kind

3. For economies and diseconomies of scale, see Appendix I.

of organisation, such as a large local authority, into those which essentially adhere to the nature of the activities undertaken by the given unit, and those which can equally or more advantageously be operated by another organisation external to it. The first are called internal economies and the second, external. Examples of the first are the tools, machinery and division of labour employed in a factory; and of the latter are the telephone and electricity services, technical education or specialised markets dealing in certain commodities and raw materials. Some economies, however, may be internal to one set of firms and external to another. Typing pools, advertising and marketing departments, drawing and design offices situated inside an organisation using them exclusively are the causes of internal economies; but typing, advertising and marketing agencies, drawing and design centres operated independently and used by a number of firms are the causes of external economies.

The second example shows that a great many economies at present operated internally can be externalised for the benefit of many similar firms or for a whole industry. The functions corresponding to each economy can be exercised either by independent agencies or by cooperatively owned joint service organisations of many different sizes operating at many different levels. (Appendix II sets out these proposals in greater detail.) Such bodies do in fact already exist in the armed forces and also in industry. There is, for example, a Defence Staff College common to all three services as well as specialised corps shared by all three. Many firms in industry share a joint computer-based statistical unit, or joint warehousing and transport services; some share the same marketing organisation. Other external economies are exercised by very much larger bodies : the government itself, some nationalised industries, the Post Office, for example, and by some international agencies such as UNCTED (United Nations Committee for Technical, Educational Development).

There are, however, some internal economies of scale that cannot be advantageously externalised. These are known as the physical economies, and are mostly associated with the use of very large plants and machinery entailing large production runs, or with what are known as the benefits of integrated planned production whereby various components of the same finished product are made and assembled in the same or adjoining factories.

Another physical economy which might be considered separately in a class of its own is that obtained from the fully automated production of a single product. Thirty or forty men can perform the same functions with one machine or set of machinery that before as many as a hundred performed.

These three classes of internal economies – those that can be advantageously externalised, the physical economies that adhere to large firms and the economies of fully automated production – correspond to the three tiers of an industrial structure that as a result might be envisaged. This would provide for a tier consisting of the 'Weil-sized' firms or collectives, or small- and medium-sized private enterprise firms liberally conceived, co-ordinated and serviced by joint-service organisations at various levels; another made up of the larger firms necessitated by the physical economies, and a third of fully automated industries. Outside this structure, but related to it, would exist the financial institutions needed to supply the capital; some socialised investment bodies[4] such as industrial banks and trusts, borrowing from the public and lending to, or investing in, industry : others, private institutions such as merchant banks and investment trusts, as now. This would be realised in Keynes' prediction. 'It is not the ownership of the instruments of production which it is important for the State to assume. If the State is able to determine the aggregate amount of resources devoted to augmenting the instruments and the basic rate of reward to those who own them, it will have accomplished all that is necessary.' As he foresaw : 'A somewhat comprehensive socialisation of investment is all that is necessary to bring about a more just state of affairs.'[5]

Once investment has become institutionalised in a social manner as Keynes foresaw, all kinds of organisation become possible. Indeed organisations will take the form needed to answer the skills, personalities and pursuits of those wishing to form them. There will be small- and medium-sized firms, cooperatives and collectives of workers standing beside other more conventionally directed enterprises. Moreover, once the models have been established in industry they will be imitated in all other sectors of the economy and community.

4. See my *Impact of Size*, Chapters 5, 7, and 8.
5. J. M. Keynes, *General Theory of Employment, Interest and Money.*

Manufacturing industries employ no more than about a third of the working population. The same principles can be applied with suitable adaptation to most other categories of work; retail trade, the service industries, the civil service, local authorities, trade-union organisation, education and so on. From this list the most important to select for early attention are those in the public sector. The structures of the nationalised industries and of central and local government, especially those departments administering the social services, are too large, authoritarian, impersonal and inflexible to adjust to demands for participation by ordinary citizens and interested workers.

A MORE GENERAL PICTURE

The above are, of course, only a few of the possible practical applications of principles raised in earlier chapters. They point, it is hoped, to a foreseeable time when there will be interesting work to do at most levels of industry for those who want to do it. Weil-sized firms will devise, or demand, of machine-tool manufacturers, the tools to correspond to the skill and thought-content of their work. Larger firms will be made up of purposive groups participating by means of orderly and imaginative understanding of the processes of the firms as a whole, employing Weil-like principles where possible, and, where not, casting further boring work on to machinery. Then there will be the automated sector manned by a few highly skilled and competent operatives. Thus, as Camus foresaw: 'The day comes when machines capable of a hundred operations, operated by one man, create one sole object. This man on a different scale will have partially redis-covered the power of creation which he possessed in the days of the artisan.'[6] Reinforcing the efforts of individual firms in each of the first two tiers will be the joint-service organisations and agencies, all with specialised work to do to correspond with each of the many economies of scale.

There will remain, of course, many boring and irksome jobs to do. Those working at the most irksome, at present the less well-paid, might justly be compensated by higher pay and shorter hours. Clearly there will be many aspiring writers, artists, social workers and curates minding the repetitive machines, emptying

6. Camus, *The Rebel*, p. 259.

the dustbins, sweeping the streets, doing clerical work and tightening the bolts of railway lines to sleepers. These are not intended as flippant suggestions. In Italy most *artigiani* and many artists are employed in the mornings to do remunerative routine work and, after a siesta, spend the rest of the day at the work they really enjoy doing, the *artigiani*, especially, often being surrounded by their family and friends as they do it. Besides those who might be willing to do routine work in compensation for the means to follow, or as a way of relaxing from, their chosen pursuits, there are others, possibly hundreds of thousands, who actually like monotonous employment and perhaps even more who enjoy the security of working for large organisations.

Most of the schemes for the reform of industrial structures and other ideas put forward have been presented purposely within a framework that is consistent with either the private or public ownership of the means of production, distribution and exchange. What matters is that the concept of ownership should be seen to be divisible and qualifiable, so that all work in whatever capacity done on material things to enhance their reality, to make new things of them, or to bring them from workshops and factories to consumers, as well as to provide other kinds of services, should give rise to rights corresponding to functions, and that these rights should entitle their owners to a just proportion of the new value which they have helped to create. If all forms of ownership, that of the physical entity itself and those created out of it – whether owned by the state, corporations, syndicates, partnerships, small or large firms, collectives, cooperatives or private individuals – are restricted and qualified in accordance with the principles of liberal revolution; then actual physical ownership, residuary ownership, of an asset will become of little interest.

In many respects the outcome of all these policies will be the opposite of the kind of socialism that has been shaped by the influences of the modern utilitarian outlook. The central government will have many fewer direct functions of initiative : its powers will be residuary. The automated industries, for example, might well be placed under statutory control rather than nationalised, and this form of control will ensure workers' participation and a share of the profits commensurate with their responsibilities. Many of the existing nationalised industries might well be split up into local or regional units and subsequently reorganised in one of the ways already described. Then again the state will aim at achieving a just distribution of benefit from the economic system; but will do this through policies of creating decentralised rights. Marx's strictures against exploitation are, of course, valid : but he did not live to see either the growth or the exploitative capacity of the typical modern economic and administrative giant. The point is to restrict and limit the powers of organisation, ownership and rights of all kinds; not to transfer them in undivided and unqualified form from one class of exploiter to another.

A NEW ATTITUDE TO THE PRODUCTIVE SYSTEM

Men's concept of the role of the industrial system will be different. They will no longer want it to be maintained as a continuing self-replenishing process, tied to the psychology of material incentives, with advertising as an auxiliary arm to create artificial demands for everything that arrives at the end of its production lines. Instead, they will wish it to become more and more subservient to the priorities of the outlook itself. Thus the gimmickry of artificial utilitarianism will disappear and only those novelties will be introduced which are acceptable to the changed order of social values. In this sense, it is true that the adoption of the alternative outlook will entail the loss of much variety : deliberately so. If, for example, the mass production of items such as washing powders and many kinds of consumer durables were to be automated, then there would be many fewer improved products of these types entering the market every year. Mass-produced motor cars, refrigerators, washing machines and electrical and gas appliances of many kinds will be built to last. Once an automated production line is laid down, it will be very costly to dismantle and substitute another. The pioneering of new models will be left almost entirely to bespoke manufacturers catering for the enthusiast and the wealthy. The question may be asked, however, how many consumers really want, still less need, new models and faster motor cars every year, or gas stoves with fresh gadgets, or electrical appliances more difficult and costly to repair; and is it really important which detergent washes whiter? Rather it matters that their washing powder should be cheap, effective and not destroy what it is intended to clean; that motor cars should be safe and reliable to drive, that repair bills should be minimal, and that the life of the car itself should last longer than the spread of the hire purchase liabilities incurred in buying it. Better far than yielding to pressures created by advertising techniques to abandon year by year old model cars, stoves, fires, refrigerators, and domestic equipment and replace them with new, will be to buy in the first place a reliable model of proved performance which will last for many years.

There is also a valid social point to make in connection with planned obsolescence. It is one to which Schumpeter drew attention.[7] Capitalism (and no less socialism imitating capitalism) is exceedingly wasteful and destructive of the wealth it has created. Manufacturers are constantly forced, by the pressures of competition and fashions and novelty, to lay down new production lines or to install new plants, before the useful life of the old is anywhere near exhausted. The loss of real capital value to the community is enormous.

These remarks should not be taken to cast doubt or scorn on all technological achievements; but rather to suggest that technology should be used discriminatingly. It should serve men's priorities and not create its own for them to serve. Hardly any form of modern work better illustrates the marriage of interest and technology for the satisfaction of human need than such engineering projects as motorway and bridge building. Here one imaginative concept combines the separate exercise of many skills towards a common end which is aesthetically pleasing and of great advantage to the communities they bring together. In such an undertaking one firm of civil engineers coordinates the skills and specialisms of many separate firms.

Another cause of less variety, as has already been suggested, will arise from the control of wasteful processes. The urgent examination during the last few years of issues such as pollution and conservation has shown that the damage to environment, natural resources and the human body caused by many industrial processes is enormous. If this is so, then men will be increasingly willing to measures their real standards in much wider terms than they have done before. The cost of saving the environment will enter into their reckonings as much as any more tangible item

7. Joseph Schumpeter, *Capitalism, Socialism and Democracy* (London, 1943), Chapter 7 especially.

already included in the cost of living index. Any hesitation people may feel about these questions ought to be dispelled quickly if they try to envisage a world and a time when as many nations in the East achieve a fully fledged industrial system as in the West. If the West does not reduce its greed and gimmickry voluntarily and with grace, it is easy to believe that it will be forced to do so.

In compensation for whatever losses there will be in terms of certain forms of variety, novelty and gimmickry in mass markets, there will be many advantages. Goods produced in the small-firm sector will be of greater intrinsic quality and workmanship. The effective unit of work and decision-making will be close to its local market, and therefore responsive to consumers' detailed needs and specifications. Manufacturers will be able to consult their retailers, and their eventual customers. As a result there will be more, not less, variety. Many items of equipment at present mass-produced will disappear from the shelves of shops, for example, standardised hi-fi and stereo sets, and in their places will be products put together – of course, many of the parts will be made in considerable quantities by different precision manufacturers – ready to meet the particular needs of different consumers. They will probably be cheaper too. Producers will no longer have to bear all the expenses of national advertising, seductive packaging, and the very considerable overhead costs of remote head offices. There will of course be advertising; but this will be informative rather than exaggerated, and the money paid for it will enable local communication media to stand on their own feet. An additional advantage not easy to over-estimate as part of the creating of the new social outlook will be that producers will get to know the consumers for whom they are doing things and be able to talk intelligently with them.

Then as to inventiveness; it can be argued that surely such a society will tax the ingenuity of the inventor and of other classes of creative people too. Released from his dependency upon the artificial utilitarian system of production, the inventor will be placed in a fresh relationship of having to meet the challenge set by purposive groups and ordinary people needing the means of achieving fulfilment of their projects in ways typical of their particular characteristics. Then, too, in a country such as Britain or Italy, he will have the challenge of inventing items such as means of transport more suited to their indigenous small-scale needs than those of vast countries with enormous resources such as the USA or USSR: small cars suited to the layout of old towns and cities – indeed, the Fiat 500 and the Volkswagen already exist to illustrate this point – or medium-sized aircraft not requiring vast airports for their reception. In countries with ancient cultures resting on peasant and small-holding economies, such as many in Africa and Europe, he will be set the task of inventing the appropriate, efficient machinery for use by balanced communities, and of bringing industries on a small scale into the country. This will frustrate the pundits of the large-scale from persuading the populations of these countries of the need to use large and expensive machinery in new mass centres of population, thus destroying their characteristic ways of life.

PRIORITIES

Critics might argue that, freed from the pressures of an affluent society and no longer goaded to an endless flow of goods, producers under the influence of a more human outlook would cease to be efficient or resourceful, and ordinary people such as workers, managers and executives would work less industriously if the incentives to do so were lacking. Critics might claim, too, that questions such as 'Abundance for what?'[8] repeatedly asked in a critical spirit, undermine all the genuine achievements of modern society's meeting mass need and overcoming destitution.

The destruction of artificial utilitarianism will not destroy people's wills to support themselves, to enjoy a rich life, or, as far as possible, to gain the means of obtaining their personal fulfilment within a society of greater warmth and fellowship. Nor will it destroy their efficiency. On the contrary, artificial utilitarianism only promotes efficiency in certain ways; its chief priority is an unending production of goods with which to satisfy the senses or to support the alienated individual's yearning for tangible evidence of status. It is possible to do this very efficiently, yet there are at least two reasons why it is not always so. The first is that, if production is maintained as an unending stream, then the goods themselves, as we know, have a short life; in fact, their very design must incorporate the need for them to wear

8. David Riesman, *Abundance for What?* (London, 1964).

out quickly. The second is that in time the workers themselves become corrupted by the size of the wage and overtime packet which comes to be of greater importance than workmanship or any other pride or incentive.

The better priority is a society devoted to the 'production' of more rounded, more 'truly human' men and women, and communities in which they can live fuller and more spontaneous lives. If this were accepted, then the more valuable efficiency would be that kind which is measured against these goals. We should get lasting, less shoddy goods with more attention paid to their design, their appearance and to the true needs of the community. We should also get a society in which all had the capacity to enjoy them. In such a society, too, many items would disappear from the list of what are at present regarded as essentials either at home or in society as a whole. This point may be reinforced by one's observations of how quickly, under stress of the more urgent interest, a strike or national emergency or a more personal aim, the ordinary worker is willing to dispense with many of the items previously deemed essential. Thus, by de-emphasising the value of productivity for production's sake and the money norm as an incentive for achieving it, and by stressing the importance of a more creative set of 'truly human' values, resources of all kinds would be left over for the pursuit of more important ends – education, leisure and a whole host of other intrinsic satisfactions. But even more urgent for the sake of the present argument, they would be available both to improve the basic standards of the less affluent nations and to make possible an altogether different productive system in which an altogether higher level of efficiency would be required. In this system the present prestigious standards of our affluent societies would count for less and less; and the requirement that work should satisfy simultaneously material and creative needs, for more and more.

Existing tendencies of industry and technology cannot, of course, be suddenly reversed. Changes can only come about when scientists, inventors and organisers, reacting to human demand, have pioneered new techniques, new tools and forms of production. These will take time and will be part of a continuing dynamic process phased over many years, some of them perhaps as long as a generation. Within these limitations, and to some degree taking advantage of them, the picture presented of a more creative society can be shown to be no mere daydream. It is possible to show, too, that the order of priorities it postulates are shared by a great many ordinary people. If, for example, the questionnaire formulated at the end of Chapter 1 were to be used, the answers and the discussions following them would in all probability take the form predicted. Granted the assumption that theoretically it is possible that production can be doubled in the next generation, most ordinary people would prefer to use at most some of the potential increase to live fuller, more creative lives rather than to go on adding to their list of 'essentials'. Affluence is not an end in itself. Some would place their emphasis upon using a high proportion of the increased productivity to make work itself a more realistic reflection of their skills and interests, others upon their desires for all their capacities to be involved in all the processes of work from planning to execution of the final product; others, upon giving more time to political and social activities, upon a fuller leisure life; and yet others, upon the needs of the worst off – internal and external proletariats. There would, of course, be a dull and un-adventurous minority who would simply state their preference for routine and mass-production methods of work – or for machinery and automation to be used to give them even better living standards. The discussion solely concerns a cake not yet mixed, let alone in the oven or on the table. This makes the policies of a long-term political outlook very much easier to discuss than, say, the immediate programme of a political party.

Finally, we have to be realistic about the relationship between freedom and material security. The great masses of mankind worry immensely about their security and for most this comes first – if intellectuals and creative people wish to have true freedom in industrial society they must see to it that a man who works hard, skilfully and creatively can earn good money and keep it safely. Such, then, is a sketch of the kind of industrial society to which the principle of liberal revolution might lead. The new society has no name. It is almost certain that it will be neither capitalist, socialist nor communist. People are disillusioned with these forms of organisation and their excesses. It will probably not be called liberal either, but its pedigree will almost certainly be traced to freedom and justice working through a policy of liberty.

Prior to the need for thinking out new policies, however, is that of a new outlook. And this outlook must be based on the image of the whole man, the truly human man and woman, and it must have priorities. It must condemn utilitarianism and the standards of greed, appetite and sensation. It must return to the ideals of a rounded, balanced life and use science to attain these ideals. It must proclaim the duty of everyone to be concerned for the whole world, its plants and organic life as well as the human. Such an outlook must have a starting-place and a place to which it can always go to replenish itself. This is the small community and a creative fellowship of men and women sharing similar values, standards and priorities.

Who owns the capital in any particular circumstances – individual, state, finance house or corporation – must increasingly become an unimportant question, provided that all capital is shorn of its power to exploit or tyrannise, and provided that individuals have the rights in it which enable them to maintain their freedom and express their chosen ends. What is the nature of the work done, how it is done, in what sized units it is done and by whom it is done and organised – these are the important questions that the future must answer in positive, definite and creative terms. Violence and despair, alienation and boredom are but the manifestations of thwarted creativity. To be creative in some meaningful way is to be human and everyone should have the means to be this and thereby to enjoy a full life.

Live unto the dignity of thy nature, and leave it not doubtful at the
last that thou has been a man.

(Thomas Browne, *Religio Medici*)

Conclusion

HUMAN SIGNIFICANCE AND MATERIAL TENDENCY

The more creative and hopeful outlook that has been described
here does not suggest that it is either desirable or possible to go
back on any of the genuine and very great material achievements
of modern utilitarian techniques, although of course it does
demand a searching review of what those achievements are and
a rejection of many that have no real value. Neither does it deny
the existence and likely persistence of many of the material
tendencies which modern utilitarianism has cited and adapted
to support its prophecies, form its artificial 'laws' and construct
its plans. On the contrary, high on the list of the purposes of the
more human outlook is the desire to make use of both achievement and tendency for the sake of a fuller, more natural human
life. In these respects, it values highly (as indeed does Marx) the
human abilities to conceptualise and form intentions. It also
rates very highly the human capacities to respond to emergencies,
to repair and, when occasion demands, to improvise.

The present time is one of great emergency. Men have invoked
the forces of the universe and the elements of the earth in order
to create the golden image of the machine to do their will and to
realise for them their dreams of paradise. But it has not done so.
Instead they have discovered the machine, as well as the forces
and elements which they have invoked, being used to do the will
of these other artefacts of their desires, the Monster of Frankenstein and the corporate mechanisms that have issued from him :
the modern bureaucratic, autocratic state and the vast, soulless
corporations and *kombinats* of artificial utilitarian society,
capitalist, socialist and communist alike. One day, perhaps, these
monsters, like the dinosaurs of old, will become all body with an

ever smaller head, and so go their way to extinction. But human-kind cannot wait for the slow pace of evolution to do justice. It must act now. The monsters already threaten humanity. And although men's appetites are boundless, and machinery might possibly be devised to stimulate and satisfy them indefinitely, the bounty of the earth, that mother of their mortality, is not. Nor can human beings allow mechanised, over-organised civilisation indefinitely to sap their own creativity and resourcefulness. The silhouette of the antheap and the beehive together serve as a symbol to warn them. Appetite and instinct can serve as the motive power of an artificial society, but that will be the price.

It is such a situation to which human beings must respond. They must declare what fundamentally they value most and reassert their essential and most distinctive qualities. Then they must be ready, if necessary, to improvise new ways of life or adapt old attitudes, to devise new institutions, or simply to repair the existing.

Men are not completely free. Far from claiming them to be so, this alternative outlook points to the actual limitations imposed by a combination of physical nature and human nature that restricts all their activities and limits the realisation of all their ideals. Yet their attempts to give independent value to what they do distinguishes these activities as human and increases the area of their practical freedom. One aspect of the very real and practical freedom that men have is to negotiate the images of their thoughts with the concrete facts of history and of material developments. The media of these negotiations are their every-day intentions, projects and activities – their active lives and common existence. As the limiting boundaries of this common life expand, so will it become possible for all men to have greater freedom, and to realise more of their intentions in practical forms. The apogee of men's collective ambition – the end of liberty considered as public policy – is so to extend the boun-daries of this common existence in a field of such generous proportions that every man living in it can fulfil the good he has set himself.

But men are ambiguous. Sometimes they deal with the crisis on their hands as though it were exclusively economic and material; sometimes as exclusively political, and sometimes as part of a crisis of history in which the spiritual has intervened.

Rarely do they relate the three. This ambiguity is even at the core of human good itself. It is impossible to define it as a single good, or to locate it in one state or condition. It is a craving for goodness which sets up in different people, and in the same person at different times, changing goals, and according to the goal so the methods of attaining it vary. Choice is nearly always possible and decision-making necessary. Ambiguity is also at the core of human personality. As a member of different groups and associations, in family and friendships, at work and in his wider social activities, each man shows a different aspect of himself, and, superficially at least, often appears as a different person; so, too in different situations, or facing different aspects of value and reality. Upon all this, whilst he is living, he has continuously to impose a unity; and it is from the way in which he organises his experiences into a unity that he is uniquely recognisable for what he is and who he is. In every single one of these activities, he affects other people's lives and they react to him, causing a chain of circumstances that bring yet others into the same area of personality. In every item of personal as well as public life, therefore, each individual, although nearly always in an unconscious way, is a maker of history. His fingerprints mark the door he opens; his footprints leave impressions on the ground and these with those of others merge into significant social patterns and into a causal sequence of past and present which lead into a future, to which he has already helped to give shape and direction.

All human actions are significant. The free and the determined ride together. Who directs which, and which influences the more, we shall not know until the end of time. But the more we ponder the facts of human ambiguity, and the possibilities of action that this, when mixed with the immense power of modern knowledge, affords to each human being, so the more open history seems to be. This openness is not caused by any single human, individual or collective decision to make a precise course of events go this way or that, for clearly the hidden forces, the imponderables, are too great; but by the infinite number of little and big decisions in favour of certain definite values when men have to face the particular direction of the value for which they decide. It is these decisions and the actions resulting from them which have helped give history its shape and direction:

political, social and religious outlooks are effective shapers of history.

The view of human freedom expressed here is interestingly paralleled by what the theologian Karl Barth had to say about human freedom in quite different terms. God, he proclaimed, has given man his freedom and made him his partner to shape his own history : 'he [God] is the free One, in whom all freedom has its ground, its meaning, its prototype . . . He is also the creator of him who is his partner.'[1] Thus, freedom is not something merely negative – the formal protection of declared rights. It is some-thing positive, that, in partnership with the given of physical nature and the tendencies set in motion both by history and the applied sciences, leads to human creativity.

The acceptance of Barth's existential statement as a literary device to express an optimistic conviction of the value and nature of human freedom, of man's power to innovate, draws attention to the fact that the forces of history, of materialism and of the technology which man himself has been the agent in raising to artificial existence are not all-powerful and deterministic. Man, too, is a reality, a partner with them; his affections, his values, judgments and purpose, as well as his will, are creative, innovat-ing agencies. The material and the human, impersonal tendencies and personal values, combine to shape human history. As man grows up, his conceptualisation of purpose, his awareness of his own powers and of the reality of other men's missions, as well as his insights into physical nature and his vision of a greater liberty for all mankind, can have an ever-increasing role in determining his own future.

In these processes the pleasure-pain calculus, whether as satirised in Chapters 2 and 3 or whether in the more mathe-matical way that Bentham intended, can in fact play no part at all. Men do not always deliberately avoid pain; nor can they do so. It is often impossible to include its avoidance in any cal-culation of voluntary choice. Most doctors, nurses and priests attending the sick would say that the human capacity to recognise pain and to bear it consciously as the accompaniment or sign of injury or impairment of the body, are two of the most typical marks of the truly human. 'Only in pain', one has said, 'do the

1. Karl Barth, *The Humanity of God* (London, 1961), p. 41.

weak meet the strong.'[2] Men become their eventual selves through pain as much as through any other experiences. Nor were Bentham and the Philosophical Radicals – the Utilitarians – right in associating work with pain. Some forms of industrial work when Bentham wrote may well have been painful, indeed almost unendurable; just as today an enormous quantity of work is boring. But neither kind is a fitting occupation for the whole man. Work, fully and properly understood, is the coordination of mind and limb directed to the achievement of a precise purpose. And a man's work is free when he has full control over these items. So understood, most men and women find work, or would find it, intensely enjoyable.

Mortal life is short. Only through purposeful activity of some kind can most men hope to begin being more fully themselves and to serve others well. In such activity and in what little time is left over, they can encounter each other by seeking the conviviality of fellowship or the serious purposes of politics and social work. They can encounter each other, too, through recognition of their common qualities, through the exchange of general ideas and through the range of their affections. It is fitting, therefore, that we should begin finding our way to true freedom by attempting to introduce our understanding of it into our modes of working, into our toolmaking and into our economic structures. From here the creativity implicit in it will spread to the rest of our lives and to the rest of society.

Whether at work, in politics, in the community or in leisure, we can value each other as ends and no longer as means or mere productive tools. We can respect each other's different and unequal powers. But we can at the same time respect the common humanity of the propensities that each of us bears in himself, as well as the values that bind us as persons. Let us stop belittling the scope of the freedom that this has given us to shape our common future. Instead, let us cherish it for the opportunities it gives us, to make all we do and the way we live together more and more the projection of what we value most. On the assumption that we shall do so is founded the hope that man will find the means of his freedom in modern society. Humans can find that for which they seek. They can find good when they give up

2. Archbishop Bloom, in a television interview.

their fascination with the artificial, turn away from the dereliction of purpose that it has caused, and face the direction of their freedom.

> These are the spells by which to re-assume
> An empire o'er the disentangled doom.
> To suffer woes which Hope thinks infinite :
> To forgive wrongs darker than death or night;
> To defy Power which seems omnipotent;
> To love and bear; to hope till Hope creates
> From its own wreck the thing it contemplates;
> Neither to change, to falter or repent;
> This, like thy Glory, Titan, is to be
> Good, great and joyous, beautiful and free;
> This is alone – Life, Joy, Empire, and Victory.
>
> (Shelley, 'Prometheus Unbound')

Men can afford to be hopeful. As soon as they have recovered a proper sense of their own worth and abandoned the utilitarian outlook, they have all the amazing possibilities opened up by the discoveries of this century and the next to achieve true freedom and fellowship. The realisation of a very wide range of human values and purposes is possible. Creativity is possible. Such optimism must prevail, even if, for a longer time than we wish, the ugliness, distortions and artificiality of the utilitarian outlook should remain unabated and, in consequence, catastrophe cannot be avoided. In the end, proportion will be restored to the boundaries of human life and men will be able to discover their true significance within them.

Appendix I

THE ECONOMIES OF SCALE

These are the advantages attributed to large-scale operation. They may be external (a telephone system; a technical college specialising in say the teaching of steel technology in a steel-producing area; a socially or cooperatively-owned computer; markets specialising in particular commodities or not). Or they may be internal, (advantages accruing to an organisation from certain functions performed under its own roof or roofs). Many economies are external to some firms and internal to others: e.g. typing pool is an internal economy; a typing agency serving several firms, an external economy. All but the first three listed below may be considered in this way: i.e. internal in one set of circumstances (those of big business) and external in others (those of small firms), i.e. 'coordination through the market'.

Based upon the economies discussed in E. A. G. Robinson's *The Structure of Competitive Industry* (London and Cambridge, 1931) it is convenient to draw attention to ten classes under which the economies of scale can be discussed. (See my *Impact of Size* for a more detailed explanation.)

1. *Physical.* Large and costly physical items, plant and equipment, the employment of which postulates a large organisation: a motor car assembly line. But note, not all large and costly plants require the employment of large numbers of workers; e.g. a modern automated petrol refinery needs only forty or fifty men to run it. Large machines in fact tend to be *capital intensive and labour saving.*

2. *Financial.* This is the key economy of scale. It is the economy which enables the big firm to prosper in the market, expand quickly and generally 'have its way'. A large firm with valuable capital assets and a high stock exchange quotation can

borrow readily and pay a lower rate of interest than smaller firms.

3. *Managerial.* One very able director-general as managing director can (sometimes) take the place of ten or a dozen less able managers of smaller units. Also the economies related to skilled specialist management – e.g. really skilled heads of department supported by a number of well qualified and able specialists. Management techniques in recent years have improved so immensely as to make very much larger reorganisation and 'groups of companies' possible.

4. *Pool of massed reserves.* This is realised by combining with a common organisation reserves of facilities for which there is a fluctuating demand in each use, e.g. typing pools, crews, cutting rooms, film editors, research departments, libraries, location finders and so on.

5. *Coordination.* The coordination of planning of multi-activities; again the assembly line, or the manufacture of steel piping at the gates of steel foundries.

6. *Buying- and selling-economies.* Achieved by size of bargaining power in general. Bulk buying, bulk selling.

7. *General ability.* Of a large company or corporation to survive risks and uncertainties, take knocks and recover; also to be able to stand up to political pressures and make good political bargains.

8. *Research and development.* In some industries such as electronics, this is the basis of a firm's existence and research costs can be considered as 'threshold cost'. In spite of this, hardly any innovations of this century have been made by large firms.

9. *Advertising (including market research).* The better the advertising and the more the advertising, the greater the sales. But costs are often too high, so that these advantages tend to occur mainly when only a few giant firms dominate an industry.

10. *Prestige and atmosphere.* Tradition built up over years with which new employees and new departments are encouraged to identify.

There are, of course, 'diseconomies' of scale : the disadvantages of large-scale operation. These are due mainly to the human factor, as it is euphemistically called – i.e. people work better in small groups – (see Chapter 14). Solutions to the problems of scale may be described as 'devolution downwards' and 'replication across'.

From the above, it may be seen that a function will often represent an economy of scale for the producer and a diseconomy for the community in which his factory exists.

In my *Impact of Size*, Chapter 5, I set out in some detail proposals for the externalising of economies 4, 5 (parts of), 6, 8 and 9 in *Industrial Service Corporations*. I treat economy 3 as one of the sources of the human *diseconomies of scale*. And I deal separately with the *financial* or capital economies. Thus, only economy 1, the *physical* economy, is a necessary determinant of large-scale, giant-sized firms. In Chapter 8, I modify these proposals and adapt them to meet some of the conditions of the present capitalist economy characterised by rapid industrial concentration.

Appendix II

The right sizes of groups for different purposes within truly or fully human communities and societies; and the appropriate tools, techniques and methods of administration for such communities and societies and for those working or living in them

Ivan Illich's essay, 'Violence, a mirror for Americans',[1] provokes thought, reflection and self-criticism. But does he, at the cost of his own gospel being taken far less seriously than it ought, minimise very much the needs of the poor for certain material things and of the hungry for food and variety? The brave millions of Latin America only resist American investment because it will, they think, never send its fruits down to them. Nevertheless it may. Utilitarianism, artificial utilitarianism, has been so successful in seducing the North Atlantic, Japanese, Australasian and now Russian masses, because it *is* artificial; because the essence of its obsession is to relate its artificial abstractions to the process-nature of physical reality itself, and this has produced automatically a plethora of by-products that the people have either wanted or have been easily persuaded that they do. Beware, Ivan : if the artificial utilitarians can discover the pulse beat and rhythm of Latin American physical reality, they will within a generation have also their persuaders, their market men, and their radical politicians steeped in the slogans of Latin American cultures, preferences, raves and tribalistic whims. It is the prospect of this which you have to defeat, but first to understand.

You must offer an alternative. This other way and other method must start with its own critique of artificial utilitarianism, making clear exactly where amidst nature itself it takes its stance; from here too its own position of value *vis-à-vis* man – the truly

1. Ivan Illich, *Celebration of Awareness* (Harmondsworth, 1971).

human – must be stated clearly and the artificial processes which it condemns be rationally evaluated. Much of this the masses will not at first understand, be able or want to. More primitive or more basic modes of expression will have to be found. Nevertheless, common to both modes of expression is the need to be earthy, to be practical. Values exist, it is true, in being perceived and formed into ideas. But they can only be believed in praxis. A reservoir of water cannot be considered as the place for a new centre of population, a new community, until its existence has been verified by touch and its purity vouched for by analysis and actual drinking.

It is not enough simply to invent more labour-intensive tools or techniques, nor to show how the scrap materials left over by the rich can be adapted for use by the poor : the discarded cocoa and pineapple tins made into plough-shares and discarded American tyres into sandals. These come to be simply symbols of mockery, or more gravely, gifts of offence. It is the Anglo-Saxon charity-bazaar mentality immensely extended so as to bring into its scope people with too great a dignity either to say yes, or no. These goods are rarely appreciated. They are seen as the cast-off, the second hand or the inferior, the uncaring sop.

That is one form of unsound thought and overbearing masterful attitude. The other, appreciated by Schumacher[2] more realistically than by Illich, is the massive investment – the big plant and the big machine pioneered for use by the uncreative masses of artificial utilitarian society so that its by-products may be manufactured as quickly as possible in order to satisfy its members' appetites and sensations on as large a scale as possible. This is the capital intensive machine operated by a minimum of highly paid, knowledgeable men. It is the creator of an elite of technocratic workers. Their wages do not circulate throughout the society in the same way as would the same aggregate amount paid out in lower wages to say a hundred times as many workers employed in skill-intensive or thought-intensive work. The recipients instead become at once customers for the comparatively luxurious goods of the utilitarian manufacuring nations – the ice box, the confectionery and the seductive-smelling deodorants.

2. E. F. Shumacher, *Small is Beautiful* (London, 1973).

The alternative to a few very expensive, capital intensive plants – the petroleum refinery, the row of repetitive and automatically controlled dye casting machines and the assembly line – is the same as the alternative to Schumacher's tidy schemes. It starts at the same place too – the meeting-place of men desiring to undertake skilful, purposive activity, and men and women desiring true liberty and a more considerate caring attitude to nature. Moreover it joins these prerequisites of a more fully human society to the carefully considered, legitimate economic and material needs of the masses indigenous to each country and culture. This alternative is the small, relatively inexpensive – but skill-demanding – tools and machines that can be operated in groups of 10–20, 60–100 and 250–600 men. These workers will not necessarily be highly paid at first, but they will participate in a method of remuneration that will improve their material standards as they themselves improve the material standards of the communities in which they live. Both goods and money will circulate at the level of the ordinary worker. Investment therefore is right; but investment that will cause the spread of new wealth evenly and justly throughout the society in which it is invested. Capital is not neutral. Nor need its influence be biased towards its possessors. It can either create monopolies of wealth and privilege or something approaching genuine conditions for material equality, at least of opportunity and the means of meeting basic needs.

But mankind needs skill-intensive tools and techniques for a yet more valid reason. It is to obtain their true freedom; the freedom to express precisely in material form that which they conceived first in their minds and imaginations; the power to transpose their own particular being into visible terms, into forms made by them from world's resources. Schumacher's early essay reflects this need, but as far as is known none of the tools and machines which his organisation has designed express it.

Man as material being has only one right – the right to the means of existence of himself and those for whom he is responsible. Man as creature in the vast order where the spiritual and universal meet has only two items to claim as the condition of his existence – freedom and justice. A civilised human outlook must see that these three abstractions meet in each other, and achieve their best, their most appropriate human form; that is to say not neatly in an abstract, praiseworthy pattern, but actually, really and truly, completely and fully in universal practice. The first item on the agenda of radical or revolutionary fully human politics must be, therefore, the means of making the tools, machines and techniques for meeting men's more simple material needs and at the same time satisfying the skills and aesthetic pleasures as well as expressing the mental blueprints of the workers making things. Culture as well as skills, local as well as universal values would enter this picture.

These tools, techniques and machines are needed in at least two realms : industry and agriculture. This fact points to two other areas of great importance for thought. One is the local, decentralised community with its corresponding needs of co-ordination and integration, and also of institutions of justice, distribution and exchange that can only be exercised centrally, besides other proven economies of scale too. The other is administration itself. The search has now to be begun for more simple, more genuine, face-to-face methods of administration suitable for the more fully human society. Although areas for both these investigations exist in the societies of northern Europe, Japan and the United States, they may be most apparent in the ex-colonial societies of Africa and Asia. Perhaps in Latin America too.

In the vast sparsely populated areas of Africa, the room for the ideal geographical decentralisation is immense. Intermediate technology in for example providing small community-size electricity generating plants has, as Schumacher explains, a great part to play. By creating living centres in the midst of agricultural areas the natural cycles between man and nature can be restored; the cycle of crops being grown, eaten, digested and their unwanted parts being rejected in excrement for the fertilisation of fresh crops. Here too the right balance as well as size of community living group – village, town and city – can be realised. Those educated in different disciplines, in science and arts, in rural pursuits as well as in the applied sciences can meet and set up demands for cafés, cinemas or theatres appropriate to their needs and to their living rich, convivial lives together. Professional men will be attracted as well.

But none of this can come about effectively unless there come into being the appropriate methods of local administration – the administration primarily of people, not of things. It is at this point that some rigid versions of Marxism must yield to the experience of enlightened liberal societies and come to terms with some of the human failures of communism in the Soviet Union and countries of eastern Europe.

One of the greatest weaknesses of British colonial government was that it created, on the whole, sound central government; but very little local at all (it has to be admitted that this was out of respect for local custom and culture). Parallel was the defect of the great nineteenth-century utilitarian pioneers of administration: they were concerned solely with method and its consequences; never with those whom their method affected. (The admission to be made on their behalf is that they set themselves successfully against the creation of bureaucracies – a fact to which Marx paid handsome tribute, but which failed entirely to be emulated by their twentieth-century successors.) The problem remains, therefore, of discovering what fully-human administration may mean. How can there be simple face-to-face government of equals, by equals, for equals? There must be order; there must be authority. Both have to be just and intelligible, but both must also be approachable and ready to justify by reason and argument.

If Africa and possibly parts of Asia too offer the most immediate opportunities for thinking about problems of decentralisation, the older colonies, the dominions of Australia and Canada, may better be the first places for pioneering to take place. The balance of the argument between the claims of the two is nice; but the advantages of salesmanship are probably decisive. Decentralised communities with the expertise required will almost certainly need to be mixed communities – racially mixed. Racial and religious toleration, in the true sense of people being willing to bear the weight of those things that carry them and maintain them apart, their differences, will be needed to be practised with renewed conviction. These gestures must come from the longer formally educated and from those whose ancestors considered themselves ethnically superior. Offence must be avoided and redemption offered. The spaces of Australia and Canada, therefore, must invite first. Time is pressing, simply because it is the spaces of Africa that most urgently need draining, afforestation, cultivation, peopling and stocking with herds as well as with the installations of industry. But example has to be pioneered before men can be wise enough to be practical.

Another reason makes it urgent for the pioneering to be done in the affluent countries. It is this : the new way of making things may well entail a lower level of production. The artificial utilitarian process is so wasteful of human resources and potentialities that we cannot be sure. However, we can be sure that its rejection and the adoption of skill-intensive techniques operated in human-sized groups will mean that many items of the artificial utilitarian process will not be made. The gimmickry, the novelty and the pandering to many sophisticated appetites will cease. There will be novelties of new kinds, creative novelties. Bearing this in mind, we must see how wrong it would be to demand that the populations of the developing countries should be asked to be the pioneers, to give up their expectations; never even to have the choice of saying yes or no to the goods that even now lie on the counters of the self-service emporia of the United States, Japan, Germany, France, and Britain and with which the leaders of the Soviet Union have just begun to ensnare their people by their deeds in Moscow and Washington – perhaps, but we hope not, in Peking too. Schumacher would have the developing countries to do the pioneering. Give them the knowledge and small grants, he says and in effect let them develop their own techniques.

Are there to be any exceptions to this policy of priorities, and ought there to be ? To both questions we can answer an unqualified yes. This answer comes about of itself. Ideas are produced in response to needs, spiritual or material; the fully human is always a combination of each. For that is man; a mixture of both. Should there be in Africa or Asia countries which have rejected the artificial way of life, whether in capitalist or socialist context; should they have decided for a decentralised society where power is dispersed and people seek to find true community of living; then such people are already seeking the tools and methods to better their material conditions and to make things for each other which are both needed or contain within them the love, the personality and mind of their makers.

K

Background Reading and General Sources

Introduction

Leslie Stephen,   *The English Utilitarians* (London, 1900)

Chapter 1

Hannah Arendt,   *The Human Condition* (Chicago, 1962)

David Riesman,   *Abundance for What?* (London, 1964), and *Individualism Reconsidered* (London, 1964)

Rex Warren,   *Letters on Purpose* (London, 1963)

Chapter 2

Hannah Arendt,   *The Human Condition* (Chicago, 1962)

M. M. Goldsmith,   *Hobbes' Science of Politics* (Columbia, 1966)

Elie Halévy,   *A Bentham Reader* (New York, 1969)

Mary Peter Mack,   *The Growth of Philosophic Radicalism* (London, 1928)

Leslie Stephen,   *The English Utilitarians* (London, 1900)

Chapter 3

James Burnham,   *The Managerial Revolution* (New York, 1941)

Alan Coddington,   'Cost-benefit as the new utilitarianism', *The Political Quarterly* 42, 1971

G. H. Copeman,   *The Laws of Business Management* (London, 1962)
Lionel Robbins,   *Economic Planning and International Order* (London, 1937), and *An Essay in the Nature and Significance of Economic Science* (London, 1932)
J. M. Samuels (ed.),   *Readings on Mergers and Takeovers* (London, 1972)
Peter Self,   'Nonsense on stilts: cost-benefit analysis and the Roskill Commission', *The Political Quarterly* 42, 1970
Peter F. Drucker,   *The Practice of Management* (London, 1955)

Chapter 4

Erich Fromm,   *Freedom from Fear* (London, 1956), and *The Sane Society* (London, 1956)
F. R. Leavis,   *Bentham and Coleridge* (London, 1950)
Theodore Roszak,   *The Making of a Counter Culture* (London 1970)

Chapter 5

Isaiah Berlin,   *The Two Concepts of Liberty* (London, 1958)
H. L. A. Hart,   *The Concept of Law* (Oxford, 1961)
G. H. F. Hegel,   *The Philosophy of Right* (London, 1821)
T. M. Knox and Z. A. Pelczynski (trans. and introd.),   *Hegel's Political Writings* (London, 1964)
Harriet Martineau,   *The Positive Philosophy of Auguste Comte*, 1875
W. G. Runciman,   *Relative Deprivation and Social Justice* (London, 1966)
John Stuart Mill,   *On Liberty*, 1858; and *Auguste Comte and Positivism*, 1865

Chapter 6

Jeremy Bentham,	*Fragment on Government* (1776) *An Introduction to the Principles of Morals and Legislation* (1789)
Maurice Cranston,	*Freedom* (London, 1967)
G. H. F. Hegel,	*Philosophy of Right* (1821) *Philosophy of History* (1831)
Herbert Marcuse,	*Reason and Revolution: Hegel and the Rise of Social Theory* (London, 1941)
John Stuart Mill,	*Utilitarianism* (1863)

Chapter 8

Karl Popper	*The Open Society and Its Enemies* (London, 1945) *The Poverty of Historicism* (London, 1957)
B. Malinowski,	*A Scientific Theory of Culture* (Chapel Hill, 1944)
J. R. Ravetz,	*Scientific Knowledge and its Social Problems* (Oxford, 1971)

Chapter 9

All existentialist literature is relevant, but see especially Majorie Grene, *Introduction to Existentialism* (Chicago, 1959) and Jean-Paul Sartre, *Existentialism and Humanism* (London, 1948) and *L'Être et le néant* (Paris, 1943). Also Maurice Cranston, *Sartre* (Edinburgh, 1962) and R. D. Laing, *The Bird of Paradise* (Harmondsworth, 1967).

Chapter 11

Simone de Beauvoir,	*Pour une morale de l'ambiguité* (Paris, 1957)
William Empson,	*Seven Types of Ambiguity* (London, 1953)
C. G. Jung,	*Two Essays on Analytical Psychology* (New York, 1928)
Konrad Lorenz,	*On Aggression* (London, 1966)

Chapter 12

T. E. Hulme,	*Speculations* (London, 1924)
Eugene Kamenka,	*The Ethical Foundation of Marxism* (London, 1973)
Spinoza,	*Ethics*

Chapter 13

Edward Goodman,	*The Impact of Size* (London, 1969)
Antony Jay,	*Corporation Man* (London, 1972)
Gerald Leach,	*The Great Doomsday Debate* : Barry Commoner, Alvin Weinberg, George Borgstrom and Norman Borlaeug, *The Observer,* March 1972
Theodore M. Mills,	*The Sociology of Small Groups* (Englewood Cliffs, 1967)
E. J. Mishan,	*The Costs of Economic Growth* (London, 1967)
Robert I. Rotberg,	*The Rise of Nationalism in Central Africa* (London, 1963)
A. K. Sen,	*Choice of Technology* (Oxford, 1968)
W. J. H. Sprott,	*Human Groups* (Harmondsworth, 1958)
Elias Canetti,	*Crowds and Power* (London, 1962)

Chapter 14

Robert Benewick and Trevor Smith (eds.),	*Direct Action and Democratic Politics* (London, 1973)
Bhikhu Parekh and R. M. Berki (eds.),	*The Morality of Politics* (London, 1972)
Pierre Teilhard de Chardin,	*The Phenomenon of Man* (London, 1959)

Chapter 15

Preston King and B. Parekh (eds.),	*Politics and Experience* (London, 1968) See especially King's essay 'An ideological fallacy' and Samuel Coleman's 'Is there reason in tradition?'

| Krishan Kumar, | *Revolution: The Theory and Practice of a European Idea* (London, 1971) |
| Alec Nove, | *The Soviet Economy* (London, 1961) |

Chapter 16

Nicholas Berdyaev,	*The End of Our Time* (London, 1933)
L. T. Hobhouse,	*The Elements of Social Justice* (London, 1922)
Bertrand Russell,	*Power: A New Social Analysis* (London, 1938)

INDEX